Human Architecture: Journal of the Sociology of Self-Knowledge

Monograph Series: Tayyebeh Series in East-West Research and Translation

About OKCIR

Omar Khayyam Center for Integrative Research in Utopia, Mysticism, and Science (Utopystics)

www.okcir.com

OKCIR (est. 2002) is an independent research, pedagogical, and publishing initiative dedicated to exploring, in a simultaneously world-historical and self-reflective framework, the human search for a just global society.

Since the world's utopian, mystical, and scientific movements have been the primary sources of inspiration, knowledge, and/or practice in this field, OKCIR aims to critically reexamine the shortcomings and contributions of these world-historical traditions—seeking to clearly understand why they have failed to bring about the good society, and what each can integratively contribute toward realizing that end.

The center aims to develop new conceptual (methodological, theoretical, historical), practical, pedagogical, inspirational and disseminative structures of knowledge whereby the individual can radically understand and determine how world-history and her/his selves constitute one another.

OKCIR promotes creative exercises in liberating sociology and alternative pluriversities of knowledge production and publication in the global cyberspace. As a virtual research center, its publications are available in part freely online in its open-stacks digital library, in part via subscription to its own or other academic database member-stacks, and others for purchase online via the Okcir Store and other online distributors. Selected publications are also available in print for online purchase by libraries, institutions, and interested print readers.

OKCIR pursues innovative editorial, digital, and print publishing practices reflecting its substantive goals, and is the publisher of *Human Architecture: Journal of the Sociology of Self-Knowledge* (ISSN: 1540-5699, est. 2002) which explores issues pertaining to the center's interests. *Human Architecture* is a hybrid scholarly journal whose edited and monographed issues are simultaneously published also as individual books in hardcover, softcover, and pdf and/or epub ebook formats (with separately assigned ISBNs).

Tayyebeh Series in East-West Research and Translation (2014-) and Ahead Publishing House (imprint: Okcir Press) (1991-) respectively honor Tayyebeh Tamjidi (1928-2020) and Mohammed (Ahad) Tamjidi (1930-2007) whose parental love and support made the life and works of Mohammad H. (Behrooz) Tamdgidi, the founder of OKCIR, possible.

Published to Date in the Series

Omar Khayyam's Secret: Hermeneutics of the Robaiyat in Quantum Sociological Imagination: **Book 1**: *New Khayyami Studies: Quantumizing the Newtonian Structures of C. Wright Mills's Sociological Imagination for A New Hermeneutic Method* (Okcir Press, 2021)

Omar Khayyam's Secret: Hermeneutics of the Robaiyat in Quantum Sociological Imagination: **Book 2**: *Khayyami Millennium: Reporting the Discovery and the Reconfirmation of the True Dates of Birth and Passing of Omar Khayyam (AD 1021-1123)* (Okcir Press, 2021)

Omar Khayyam's Secret: Hermeneutics of the Robaiyat in Quantum Sociological Imagination: **Book 3**: *Khayyami Astronomy: How Omar Khayyam's Newly Discovered True Birth Date Horoscope Reveals the Origins of His Pen Name and Independently Confirms His Authorship of the Robaiyat* (Okcir Press, 2021)

Omar Khayyam's Secret

Hermeneutics of the Robaiyat in Quantum Sociological Imagination

---

BOOK 1

New Khayyami Studies

Quantumizing the Newtonian Structures of
C. Wright Mills's Sociological Imagination
for A New Hermeneutic Method

About this Book

Omar Khayyam's Secret: Hermeneutics of the Robaiyat in Quantum Sociological Imagination is a twelve-book series of which this book, subtitled *New Khayyami Studies: Quantumizing the Newtonian Structures of C. Wright Mills's Sociological Imagination for A New Hermeneutic Method*, is the first volume. Each book is independently readable, although it will be best understood as a part of the whole series.

In the overall series, the transdisciplinary sociologist Mohammad H. Tamdgidi shares the results of his decades-long research on Omar Khayyam, the enigmatic 11th/12th centuries Persian Muslim sage, philosopher, astronomer, mathematician, physician, writer, and poet from Neyshabour, Iran, whose life and works still remain behind a veil of deep mystery. Tamdgidi's purpose has been to find definitive answers to the many puzzles still surrounding Khayyam, especially regarding the existence, nature, and purpose of the Robaiyat in his life and works. To explore the questions posed, he advances a new hermeneutic method of textual analysis, informed by what he calls the quantum sociological imagination, to gather and study all the attributed philosophical, religious, scientific, and literary writings of Khayyam.

In this first book of the series, following a common preface and introduction to the series, Tamdgidi develops the quantum sociological imagination method framing his hermeneutic study in the series as a whole. In the prefatory note he shares the origins of this series and how the study is itself a moment in the trajectory of a broader research project. In his introduction, he describes how centuries of Khayyami studies, especially during the last two, have reached an impasse in shedding light on his enigmatic life and works, especially his attributed Robaiyat.

The four chapters of the book are then dedicated to developing the quantum sociological imagination as a new hermeneutic method framing the Khayyami studies in the series. The method builds, in an applied way, on the results of Tamdgidi's recent work in the sociology of scientific knowledge, *Liberating Sociology: From Newtonian Toward Quantum Imagination: Volume 1: Unriddling the Quantum Enigma* (2020), where he explored extensively, in greater depth, and in the context of understanding the so-called "quantum enigma," the Newtonian and quantum ways of imagining reality. In this first book, he shares the findings of that research in summary amid new applied insights developed in relation to Khayyami studies.

In the first chapter, Tamdgidi raises a set of eight questions about the structure of C. Wright Mills's sociological imagination as a potential framework for Khayyami studies. In the second chapter, he shows how the questions are symptomatic of Newtonian structures that still continue to frame Mills's sociological imagination. In the third chapter, the author explores how the sociological imagination can be reinvented to be more in tune with the findings of quantum science. In the last chapter, the implications of the quantum sociological imagination for devising a hermeneutic method for new Khayyam and Robaiyat studies are outlined. In conclusion, the findings of this first book of the *Omar Khayyam's Secret* series are summarized.

Omar Khayyam's Secret

Hermeneutics of the Robaiyat in Quantum Sociological Imagination

BOOK 1

New Khayyami Studies

*Quantumizing the Newtonian Structures of
C. Wright Mills's Sociological Imagination
for A New Hermeneutic Method*

Mohammad H. Tamdgidi

Human Architecture: Journal of the Sociology of Self-Knowledge • XIV • 2021

Monograph Series: Tayyebeh Series in East-West Research and Translation

Okcir Press

About the Author

Previous books beside this series by Mohammad H. Tamdgidi

Liberating Sociology: From Newtonian Toward Quantum Imaginations Volume I: Unriddling the Quantum Enigma (Okcir Press, 2020)

Gurdjieff and Hypnosis: A Hermeneutic Study (Palgrave Macmillan, 2009)

Advancing Utopistics: The Three Component Parts and Errors of Marxism (Routledge/Paradigm, 2007)

Mohammad-Hossein (a.k.a. 'Behrooz') Tamdgidi (pronounced "tamjidi") is the founder and editor respectively of OKCIR: Omar Khayyam Center for Integrative Research in Utopia, Mysticism, and Science (Utopystics) and its publication, *Human Architecture: Journal of the Sociology of Self-Knowledge* (ISSN: 1540-5699) which have served since 2002 to frame his independent research, pedagogical, and publishing initiatives. Formerly an associate professor of sociology specializing in social theory at the University of Massachusetts (UMass) Boston, he has also previously taught sociology as full-time lecturer at SUNY-Oneonta, and also as adjunct lecturer at SUNY-Binghamton. He has published numerous books and edited more than thirty journal collections, in addition to other peer reviewed articles and chapters.

Tamdgidi's areas of scholarly and applied interest are the sociology of self-knowledge, human architecture, and utopystics—three fields of inquiry he invented in his doctoral studies and has since pursued as respectively intertwined theoretical, methodological and applied fields of inquiry altogether contributing to what he calls the quantum sociological imagination. His research, teaching, and publications have been framed by an interest in understanding how world-historical social structures and personal selves constitute one another. This line of inquiry has itself been a result of his longstanding interest in understanding the underlying causes of failures of the world's utopian, mystical, and scientific movements in bringing about a just global society.

It was during his undergraduate studies at U.C. Berkeley and in the course of his mentorship by the painter and design architect Jesse Reichek (1916-2005) that Tamdgidi's notion and project "human architecture" was born. During his graduate studies at SUNY-Binghamton, he was mentored in methods, theory, and world-systems studies by Terence K. Hopkins (1928-1997) and Immanuel Wallerstein (1930-2019), and further in dialectics by Dale Tomich and on space and society by Anthony D. King, amid a uniquely autonomous and flexible transdisciplinary Graduate Program in Sociology founded by T. K. Hopkins.

Tamdgidi holds a Ph.D. and M.A. in sociology in conjunction with a graduate certificate in Middle Eastern studies from Binghamton University (SUNY). He received his B.A. in architecture from U. C. Berkeley, following enrollment as an undergraduate student of civil engineering in the Technical College of the University of Tehran, Iran. In Dec. 2013 he retired early from his tenured and promoted position at UMass Boston in order to pursue his independent scholarship in quantum sociological imagination and its application in Khayyami studies through the conduit of his research center, OKCIR.

In anticipation of the imminent millennium of birth and the forthcoming ninth centennial of passing of Omar Khayyam

for my mother,
Tayyebeh Tamjidi
(March 20, 1928 - December 31, 2020)

OMAR KHAYYAM'S SECRET
Hermeneutics of the Robaiyat in Quantum Sociological Imagination
*Book 1: New Khayyami Studies: Quantumizing the Newtonian Structures of C. Wright Mills's
Sociological Imagination for A New Hermeneutic Method*

Author: Mohammad H. Tamdgidi

Copyright © 2021 by Mohammad-Hossein Tamdgidi

First Edition: June 1, 2021
Okcir Press • P. O. Box 393, Belmont, MA 02478, USA • www.okcir.com
For ordering or other inquiries contact: info[at]okcir.com

Okcir Press is an imprint of Ahead Publishing House, which is a division of OKCIR:
Omar Khayyam Center for Integrative Research in Utopia, Mysticism, and Science (Utopystics)

Library of Congress Control Number: 2021906754

Publisher Cataloging in Publication Data

Omar Khayyam's Secret: Hermeneutics of the Robaiyat in Quantum Sociological Imagination
*Book 1: New Khayyami Studies: Quantumizing the Newtonian Structures of C. Wright Mills's
Sociological Imagination for A New Hermeneutic Method* / Mohammad H. Tamdgidi, 1959- /
First Edition: June 1, 2021
Human Architecture: Journal of the Sociology of Self-Knowledge • Volume XIV • 2021
Monograph Series: Tayyebeh Series in East-West Research and Translation

284 pages • 6x9 inches • Includes illustration, references, bibliography, and index.
ISBN-13: 978-1-64098-002-0 • ISBN-10: 1-64098-002-4 (hardcover: alk. paper)
ISBN-13: 978-1-64098-003-7 • ISBN-10: 1-64098-003-2 (softcover: alk. paper)
ISBN-13: 978-1-64098-004-4 • ISBN-10: 1-64098-004-0 (EPub ebook)
ISBN-13: 978-1-64098-005-1 • ISBN-10: 1-64098-005-9 (PDF ebook)

1. Omar Khayyam. 2. Sociology. 3-Sociological Imagination. 4. Quantum Science.
5. Newtonianism. 6. Hermeneutics. 7. Robaiyat (Rubaiyat). 8. Khayyami Studies.
I. Mohammad H. Tamdgidi, 1959– II. Title

First Edition: June 1, 2021
Licensed cover images below from Dreamstime
Front cover images: light wave (118030391)
Back cover: mechanical mind (23656479) and light wave (118030391)
Cover/Spine/Jacket: Statue of Omar Khayyam, by Abolhasan Seddiqi, Laleh Park, Tehran, Iran (author)
Cover and Text Design: Ahead Publishing House, Belmont, MA, USA

The paper used in the print editions of this book is of archival quality and meets the minimum requirements of ANSI/NISO Z39.48-1992 (R1997) (Permanence of Paper). The production of this book on demand protects the environment by printing only the number of copies that are purchased.

هر راز که اندر دل دانا باشد

باید که نهفته تر ز عنقا باشد

کاندر صدف از نهفتگی گردد دُرّ

آن قطره که راز دل دریا باشد

عمر خیام

Any secret that is in a sage's heart sealed
Must be even more than phoenix from all concealed,
Since it's from shell-hiddenness that becomes a pearl
That drop which is the ocean heart's secret, congealed.

— Omar Khayyam (Tamdgidi translation)

Contents

List of Figures

Note on Transliteration

In the English edition of this book and its parent series, texts in languages using diacritics in their Latin alphabet are rendered as in the original.

When quoting Persian and Arabic texts transliterated by others, I will render them (including their diacritics) as found in the source, whatever transliteration system the source has used, which can vary from one source to another.

My own transliterations of Persian and Arabic texts will follow their pronunciation in Persian; that is, Arabic (or any other language) words internalized in Persian language will be transliterated according to their Persian pronunciation, except for the commonly transliterated words that have already been established in public discourse, as further explained below.

The main goal of the transliteration system newly designed for and applied in this series as explained in the appendix to each book is to make it possible to pronounce Persian words and those in Arabic (or in other languages) internalized in the Persian language the way a native Persian speaker would usually pronounce it (local dialects of Persian notwithstanding). Fulfilling this need is important, since otherwise we would lose the Persian pronunciations of Persian and its internalized (including Arabic) words over time. In reading Persian poetry, in particular, we need to produce Persian, and not Arabic, pronunciations of the words.

In Persian transliteration systems prevalent today, at times native and internalized words in Persian are transliterated in ways that result in Arabic pronunciation. The word "Rubaiyat" (used for رباعیّات which is actually an Arabic word), for instance, does not readily produce the Persian pronunciation of the word, which is Robāʿiyāt; Khayyam should be pronounced as Khayyām (not Kayam), Isfahan as Éṣfahān, Ibn Sina as ébn-e Sinā, Iran not as "I ran" but as Earān (Ear+ān), Ramadan as Rameẓān, Islam as Éslām, and so on.

Some of the above word examples have been already transliterated in Western languages in common forms (such as Iran, Islam, Isfahan, etc.), so I will maintain the same spelling in the main text while providing their full Persian transliteration in a cumulative glossary following the transliteration system introduced in the appendix of each book of the series. In others, when needed or found substantively needed, I will render the word in a way that emphasizes the Persian pronunciation. In doing so, however, in the main text I will strip it of diacritics, while providing its full transliteration in the cumulative glossary placed in the appendix to each book. This is to avoid cumbersome experiences of reading and writing native and internalized Persian words; even in English, we do not use diacritics to distinguish how 'u' sounds differently in "bus," "busy," "cute," or "mouse."

The use of diacritics in the main text, following one or another transliteration system, poses its own challenges. The difficulties generated by a confusing and at times conflicting diversity of transliteration systems used today for Persian and Arabic do not in my view warrant making the reading and writing of the text itself cumbersome. In this age of the Internet, such diacritics also make online rendering of the texts, and digital searching for them, often challenging, if not impossible and unsuccessful. Moreover, at times, rare diacritics make the words in which they appear impossible to render online depending on browsers used, resulting in their being replaced by wrong or distorted words.

It is for the above reasons that in this series I will avoid using diacritics for the words transliterated in the main text, but will offer full diacritics for them in a glossary following the transliteration system explained in the appendix to each book. So, for instance, while in my proposed system رباعیّات is transliterated as Robāʿiyāt, in the main text I will simply render the same as Robaiyat. If خیام is fully transliterated as Khayyām, in the main text I simply render it as Khayyam. ʿOmar is simply rendered as Omar. All diacritics, including ʿein (ع) and hamzeh (ء) are omitted to simplify the renderings of the words (such as Arouzi, Ismaili, or Shafa), while the transliteration system as described in the appendix is used as a guide to make sure the Persian pronunciations of native and internalized words in Persian are rendered. As noted, for established words such as Isfahan, Iran, Islam, etc., I will just use the common form in the main text.

For substantive reasons, the word "Rubaiyat" will only be used when referring to the particular tradition arising from the FitzGeraldian and Western translation efforts, while I will use instead "Robaiyat" to distinguish the new tradition I hope to engender by advancing the new Khayyami studies as initiated in the present series.

Where it is needed in the main text, such as when sharing of transliterations of poetry, for the readers' convenience I will include them in full transliteration next to the original Persian and my English translations in the main text itself.

Acknowledgments

Without the contributions of countless scholars and writers, past and present, in Iran and abroad, who have explored the life and works of Omar Khayyam over the many centuries, the conduct and results of this study would have been impossible. The list of these individuals is long, and I hope my specific engagements with some of their works throughout this series may serve as expressions of my deep appreciation for their valuable contributions.

I thank my wife Anna Beckwith for her patience and encouragements during the many decades it took me to conduct this research on Khayyam. I also thank Ramón Grosfoguel for his kind interest in my work, including that on Khayyam, and for inviting me to offer a seminar presentation on Khayyam in March 2011 at U. C. Berkeley.

I further thank the staff of the Interlibrary Loan at UMass Boston's Healey Library for their professionalism and timely processing of my requests.

My sabbatical year (2010-11) after being granted tenure and promotion at UMass Boston allowed me to spend more focused time on earlier phases of this research. Ironically, the sabbatical gave me a sense of the enormity of the effort needed for this research, resulting in my decision to retire early, in Dec. 2013, from my academic position so as to devote full-time to this urgent study while also attending to the needs of my mother in Iran, who unfortunately passed away on the last day of the year 2020, from natural causes in old age.

What ultimately made this study possible have been the love, support, and sacrifices of my parents, Tayyebeh Tamjidi (1928-2020) and Mohammed (Ahad) Tamjidi (1930-2007). My only wish and hope is that this engagement with the immortal spirit of Omar Khayyam will keep the names and memories of both my parents, and my endless love for them, alive forever.

This series as a whole is dedicated, beside Omar Khayyam himself, to the memory of my mother and in celebration of the universe of love, search for justice, and spiritual curiosity she bequeathed to me. I have already shared, in an extended acknowledgement in my recent work *Liberating Sociology: From Newtonian Toward Quantum Imaginations: Volume 1: Unriddling the Quantum Enigma* (2020), her life's story in the context of the broader history of contemporary Iran, so I refer interested readers to consult that writing for further insights into the motivations behind this series. It may suffice here again to say that this series is entirely a work of her life as well, as superposed with mine, in search of understanding by way of Omar Khayyam the enigma of our common human existence.

Despite her progressing Alzheimer's in the last decade or so of her life, during which she became oddly a love poet reliving her younger years, Tayyebeh lived long enough to walk me through the last day of the calendar year 2020 into 2021. Her 94th birth day on March 20, 2021, would have fallen also on the last day of Iran's calendar year and nominal century 1399 (SH), just a day before the 1400 SH Nowrooz holidays began. So, I see this book and series as also a Nowrooz gift from and to her as well.

I wish to thank my mother's kind nurse and caretakers in Iran, Mrs. Sakineh and Mr. Qasem Rahimi, and also Mr. Ashtiani, for providing me with the peace of mind needed to carry out this research, during the recent years I frequently traveled to Iran to attend to my mother's needs.

As the studies being reported in this series demonstrate, the timing of the simultaneous publication of the first three books of this twelve-book series ahead of June 10, 2021, or Khordad 20, 1400 SH, at sunrise, Neyshabour's time, of the Iranian Islamic solar calendar (one that Khayyam himself and his team of astronomers reformed centuries ago) is uniquely significant as far as Omar Khayyam and new Khayyami studies are concerned.

As expressed in one of his quatrains, Khayyam wished to be reborn like a green after a hundred thousand years. Now we know exactly when those hundred thousand years began, and on what day and time exactly its first millennium falls. So, I dedicate this series to him toward that aim, hoping that it will serve to renew interest in ever resurrecting his legacy as a wonderful gift from Iran's rich culture for 99 more and counting millennia to come. Perhaps somebody then will remember me too!

The astrological charts used in this series were prepared by the author using the Swiss Ephemeris database using software Time Cycles Research (TCR) for which he holds license. The online resources and the Swiss Ephemeris database available also on the online resources of the site Astrodienst were also helpful in the research conducted for this book. I thank them both, and also the site Medieval Astrology Guide, for providing their online resources and services.

The images used for book covers (including any inside from Dreamstime) have also been licensed for use. Many sources on which this study has drawn are old, out of print, and freely available online. Other acknowledgments and credits are given in the text itself or in footnotes. I draw on others in the spirit of fair use for educational and research purposes.

Preface to the Series: Origins of This Study

While a simple expression of interest may suffice for explaining why I became interested in this research on Omar Khayyam, I think a prefatory note in that regard and on how it relates to my prior and forthcoming works is necessary here since it will shed light on why I launched this study and how it is itself a moment in the trajectory of a broader research project.

The origin of this series on Omar Khayyam goes back to my graduate doctoral research in sociology resulting in a dissertation titled "Mysticism and Utopia: Towards the Sociology of Self-Knowledge and Human Architecture (A Study in Marx, Gurdjieff, and Mannheim)," which I deposited at Binghamton University (SUNY) in 2002. Even though engagement with Khayyam's works was not explicitly made in that dissertation beyond brief commentaries, it was during that research that I encountered Khayyam in an entirely new light.

There seemed to be a strange coincidence between my research findings and what I found newly meaningful about Khayyam's works and life, even though much about him remained understudied or misunderstood. My research was increasingly making clear in a deeper sense than before much that had been obscure and puzzling to me about Khayyam until then. Looking back, had I not been pressed with the need to complete my doctoral studies, and with a dissertation already growing too long at the time, I would have added a significant new part on the study of Khayyam to that work, and the dissertation subtitle would have then ended up including the name of

Khayyam, following those of Marx, Gurdjieff, and Mannheim.

My doctoral research had been basically about exploring why humanity has hitherto failed in bringing about a just global society. To pursue this research interest, which was simultaneously world-historical and biographically self-reflective in terms of exploring worldviews that had one way or another shaped my own thinking, I conducted an in-depth, comparative study of the works of three representatives—Karl Marx, George I. Gurdjieff, and Karl Mannheim—from the world's utopian, mystical, and social scientific traditions respectively. The study led to the insight that the mutual alienations of these traditions from one another (as part of their parent philosophical, religious, and scientific paradigms respectively) were key explanatory factors. These fragments of an otherwise unitary humanist search for a good life signified at a deeper level a substantive separation between the personal self and the broader social dimensions of human efforts at understanding and transforming human reality—itself rooted in a dualistic outlook that consciously and/or subconsciously, that is habitually, perpetuated these mutually alienating traditions and their parent paradigms.

To put this in more familiar terms, we often try to know and change the world, but do not understand and change our own selves and the role we personally play in shaping broader social life; or, conversely, we aim at knowing and changing ourselves personally but disregard the role played by broader social contexts in shaping our everyday lives. Moreover, the distinction itself signifies a dualism that has been consciously and/or subconsciously perpetuated for a long time through a simultaneously personal and mass hypnotic process, one that needs to be understood and transformed in its intricate socio-psychological complexity. It is as if we have fallen asleep to a personally and world-historically perpetuated dualistic way thinking, feeling, and sensing our selves and broader social world, one that consequently affects and fragments even the various efforts we make at understanding and changing that reality in personal and world-historical contexts.

Our inner fragmentations result in ways of knowing and changing that separate, in reductivist ways, the body, the mind, and feelings from one another personally, while our broader efforts at social transformation reductively separate economy, culture, and polity from one another. Both of these self and broader social tendencies are rooted in the same dualistic outlooks which shape and are in turn shaped by the fragmentation of human search for a good society into a philosophically perpetuated separation of religion and science—becoming manifested in the alienations of utopian, mystical, and social scientific paradigms from one another.

Utopians criticize mystics for being self-indulged and forgetting to change the larger social world while charging scientists for not being imaginative in seeking better worlds due to their subservience to a "realistic" attitude toward the world. Mystics charge utopians and scientists for seeking salvation or improvement in a world of inescapable suffering, a more or less unchangeable ground where calm or peace can be achieved at best only in inner/private personal and/or other worlds beyond. Scientists disparage both utopians and mystics for not being grounded in reality, not being "objectively realistic" in their understanding of the world. And yet, despite their failures, the traditions have accumulated wealth of knowledge and experience in their respective fields which remain fragmented and not adequately shared and integrated with one another because of their mutual alienations from and suspicions toward one another. Therefore, their contributions still remain unintegrated into a unitary approach that can show a way out of the status quo toward more liberating and just outcomes in inner and global human realities.

I concluded then that human liberation in favor of a just global society could not be a one-sided philosophical, religious, or scientific endeavor. The good society cannot result from the actions of a wise few from the above, divine intervention(s) from the beyond, or supposedly objective laws of motion of society and/in nature. It can only be the result of humanity's own *creative* activity, to advance which I proposed pursuing three overlapping projects that relate to one another in terms of whole-part dialectics:

1) The methodologically motivated project, *Human Architecture*, which involves a spatiotemporally conscious and intentional effort at rethinking and reconstructing methodological (along with their underlying ontological and epistemological) dualisms in favor of a nonreductive, creative dialectics of part and whole with particular attention paid to the role played by the human subconscious mind mediating conscious and unconscious realms of matter;

2) The theoretically motivated project, *the Sociology of Self-Knowledge*, which involves rethinking the dualistic notion of personal self and broader society in favor of a unitary conception that fosters a simultaneity of human efforts at self and broader social knowledge and change with a particular emphasis on recognizing the multiplicity of personal selves in the micro and the singularity of human world-history in the macro spheres;

3) The practically motivated project, *Utopystics (with a 'y')*, which involves critical and comparative fusing, in a simultaneously self-reflective and world-

historical framework, of the most valuable contributions of utopianism, mysticism, and social science—arising respectively from their parent philosophical, religious, and scientific paradigms—into a unified liberating paradigm that aims at bringing about change creatively, beginning from the intra/inter/extrapersonal here-and-now, and expanding to ever broader social spheres *always by own example*, that is, not through destructive antisystemic, but through constructive, creative, what I call "othersystemic," behavior.

In other words, human efforts at knowing and changing the world (beginning from personal and spreading to broader communities of selves) are directed at creative, conscious and intentional design and building of the alternative/desired reality in the here and now as the most effective way of transforming the status quo. In fact, I argued, if we look at major transitions in world-history from one social formation to another, we will find that their relative success had more to do with the gradual formation of the new formation amid the old reality for a long while, rather than through spending energies merely to overthrow the status quo overnight.

So long as we postpone seeking a better world because of being focused on antisystemic acts rather than building *othersystemic* realities—which take patient, creative, constructive, long-term, and self-determined efforts at building new social realities amid the everyday life and structures of the existing selves and societies—we would be engaging in a self-defeating movement. It is the goodness of the alternative order by its own example that offers, and should offer, the conditions for the withering away of the old order more or less on its own. And this applies not only to efforts at understanding and transforming macro social processes, but also to efforts at understanding and changing our own everyday intra/inter/extrapersonal realities. It is the apprehension and application of the simultaneity of self and broader social transformations that make the creative building of the new amid the old both possible and necessary.

In the efforts noted above, I argued, special attention must be paid to the problem of human subconscious habituation in personal (body, mind, and feelings) and social (economic, cultural, and political) realms, for which a working knowledge of self-, interpersonal, and mass hypnosis must be critically cultivated and used in ways that enable our understanding of how our own and others' personal and social habits are formed, and how they can be self-consciously and intentionally transformed beyond established habits in favor of desired outcomes. Understanding the nature of self-hypnosis (or, rather, self-dehypnosis, that is, self-awakening) and applying its techniques can empower us to always remain on guard against subconscious personal, small-group or large-group/institutional and habitual conditioning in favor of fostering human awakening in favor of personal and broader social critical thinking, freedom and self-determination. In pursuit of learning and practicing such techniques, critically learning, but also dehabituating, from the world's diverse meditative traditions play key parts in helping us find ways of understanding and transforming our personal self and social habituated structures of living in favor of personally and socially liberating outcomes.

It is important to note in considering the above that the proposition of *creativity* as a key explanatory and transformative factor in human liberation is not based on the rejection of the philosophical, religious, and scientific attitudes per se, but on the rejection of their disciplinary and cultural *fragmentations*, without and within. On the contrary, the effort aims at creatively uniting the rational and useful elements of these approaches and the best they have contributed to a unitary process reconceived in terms of the dialectics of wholes and parts. The point is to pursue creativity within and across philosophy, religion, and science by designing and building integrative paradigms that transcend the subconsciously rigidified fragmentations of these traditions. Neither one nor another of the philosophical, religious, or scientific attitudes, nor their utopian, mystical, or social scientific expressions, alone, can offer a solution to the human problem, since the answer lies in the *integration and unification* of their most rational elements into new syntheses uniting the otherwise inseparable parts of the human creative, artistic, attitude.

I therefore argued that the just global society would not be a result of either a philosophical, or a religious, or a scientific breakthrough. It will be an *artistic* breakthrough, through the *creative act*, in the process of which the best of human philosophical, religious, and scientific achievements can and should be integrated. Whether it will be achieved or not is not preordained in ideas, faiths, or facts. Its realization, if at all possible, depends on human willful, creative, artistic, effort. It may succeed, or it may not. If the creative act succeeds in bringing about and maintaining a just global society, then we may regard it as being simultaneously the wisest, the highest spiritual, and the greatest human scientific achievement. A creative approach that fosters nondualistic wisdom in favor of a just global society as being achievable by all and not just a few, a religiosity that considers self-determining human agency to create a good life to be what a divine power intended by its creative act, a scientific approach that includes humanity as a part of nature and thus its powers as the agency responsible for bringing about a good life, would be appreciatively open to integrating their pathways to better life, instead of fragmenting them by way of pursuing their own either/or based strategies.

The more I explored the explanatory value of the above overall thesis during my doctoral research, the more I found its echoes in Omar Khayyam's life and works. If Marx, Gurdjieff, and Mannheim represented respectively the one-sided human efforts in utopian, mystical, and social scientific liberation, Khayyam increasingly represented to me an integrative effort at overcoming mutually alienating traditions of utopianism, mysticism, and science as described above. However, the exploration of this three-fold representation required further research in the deep structures of Khayyam's attributed texts amid wider Khayyami studies, one which I decided to undertake more systematically following my doctoral studies.

This continuing research interest was reflected in my decision to establish, immediately following graduation in 2002, my personal research center OKCIR: Omar Khayyam Center for Integrative Research in Utopia, Mysticism, and Science (Utopystics)—one which has since been accessible online at www.okcir.com—and to launch its independent research and pedagogical journal, *Human Architecture: Journal of the Sociology of Self-Knowledge*, thirteen volumes (31 issues) of which have been published to date from 2002 to 2020 (also accessible at the same site). The interests fueling the issues of *Human Architecture* represented the ways I continued to pursue the overall research project as outlined above.

The first two of what would have been the four parts that comprised my doctoral dissertation (three associated with Marx, Gurdjieff, and Mannheim, and the fourth involving my alternative effort at building a unitary conceptual framework, to which I would have associated the works of Khayyam but did not due to limitations of time) were subsequently updated and published separately under the titles *Advancing Utopistics: The Three Component Parts and Errors of Marxism* (Routledge/Paradigm, 2007), and *Gurdjieff and Hypnosis: A Hermeneutic Study* (Palgrave Macmillan 2009).

My plan for publishing the third leg on Karl Mannheim of the intended works, however, was subjected to more prolonged rethinking and updating in relation to my new research on and teaching interests in C. Wright Mills's work on the sociological imagination. This involved writing and publishing new material (as various articles or chapters) in my areas of research and teaching interests during an academic career that resulted in my tenure and promotion as an associate professor of sociology at UMass Boston in 2009.

It was during this period of active rethinking of my work in relation to Mannheim and Mills that my notions of quantum sociology and quantum sociological imagination also emerged. Over the years, I came to regard human architecture, the sociology of self-knowledge, and utopystics as the methodological, theoretical, and historical-practical components of what I now called the quantum sociological imagination as an umbrella concept framing my alternative sociological perspective.

I had originally planned on publishing the third part of the works (on Mannheim and Mills) as described above before moving on to the present series on Khayyam as its fourth leg. But I now found myself increasingly engaged in two closely interrelated projects, one in Khayyami studies and another on further understanding more deeply the relevance of relativistic and quantum scientific findings for further cultivating the sociological imagination. In other words, to pursue my Khayyami studies I had to advance more deeply into the methodological grounds of quantum sociological imagination, and to pursue the latter, the study of Khayyam's works and life itself proved and served as empirically and theoretically illustrative and instructive.

It was amid such a fruitful dialectical back and forth between the two lines of inquiry that I found myself in the unenviable position of having to confront an elephant in the room, so to speak, that is, the so-called quantum enigma—needing to resolve, at least to my own satisfaction, the decades-long, nearly a century-old, puzzle.

The latter I was happy to achieve in the course of inquiry and writing over several years, resulting in the recently published first volume, subtitled *Unriddling the Quantum Enigma*, of the series titled *Liberating Sociology: From Newtonian Toward Quantum Imagination* (2020), which will serve as a basis for critically building further on Mannheim's and Mills's sociological contributions in later volumes of that series. The full details of my findings in that work can be obtained by consulting the book itself, but parts of it were will be synoptically relayed in an applied way in the present series in Khayyami studies to illuminate its methodological usefulness.

As far as the quantum sociological imagination framing the overall method of hermeneutic textual analysis applied in this study on Khayyam is concerned, therefore, I regard this overall series on Khayyam as a practical arena for its introduction and further development in an inductive and applied way, and for demonstrating its usefulness by the actual results it can achieve as an approach in sociological analysis. I do not intend to dwell too deeply in the exposition of this approach in this series beyond what I present in this book and its application throughout the *Omar Khayyam's Secret* series. The reasons are three-fold.

First, important groundwork for this approach have already been laid in previous writings, especially in detail in *Unriddling the Quantum Enigma* (2020); second, some elements are newly developed and thus demonstrated in a practical way in the course of the present series on Khayyam; and, third, I plan on retrospectively exploring further the quantum sociological imagination (as a basis for the hermeneutic method applied in this study) in future volumes of the *Liberating Sociology* series, planned for publication following the release of the present twelve-book series on Khayyam.

Instead of providing an overly general road map for the contents of the later books of this series on Khayyam, I will let the exploration itself chart their path, an approach that will be itself further elaborated upon in the chapters to follow in this first book.

Abstract

This essay, titled "Preface to the Series: Origins of This Study," is a common preface to the twelve-book series, *Omar Khayyam's Secret: Hermeneutics of the Robaiyat in Quantum Sociological Imagination,* authored by Mohammad H. Tamdgidi, included in its first book subtitled *New Khayyami Studies: Quantumizing the Newtonian Structures of C. Wright Mills's Sociological Imagination for A New Hermeneutic Method.* This preface serves to shed light on why the author launched this series on Omar Khayyam and how it is itself a moment in the trajectory of a broader research project. The origin of the series on Khayyam goes back to the Tamdgidi's graduate doctoral research in sociology resulting in a dissertation titled "Mysticism and Utopia: Towards the Sociology of Self-Knowledge and Human Architecture (A Study in Marx, Gurdjieff, and Mannheim)" (2002).

The more he explored the explanatory value of the overall thesis during his doctoral research, the more he found its echoes in Omar Khayyam's life and works. If Marx, Gurdjieff, and Mannheim represented respectively the one-sided human efforts in utopian, mystical, and social scientific liberation, Khayyam increasingly represented to him an integrative effort at overcoming mutually alienating traditions of utopianism, mysticism, and science as described above. However, the exploration of such a three-fold representation required further research in the deep structures of Khayyam's attributed texts amid wider Khayyami studies, one which he decided to undertake more systematically following his doctoral studies, resulting in the establishment of a research center in Khayyam's name and its scholarly journal and publications. Following the publication of three books on Karl Marx (2007), G. I. Gurdjieff (2009), and a transdisciplinary study in Karl Mannheim and the sociology of scientific knowledge of the quantum enigma (2020), the author's continuing interests in reinventing C. Wright Mills in favor of a quantum sociological imagination are explored in this series on Khayyam's life and works, serving as both exploratory and applied contexts.

Introduction to the Series: The Enigmatic Omar Khayyam and the Impasse of Khayyami Studies

... in the entire world and regions of its inhabited quarter
I did not see anyone, anywhere, like him ...

— Nezami Arouzi, *Chahar Maqaleh* (*Four Discourses*),
c. mid-12th century AD

Nearly a thousand years after his birth, the life and works of the enigmatic Omar Khayyam are still wrapped deeply in veil, major puzzles about him still abound, and modern Khayyami studies in Iran and abroad, after nearly two centuries of active research, have grounded to a halt, reaching an impasse.

Here we have a man whose fame has reached the highest peaks of world culture for his attributed Robaiyat (quatrains), yet his authorship of most, even all of them, some say, are increasingly in doubt.

Here is a poet—perhaps more famed, (re)translated, and published than any other—to whom no surviving accounts by his living contemporaries reportedly refer as a poet, nor do they cite any robai (quatrain) as his. Yet, starting from just decades after his passing, an increasing number of quatrains gradually, and then in the last two centuries increasingly, became attributed to him. Meanwhile, no manuscripts of any robais directly written, or attributed to have been directly written, by him have been found or claimed by others to have been read or seen.

Here we have a man who in his own writings clearly refers to Avicenna (or Ibn Sina, d. AD 1037), the major philosopher and physician of the medieval period, as his teacher with whom he had personal conversations; yet, the various prevalent dates of birth attributed to Khayyam today render such a personal association to be impossible by age.

In fact, Khayyam's dates of birth and passing are themselves still in doubt even though some believe they have been conclusively determined by way of careful considerations of his reported birth horoscope, whose results some claim to have passed precise calculations by modern astronomers. Yet, seemingly unconvinced, many scholars or sources still continue to offer a variety of other dates for both his birth and his passing.

Here is a man whom a famed biographical commentator (who met the old Khayyam as a young child, not as an adult) characterized posthumously as having been miserly in writing, setting a trend in time for others to repeat the same judgment about Khayyam as a taken-for-granted, undisputed fact. Yet, the same commentator starting such a trend failed to mention, in the *same* account offering that judgment, many works that we definitively know Khayyam *did* write and *have* reached us, including his path-breaking work on algebra indisputably authored by him.

The same commentator referred to Khayyam as having been miserly in teaching (again, as if a matter of fact), yet that very commentator himself listed many others in his *same* biographical compendium as having been Khayyam's students. This is not to mention other, grown-up, contemporaries (such as the author Nezami Arouzi whose quote epigraphs this introduction) who proudly acknowledged Khayyam to have been like a teacher to them.

Here is a man who was characterized by the same commentator to have had an angry temperament, and, yet, the same Khayyam is world-renowned for having composed the tenderest quatrains about human life and death, beauty and love, roses and gardens, the passing of time, the stars, and God. In fact, the *same* commentator reported in the *same* entry how an old Khayyam during a meeting with him as a child gently tested (as presumably kind teachers do) his knowledge of poetry and geometry and used the teaching moment as an opportunity to tenderly praise and encourage the child in the presence of the child's father.

Here is a man who was reported to have played a leading role as a member of a team of astronomers commissioned by Soltan Malekshah (of the Turkic Seljuk dynasty) and his famous Persian minister, Nezam ol-Molk, to build an observatory in Isfahan and to reform the Persian calendar so that

Nowrooz (the first celebratory day of the new Persian solar year) could fall again on the first day of Spring. But, the projects having been reportedly left incomplete due to political intrigues resulting in the assassination of the minister and the death of the king suspiciously happening shortly thereafter, nothing substantial is said to have remained of either activities to corroborate the reports, except for a single ephemeris page about some fixed stars. And yet, ironically, Khayyam's authorship of a major literary work written in a most lucid and exemplary Persian, actually bearing his name and not claimed by or for anyone else, commonly titled today as *Nowrooznameh* (*The Book on Nowrooz*), has been doubted and often ignored by some Khayyami scholars, having remained untranslated into English or other languages to this day.

The book is a literary work on the traditions and symbolisms of the Iranian New Year celebration, in the introduction of which the author at some point advises a new king (presumably a young son of the then late Soltan Malekshah) to finish the observatory project that remained incomplete by his father. The book itself, of course, is also a reminder of the tradition of the Persian New Year celebration, Nowrooz (meaning "New Day" or "New Times"), associated with the (also left incomplete) calendar reform project—a feast mentioned in some extant quatrains attributed to Khayyam.

Here is, allegedly, a global symbol of hedonism, wine-drinking excess, and questioning of faith, who was called in his own time an "Imam," a religious leader, titled Ghiaseddin ("Refuge of Faith")—one regarded as a unique and incomparable Muslim sage, who reportedly surprised even distinguished orthodox Muslim scholars of his time with his vast knowledge of the Qoran, and one who reportedly died while fasting and praying to God.

And yet, this is the same man known as the author of those Robaiyat attributed to him, their authenticity disputed, wherein wine and wine-drinking are cherished in the highest regard, wherein fasting and praying are at times subjected to critical poetic wit and sarcasm.

Here is a man who was called "The Philosopher of the East and the West" and praised in the highest regard as a man of unique wisdom in his own time. Yet, his few surviving philosophical writings are still left either unexamined, little understood, or simply dismissed by some as offering nothing new.

We have a man who became world-famous more for having written a few quatrains, still not yet firmly attributable to him, allegedly composed in his spare time, than for authoring major pioneering works in mathematics and geometry. Here is a man who, as an astronomer, presumably still in his twenties (if the existing, still doubtful estimates of his birth date are supposed to be correct), was responsible as the leader of a select team of astronomers more senior to him for calculating a solar calendar that still remains—to a day in every five thousand years—more accurate than the Gregorian Christian calendar used today in the West.

Here is a man who said in his own writings that the Sufi way is the best of four paths in search of God's truths (the other three being those of the orthodox theologians, the philosophers, and the Shia Ismailis, the latter of whom he must have taken seriously enough as a scholar to be included in his list as an intellectual trend than just an extremist resistance group). Yet, some of the quatrains attributed to him do not spare the Sufis (among others) from the sharpness of his critical tongue—leading some Sufis coming after him, including the famous fellow Neyshabourian, the poet Farideddin Attar (d. AD 1221), the author of the famous *Manteqotteir (Conference of the Birds)*, to consult what we may call today a psychic to visit Khayyam's plot so as to poetically portray him in his grave as a spiritually incomplete seeker.

This is a man who was reportedly chastised, also as an "incomplete Muslim," by Shams-e Tabrizi, the infatuating Sufi master and idol of Molana Jalaleddin Rumi (d. AD 1273), the now world-renowned Sufi poet who lived about a century and a half after Khayyam's passing. Still, most specialists have no doubt about the significant extent to which the Persian poetry of Hafez Shirazi (d. AD 1390), the undisputed master of Persian classical poetry living a generation after Rumi, is in substance and poetic tropes heavily indebted to Khayyam and his attributed Robaiyat.

Here is a man who had a problem with believing that to know God one has to follow "the one who knows," so to speak, a creed he attributes to the Shia Ismailis, yet he is regarded and praised as if a blind "follower" of Avicenna, being called the Avicenna of his own time and generation. Yet, this is the same man who himself apparently did not spare even philosophers from his criticism and declared, in an attributed robai adorning today his present-day tomb's tile work, that the foe is wrong to call him a philosopher.

And yet, here is a man reportedly reading the chapter "On the One and the Many" in the philosopher Avicenna's book *Shafa (Healing)* before pausing to put his golden tooth-pick on that specific chapter's starting page, inviting those he "trusted" to give his last, presumably secret, will.

Again, consider this: about a man whose life and simple dates of birth (and even of passing, according to some) have remained in doubt for nearly a thousand years, we know exactly what specific book he was reading, which chapter, which page, and that he marked it with a golden toothpick, before calling in his most trusted to urgently offer his "last will" and instructions, following which we are told he rose to pray and fast ("not eat and drink"). Still, some Western scholars have claimed that Khayyam was an unknown man in his own culture and land, and that they themselves are to be applauded instead for "discovering" him. And, even so, their "discovery" is based almost entirely on the oldest manuscripts, reports, and stories the people of Khayyam's *own* land have passed on through the centuries.

Here is a man about whom an Iranian writer in early twentieth century wrote that if we allow a hundred-year-old man to change his views a few times a day for his entire life, we would still not be able to account for the variety of seemingly conflicting and contradictory views, feelings, and expressions found across the Robaiyat attributed to Khayyam.

A man praised for an uncompromising integrity and independent-mindedness by many is also thought to have written letters or treatises that, others claim, cannot be relied on for understanding his true views since they may have been written to please his intended reader(s) for one favor or another, or in fear for his life. In other words, a man who himself (in the introduction to his major work on algebra) bitterly criticizes others in his time for being duplicitous, is regarded as having written his treatises duplicitously, i.e., not really meaning what he wrote at times.

Here is a man who allegedly embarked, according to a report by an observer long after Khayyam's passing, on a hurried pilgrimage to Mecca to prove his faith in fear of his life, and on the way, while stationed in Baghdad, allegedly avoided opening his door to Sufi seekers, again in fear for his life. Yet, the same man is reported to be quite peacefully enjoying a joyful gathering around that time in a meeting in Balkh, remaining still highly esteemed, as reported by writers and biographers.

This is a man who believed the Sufi path to be the best of four he lists in his writings, and, yet, about him a Sufi wrote later that he composed poems that were on the surface attractive to believers but in meaning poisonous "like snake-bites" to their religious faith.

And yet, here is a man who reportedly on his last day, reading Avicenna's book, gave his last will, began fasting and praying, and uttered his last words, presumably loudly enough for others to hear as if leaving his most important statement of will and legacy for his posterity: "O God! Thou Know that I have tried to understand Thee to the best of my ability. Forgive me, since my knowledge of Thee is my only path to Thee."

In light of the above puzzles surrounding the life and works of Omar Khayyam, I invite readers to ask why they may not consider what *they themselves already know* about Khayyam to be based on one or another myth.

Ever since Edward FitzGerald published his "free translations" in the mid-nineteenth century West of some of the "Rubaiyat" attributed to Omar Khayyam, many controversies have arisen about the historical Khayyam, about who he was, what he believed in, how he lived, and what he said, thought, or felt.

FitzGerald's contribution certainly had the result of making Khayyam world-famous, but questions still remain as to whether, first, it was FitzGerald who became world-famous because of Khayyam, and, second, that the Khayyam made famous by FitzGerald truly represents the actual historical Omar Khayyam. Was FitzGerald's a final, authentic portrayal of the historical Khayyam, or was his portrayal itself just another myth like many others from the past—this one coming from the West going through a particular period of its own history, about a man who was a famed Eastern public intellectual about whom myths, favorable or not, had already been made even before he died, and certainly for centuries after his passing?

Even the Khayyams known as such in Iran may also be myths—and I do mean to use the word "Khayyams" in plural. Some writers, based on their own interpretations of what the attributed Robaiyat meant, or which were "permissible" (to their own beliefs or to the powers or authorities of the time) to be included among the authentic quatrains and which not, decided a few decades ago that only about one hundred seventy eight or so of the attributed Robaiyat were worth his stature, discarding the rest attributed to him for being not worthy of him. The Western Orientalist portrayals of Khayyam, especially fueled by the FitzGeraldian "free translations" of his selected quatrains, were thus met with the occidentalist reactions from Khayyam's own homeland, resulting in the dismissal of whatever was deemed problematic for attribution to Khayyam in the name of seeking an "authentic" understanding of him.

The numbers of permissible Robaiyat were thus reduced from more than a thousand to a hundred and then, for some, to a handful, or even nil. His *Nowrooznameh (The Book on Nowrooz)* was readily dismissed as being suspicious regarding its authorship. His philosophical treaties were treated as being unreliable and written by a public persona in him to please this or that recipient of the letter or treatise, or in fear of his life, and thus not worthy of serious attention—the accusation of duplicity, intended as such or not, being all the more surprising (as I noted earlier) since it often came from the same observers who otherwise spared no opportunity to stress the integrity of Khayyam's personality living in troubled times. This is not to even mention how Khayyam, in a widely quoted and indisputably attributed passage in his world-famous treatise on algebra, himself severely chastises those around him who practice duplicity in the name of science.

So, we ended up with a situation where some manuscripts attributed to Khayyam became summarily dismissed in an *a priori* fashion without even a serious study of the texts themselves, before even considering why and how or whether they are authentic or not. The irony of an ever increasing world fame for Khayyam and an ever increasing evaporation of historical records about him (including his own attributed texts) that are worthy of scholarly investigation is quite paradoxical, if not amusing. It seems the violent social upheavals, catastrophic nomadic invasions, and repeated natural calamities such as devastating earthquakes, not even considering the biases and habits of the copyists and compilers of his works, or the misreading or misinterpretations of them by their contemporaries, were insufficient to deprive us of even the limited historical records available about Khayyam's life and works; now, we have to add our own subjective scholarly reservations, in fear of being branded "unscholarly" (caught amid an absurdly counter-scientific, publish-or-perish tenure-seeking culture or duplicity promoting academic "peer review" practices) to the extent of dismissing even the minimal material we have at hand for the study of Khayyam.

And yet, most of our modern "peer-reviewed" scholarships on Khayyam—amid an academic culture that still stigmatizes anything "self-published"—continue to thrive (as is the case for many ancient or even modern classics) on a series of often recycled discourses on FitzGerald's (not Khayyam's own) now world-renowned, originally *self-published* and famously-ignored-for-a-while and initially-considered-not-worth-a-penny, "Rubaiyat."

Occidentalist reservations about Khayyam's texts from Iran and the East are flip sides of the coins of Orientalist embracing of him originating in the West, both of them engaging in myth-makings about Khayyam without studying seriously the wide variety of textual materials that alone can provide a scholarly way out of the labyrinth of our ignorance about the historical Khayyam. His attributed *Nowrooznameh* dismissed and his philosophical treatises relegated to appendices, we still hold on to a circular mode of reasoning to draw an authentic Khayyam rabbit out of our magical hats full of cherry-picked robais whose authorship by him we still claim to doubt.

A school of Khayyamian thinking is then proposed by relying on quatrains that the proposers themselves elsewhere in the same book or text regard as not having been proven to be from Khayyam. Khayyam's own attributed texts are then selectively dismissed or embraced in the name of scientific and scholarly understandings of him while minute tales are told about Khayyam's childhood or growing up that no one knows where they have been plucked from.

Acknowledging that not only others', but also our own, knowledges of Khayyam are myths—that they are socially and historically constructed stories about him—can be a good beginning in the true Khayyami spirit of the term founded on healthy skepticism. Doubting what we know about him in a radical way can be a helpful starting point about gaining and developing new understandings of his life, works, and legacy. It may be that we end up constructing new myths about him, but at least we would be doing so based on more reliable studies, being aware of the social constructedness of our own knowledges or myths about him, and based on efforts that do not pretend to contrast the presumed truths on our parts with lesser-valued myths constructed by others.

It is only then that true efforts at building more reasonable and textually reliable accounts about Omar Khayyam can be made.

The trouble with any hurried attempts at offering any glimpses of Khayyam's life and works may be itself illustrated by our reaction to how I present him on the book cover or in the front matter descriptions of this book itself. Let me restate it again here.

My central purpose in the series *Omar Khayyam's Secret* is to share the results of my research on Omar Khayyam, the enigmatic 11th/12th centuries Persian Muslim sage, philosopher, astronomer, mathematician, physician, writer, and poet from Neyshabour, Iran. My aim is to find definitive answers to a number of longstanding puzzles about Khayyam especially surrounding the existence, nature, and purpose of the Robaiyat in his life and works. To explore the questions posed in the series, I apply a new hermeneutic method of textual analysis, informed by what I call the quantum sociological imagination, to comprehensively gather and study all the attributed philosophical, religious, scientific, and literary writings of Khayyam.

The above statements may seem to offer a straightforward, general portrayal of Omar Khayyam—who he was, and what he did. However, many aspects of the description will likely be questioned or disputed by one or another Khayyam scholar or enthusiast today.

To begin with, his very name may be disputed, as some may rather render it as "al-Khayyam" or "al-Khayyami" in English in order to highlight his life and contributions as part of the Arab culture. After all, they may argue, that is how Khayyam's name appeared in some of his authentic or attributed treatises written in Arabic.

For that reason, some may even question the Persian or broader Iranian ethnic origins of Khayyam's ancestry; after all, they may say, Omar is an Arab name associated with the second Caliph of Islam responsible for leading the Arab conquest of Iran, one who is moreover revered more in the Sunni rather than in the Shia branch of Islam prevalent in Iran today—that the name "al-Khayyami" is associated with Arab tribes involved in tent-making as a trade, which the word "Khayyam" denotes in Arabic, who may have migrated to Iran and its Khorasan region following the Arab conquest of Iran.

In his biographical entry on Khayyam in his *Tatemmat Sewan el-Hekmat (Supplement to the Chest of Wisdom)*, Zahireddin Abolhasan Beyhaqi, the commentator I referred to earlier, begins by stating that Khayyam was born in Neyshabour and came from generations of Neyshabouris. But, those who may wish to pursue any of the arguments above in order to culturally appropriate Khayyam's legacy for the Arabs may still find a way of arguing that being from Neyshabour does not necessarily imply not being ethnically or ancestrally Arab. It seems the Arab desire to appropriate the legacy of Khayyam and marginalize his Persian identity has become today particularly acute amid the politically charged milieu of the Middle East, especially among those wishing to turn the "Persian Gulf" into the "Arabian Gulf." And the seemingly halted Khayyami studies have provided a fertile ground for what Iranians consider to be unreflective and misguided cultural appropriations.

Of course, in response, others may note that writing treatises in Arabic was a common philosophical, religious and scientific practice following the spread of Islam which had by then taken place in the wider region for centuries. However, we should note—even if we lay aside, for instance, the controversies regarding the authorship of the Robaiyat or the *Nowrooznameh*—that Khayyam also indisputably wrote an important philosophical treatise, *Resaleh dar Kolliyat-e Vojood (Treatise on the Universals of Existence)*, in Persian, one which he himself regarded in its introduction to be despite its brevity worth "more than volumes." He was also invited at the height of his career as an astronomer in Isfahan to interpretively translate an important sermon by Avicenna from Arabic into Persian.

It should not take a nuclear physicist, or a fuzzy-thinking mathematician, nor an academic, to realize that writing in Arabic does not make an author an Arab. My writing this book in English does not make me any less a person of Persian, Azeri, or Iranian descent. Nor does my name being "Mohammad" or "Hossein," or even "Tamdgidi" (or Tamjidi)—names that are actually Arabic in origin—make me an Arab or ethnically any less Persian, Azeri, or Iranian. But then, one can be an ethnic Arab *and* an Iranian (and/or Persian, and/or Kurd, and/or Turkoman, and/or Lur, and/or Azeri, and so on, by intermarriage). There are in fact, even today when we have more defined national borders, Iranians who are of Arab ethnic origin, making the borderlands of being Iranian and Arab and/or Azeri (or any other of many ethnicities comprising the Iranian population) rather fuzzy. So, back then, a thousand years ago, when borders were even much less defined, ethnic distinctions did not necessarily imply more of an association with a distant culture than to a local one simply because of the names given to persons.

To the above, of course, one can add that there is clearly no data indicating the presence or lack thereof intermixing with the local population of the supposed Khayyami Arab tribes arriving in Khorasan, as far as Khayyam's specific family tree is concerned. So, any simplistic association of a broader tribal identity with a particular person's ethnic mix would be quite speculative. Nor does being associated with "tent-making" by name make a person one of Arab ethnic origin. In fact, the Seljuks, whose leaders dominated Iran as a colonial power during much of Khayyam's life, were known to rise from tent-dwelling nomads, so even if there is any association to be made to an ethnicity by way of "tent-making," being nomadic of the Turkic background can also be a probability to entertain. But, Khayyam was not Turkic in ethnic origin, so far as we know, even though some who cared to pass on his legacy were Azeri, one being Yar Ahmad Rashidi Tabrizi, the author and compiler of a major old Khayyami Robaiyat collection, *Tarabkhaneh (House of Joy)*.

Besides, even setting aside the Arabic context in which some of Khayyam's treatises were written and name rendered, just because the prefix "al-" is used in the name does not imply an Arab identity; after all, in the same texts, the prefix also appears before the name "Neyshabour" (also rendered then as "Nisabur" in old texts especially when written in Arabic) which is actually an Arabized version of Nishapoor (given the lack of the letter 'p' in Arabic alphabet), amid the usual rendering of Khayyam's name in old manuscripts.

The name of Neyshabour, in Iran's Khorasan, is derived from the name of Sasanian Persian king "Shapoor" (or Shahpur, literally meaning "son of the king") that is clearly referent to a pre-Islamic, Persian culture and etymology. Perhaps it is only in the mind of the Arab appropriators of Omar Khayyam that Khayyam's "al-" makes al-Khayyami an Arab as much as it makes al-Neyshabour an Arabian city. Of course, it is convenient trying to appropriate an intellectual legacy by adding an "al-" to a scholar's name when publishing materials in English (or French) about him, but that would not be becoming of scholarships open to sociological awareness of the delicate nuances of how specific persons' and peoples' ethnic and cultural identities are socially constructed and reconstructed in concrete geohistorical contexts.

The part of my statement referring to the two centuries across which Khayyam lived is obviously a compromise at this starting point of our study, on not delving into the exact dates of when he was born and when he died. The differences of opinion still linger today regarding the dates, and the dates are not merely minor details for the study of Khayyam's life and works. They may have substantive implications about whom he met, what he learned, what he wrote, and what he did.

While some consensus was reached a while ago, following the study by the Indian scholar Swāmi Govinda Tīrtha in his *The Nectar of Grace: Omar Khayyām's Life and Works* (1941), regarding the year AD 1048 as Khayyam's birth year, this is still by no means a final and generally accepted fact today. The birth dates across many serious or unserious chronicles have ranged from AD 1019 (or even earlier) to 1050, and Khayyam's date of passing has ranged from AD 1120 (or even earlier) to AD 1131 (or even later).

A consequence of this has been the casting of serious doubts, for instance, on the possibility of Khayyam's personally meeting, or having live discussions as a student of, Avicenna (d. AD 1037) despite a statement in Khayyam's own treatise *Resalat fi al-Kown wa al-Taklif (Treatise on the Created World and the Duty to Worship)* clearly conveying such a possibility. And of course the much fabled story of Khayyam's having been childhood, blood-vowing friends with young Nezam ol-Molk and Hasan Sabbah (the famed future leader of the Nezari Ismaili sect) is no longer regarded as having any merits because, it is nowadays claimed, a Khayyam who could be schoolmate with a young Nezam ol-Molk born in AD 1018 (408, Lunar Hejri, or LH), would be about 113 solar years old, say, in AD 1131 (526 LH, which some regard today as Khayyam's date of passing since they have come to assume his having been born in AD 1048), and still older (117) if considered in shorter, lunar years.

Was Khayyam an "enigmatic" figure?

Well, it depends on whom you ask.

Whether or not Khayyam was enigmatic has been disputed since some scholars wonder today whether there were actually other persons similarly named with whom the famed Robaiyat can be associated, such that the philosopher or astronomer-mathematician Khayyam may not have been the same poet of the famed quatrains. So, their argument goes, Khayyam was a straightforward, albeit brilliant, mathematician and there is nothing enigmatic about that. The enigma has arisen, they say, due to the possibility that other persons with similar names or anonymously wrote the poems—driven by one or another noble or ignoble motivation—that have now become world-famous (thanks to Edward FitzGerald) and these poems have thus been wrongly associated with Khayyam the mathematician and/or astronomer.

The attribution of poetry-writing to the scientist Khayyam, they argue, is still unverified (actually, despite otherwise reliable historical evidence that in fact offer solid second-hand proofs to the claim that he composed at least some of the famed lines); so, in their view, until it is proven otherwise, we should lay aside all such complications and implied enigmas and puzzles regarding the Robaiyat, their nature, and their true authorship, from the life and works of the astronomer-mathematician Khayyam and let others pursue their own disciplinary research on the poet Khayyam(s) as a "separate" topic of its own. Now, they say, we should just be content with regarding the historical Khayyam as the one who wrote the treatises on algebra and Euclid, who perhaps also philosophized a bit or pursued astronomy to some extent or wrote some Arabic (and a few Persian) poems in his spare time. Disciplinarity indeed can make things a lot easier, helping us avoid difficult questions by postponing them to others', if not our own, tomorrows. Yet, we allow ourselves to draw conclusions about or cast doubts on the attributions nonetheless.

What about Khayyam having been a philosopher in relation to or independently of the disputed Robaiyat?

Some scholars may in fact question characterizing one or another of the above-mentioned Khayyams as a philosopher since, except for a few short treatises and writings, they say, not much has survived to shed significant light on any distinctive school of thinking Khayyam may have professed or developed during his lifetime, other than those of Avicenna whom he is known to have read and taught.

Some more inclined to regard the famed mathematician as an occasional robai poet (who also wrote a few poems in other Persian styles of poetry, or in Arabic also, they marginally acknowledge), or those who may entertain the idea that Khayyam the philosopher is the same Khayyam who also wrote some of the attributed Robaiyat may even argue that Khayyam himself would disavow being characterized as a philosopher; after all, as noted earlier, in a famously attributed quatrain handed down through the centuries, Khayyam states that the foe is in error when regarding him as a philosopher. Or, they may note that elsewhere, in a concluding section of his *Resaleh dar Kolliyat-e Vojood (Treatise on the Universals of Existence)*, Khayyam clearly distinguished his own way of seeking to know God from that of philosophers (alongside other groups) who in his view had erred in their practice of logic.

I used the word "Muslim" in my introductory statement realizing that it provokes further controversies among the Western, particularly perhaps also Islamophobic, audiences today—not to mention among those critical of Islam in Iran and the Middle East as well. How can their cherished skeptic wine-drinker be a Muslim, they may sarcastically think?

Historical records and the authentic (and attributed) texts about and from Khayyam clearly corroborate that he lived a Muslim and died a Muslim. You will find many occasions in his own texts (when also introduced as such by copyists or his contemporaries) where Khayyam's name is preceded by the title Imam, indicating high regard of him as also a religious and spiritual leader of his time, at least by those more favorably inclined toward him. Khayyam himself, in his indisputably attributed philosophical writings, strongly eschews giving in to base bodily desires, and in an indisputably authentic passage introducing his path-breaking work on algebra, strongly condemns those who, in the name of science, sell out such pursuits in favor of base material interests.

Unless one regards Khayyam as a duplicitous liar, one should note that his own authentic scientific writings always begin and end with the most sincere and heart-felt remembering of God and his prophet(s). For the Islamophobes who regard Islam as a monolith and not capable of accommodating critical, self-critical, and diverse voices within itself, such as those found in Khayyam, it may seem paradoxical that the celebrated author of the Robaiyat, particularly in the FitzGeraldian "free translations" and interpretations of the "Rubaiyat," would have been called an Imam during his own lifetime and thereafter. In the prevalent binary myths particularly arising from the West, he is supposed to be either a heavy wine-drinker, or a skeptic that has in private renounced his belief in God or Islam, and just cleverly (or in fear) pretends in public to be a believer.

But then, Khayyam's portrayals in the most Orientalist images widespread in media are most illustrative of the Islamophilic ways the contributions of serious Islamic intellectuals and contributions are dismissed and marginalized in the eyes of the colonizing culture.

As I have explored elsewhere (2012), Islamophobia and Islamophilia are two sides of the same coin of imperial and colonial efforts in diminishing and marginalizing subaltern cultural traditions and voices. One does it by portraying a whole tradition as being fear-mongering and terroristic, another does it by cherishing it as a tradition with beautiful arts or artifacts devoid of serious critical intellectual content and anti-colonial orientation.

But when the tradition offers deep and serious critical as well as self-critical voices, such as those found in and attributed to Khayyam, they are cleverly sculpted out of their Islamic and Eastern contexts, presenting them as "deviant" or "exceptional" trends that have more affinity with a supposedly higher Western culture than their "backward" Eastern backdrop. Khayyam must have been a "materialist," a "secularist," a "non-believer," an "epicurean," and not a true Muslim, they say. So, the result is, obviously, a self-fulfilling prophecy in which anything self/critically-minded or innovating from a tradition such as Islam is sculpted out to leave the rest as what they wish to portray it to be.

But, then, such ways of dismissing and marginalizing an innovative intellect is not a modern, Western, invention. As all cultures and historical contexts are complex ensembles of different, divergent, and at times divisive and antagonistic voices, a notion that is absent in all simplistic, Islamophobic and Islamophilic, portrayals of Islam itself, efforts at diminishing and marginalizing Khayyam's life and works also had their homegrown sources.

As I noted earlier, even a century after his passing we find the fellow Neyshabourian, the famous Sufi poet Farideddin Attar, writing a poem specifically about how he supposedly took a "seer" (one whom today we may call a psychic medium) to Khayyam's grave so he could report on the "incomplete" spirit of the one buried below in the grave—being not worthy, by implication, of his Muslim faith, fame, and titles.

Or, also noted earlier, another observer writes later how Khayyam, out of fear (and allegedly not of true faith, if he actually did so) made a pilgrimage to Mecca to demonstrate his Muslim faith despite having written poems that "like snake-bites" eat at the roots (in this case, apparently the accuser's own interpretation) of Islam.

And yet, one can find ample textual evidence that Khayyam was a Muslim who was independently sympathetic toward Sufi epistemology and meditative techniques of self-purification (and, a past historical commentator interestingly notes, spiritually self-purifying "bodily exercises"), but not necessarily belonging formally to any of its sects, and who had a critical, scientific, and philosophical (and, as we shall explore, literary and poetic) mind, despite the efforts of those in the Orientalist West (or Occidentalist East) wishing to advance and build an unbeliever's mythology out of him—at times by fabricating completely odd and irrelevant translations of his attributed Robaiyat that are devoid of any or in-depth study of the authentic or attributed philosophical or scientific texts written by Khayyam.

But then, as others (supposedly more "scientific" minded) may argue, the famed scientist ("astronomer-mathematician") Khayyam could not have been in any serious way involved in such an unserious pastime as writing poetry and Robaiyat. They remind us that none of Khayyam's own contemporaries actually referred to him as a poet of quatrains (except perhaps of a few poems in Arabic, and even fewer Persian of other poetry styles, here or there), and certainly no collection of poetry has been discovered to date in any manuscript libraries that is directly written by Khayyam himself and bearing his name as their author.

They note how a contemporary, Nezami Arouzi, who sincerely tributes Khayyam as a teacher, and one whose comment about him epigraphs this introduction, did not apparently refer to Khayyam as a poet in his two biographical entries on and another reference to him in his *Chahar Maqaleh (Four Discourses)* where he devotes an entire discourse to poets but his only references to Khayyam are inserted in another discourse on astronomy/astrology regarding his astronomical interests while acknowledging Khayyam's lack of deep faith in (perhaps what he meant, conventional narratives of) astrology. His stories about Khayyam, nevertheless, ironically, evoke his astrological acumen, even though what Khayyam did in one of those stories (forecasting the weather for a king planning a hunting trip) may best be interpreted as resulting from his more down-to-earth studies of topography, seasonal climates, and meteorology.

Besides, they also insist that one of the most significant (though brief) biographical accounts on Khayyam, in Beyhaqi's *Tatemmat Sewan el-Hekmat (Supplement to the Chest of Wisdom)*, fails to mention anything regarding poetry in his entry on Khayyam—where he also omits his writings on algebra among others, by the way. The world-famous author of the "Rubaiyat," in other words, was not known (judging from the commentaries of his contemporaries) to be a poet of any significance, let alone the author of the famed Robaiyat, during his lifetime. If we follow Beyhaqi's biographical sketch, we would have to conclude that Khayyam was not even a mathematician or algebraists, because he lists nothing as such among his writings.

Khayyam's being referred to as a physician may pass critical scrutiny by some who are familiar with the reports of his having been consulted to cure a young Soltan Sanjar (a son of the Seljuk king, Soltan Malekshah) from smallpox, but for the same reasons as noted above, Khayyam's being characterized as a "writer" would certainly raise the eyebrows of some scholars, since, first of all, they may argue that Khayyam's brief biographer Beyhaqi has characterized him as someone who was not inclined to write much, regarding him as miserly in writing (and teaching). And, second, the only writing of significant length bearing his name known as *Nowrooznameh* (wherein the author actually also offers authoritative advice on both the benefits *and harms* of drinking wine) has been disputed to have been wholly or in part written by the famed scientist-astronomer Khayyam, while (the same may argue) the latter's undisputed treatises on mathematics and algebra would certainly not make him a literary "writer" in the (then or present) contemporary sense of the term—as if the disciplinary fragmentations of today are relevant to understanding how Khayyam approached his scientific work.

Even Khayyam's expertise and achievements as an astronomer are downplayed or disputed today by some, since nothing significant in writing is said to have survived his lifetime that would corroborate his involvement as a significant member of the team of astronomers reported to have been commissioned by the court of Soltan Malekshah and his famed minister Nezam ol-Molk to build an observatory in Isfahan and reform the Persian calendar. Even if he was involved in a project that according to various sources (including that offered in *The Book on Nowrooz*) remained incomplete due to the political upheavals of the time, an AD 1048 birth date would make Khayyam such a young scholar in his mid-twenties that would render him a seemingly junior partner in the team of more senior, if not more distinguished, astronomers commissioned by Soltan Malekshah's minister.

Some have even argued that what contribution Khayyam did make to reform the calendar was based on the works of another member of the team, Abdorrahman Khazeni, who actually regarded himself in his own writing as a pupil of Khayyam, and who was later involved in similar works for a succeeding Seljuk king, Soltan Sanjar.

So, as the reader may judge from the above, it is far from indisputably self-evident today who the historical Omar Khayyam actually was, when he was born, what he thought, how he felt, what he wrote, what he did, and when he died. How then can one go about seeking more definitive answers to all the puzzles surrounding him, especially regarding the existence, nature, and purpose of the Robaiyat in his life and works?

It may perhaps be considered a fate of the global, world-historical, intellectual figure such as Omar Khayyam, for his life and works to be continually mythologized, reappropriated, and reinvented by those from diverse cultures—his presumed birth date or date of passing be set by Indians and Russians, his "Rubaiyat" be made famous by a British or French, his algebra be "(re)discovered" by a French and/or an Arab, his biography by the Turkish, his legacy debated by his own homeland's scholars from diverse socio-political backgrounds, and his images nowadays portrayed at times in the most outlandish Orientalist depictions on the worldwide web, not to mention his names on those of hotels and casinos.

Omar Khayyam is a gift from Iran to the world that has not yet been adequately unwrapped. Each crowd has had or offered one or another impression of him, and made more or less important contributions in earnest (or not) in dropping the veil to reveal his enigmatic life, works, and legacy. But they have also raised new veils and added more puzzles, by making one or another error, one or another misinterpretation, one or another misconception of his works or legacies—ones which we also need to unwrap and untangle anew before reaching the actual, tightly sealed, gift Khayyam was and intended to leave behind.

So, it is not proper for us to regard existing knowledges about him to be uncontroversially authentic, factual, and official to start with. The very method we use to study him, let alone the substantive knowledges about him, are to be treated as variables, and not as taken-for-granted givens. Instead of starting with drawing on this or that scholar's portrayals of who Khayyam was and what he wrote, we must start from the scratch with revisiting and rethinking the methodological grounds and frameworks we use in our Khayyami studies. So, in the first book of the series, I will take up this task and let the exploration itself guide how the rest of this investigation in the future books of this series will be organized and conducted.

In my view, no one still properly knows who the historical Omar Khayyam was, because, in part, for one reason or another yet to be adequately understood, Khayyam himself also chose to live in a thick secretive tent of his works. He wished to live immortally in spirit and to be unmasked, but only as a result of persistent efforts like how he himself had become accustomed to when seeking an understanding of the nature and purpose of existence. His pedagogy was certainly not that of offering the answers ready-made. He wished those interested in him do the hard work, and it seems that centuries of hard work have still not born adequate fruit.

Khayyam had a message for the world, including the Iranian and the Islamic cultures, that has still not yet been deciphered. We need to take a sip of his Wine's bittersweet wisdom to understand him anew. Nearly a thousand years after his birth, it is time to bring Omar Khayyam home.

Abstract

This essay, titled "Introduction to the Series: The Enigmatic Omar Khayyam and the Impasse of Khayyami Studies," is a common introduction to the twelve-book series, *Omar Khayyam's Secret: Hermeneutics of the Robaiyat in Quantum Sociological Imagination,* authored by Mohammad H. Tamdgidi, included in its first book subtitled *New Khayyami Studies: Quantumizing the Newtonian Structures of C. Wright Mills's Sociological Imagination for A New Hermeneutic Method.* In the essay, the author argues that nearly a thousand years after his birth, the life and works of Omar Khayyam are still wrapped deeply in veil, major puzzles about him still abound, and modern Khayyami studies in Iran and abroad, after nearly two centuries of active research, have grounded nearly to a halt, reaching an impasse.

Overviewing a series of paradoxes, puzzles, and questions still left unresolved about Omar Khayyam's life and works, Tamdgidi invites readers to ask why they may not consider what *they themselves already know* about Khayyam to be based on one or another myth. Acknowledging that not only others', but also our own, knowledges of Khayyam are myths—that they are socially and historically constructed stories about him—can be a good beginning in the true Khayyami spirit of the term founded on healthy skepticism. Doubting what we know about him in a radical way can be a helpful starting point about gaining and developing new understandings of his life, works, and legacy. It may be that we end up constructing new myths about him, but at least we would be doing so based on more reliable studies, being aware of the social constructedness of our own knowledges or myths about him, and based on efforts that do not pretend to contrast the presumed truths on our parts with lesser-valued myths constructed by others.

So, it is not proper for us to regard existing knowledges about him to be uncontroversially authentic, factual, and official to start with. The very method we use to study him, let alone the substantive knowledges about him, are to be treated as variables, and not as taken-for-granted givens. Instead of starting with drawing on this or that scholar's portrayals of who Khayyam was and what he wrote, we must start from the scratch with revisiting and rethinking the methodological grounds and frameworks we use in our Khayyami studies. So, in this book, Tamdgidi sets himself this task in order to let the exploration itself guide how the rest of this investigation in this and future books of the series will be organized and conducted.

CHAPTER I—The Promise and the Classical Limits of C. Wright Mills's Sociological Imagination

The secretive style of writing any text, which then calls for hermeneutic analysis to interpret it, adds an additional layer to the task of understanding the views of its author. However, whether or not the secretive element is present as an essential or a contingent layer requiring hermeneutic analysis, the problem still remains as to how one can most effectively go about understanding an author and what he or she intends to convey through his or her text.

In the context of our research on Omar Khayyam being conducted in the present series, let us first assume that there were no elements of secrecy involved in his writings.

Let us further assume he left behind ample writings, in manuscripts verifiably his own, sharing in a straightforward and direct way all the knowledge and wisdom he wished to impart to others.

Let us also assume that all his contemporaries knew of the details of his life and works and shared their indisputable accounts of him in easily accessible and understandable manuscripts.

Let us even further assume that we can have access to all the information about Khayyam's time amid local, regional, and global contexts within which he lived and worked.

Even assuming all the above, there still remains the question of how we can successfully gain the best and most truthful knowledge about Khayyam's life and works through studying all the manuscripts assumed as such to be amply and accessibly available to us by and about him.

The study of texts to understand their meanings in social context falls in the subdisciplinary field of the sociology of knowledge, broadly defined as a branch of social scientific inquiry concerned with understanding how knowledge and social reality relate to one another. Studying Khayyam's attributed works and those of others about him in order to understand his views and life in historical context, therefore, can be framed as a study in the sociology of knowledge, broadly speaking.

Many diverse approaches have emerged in the history of the sociology of knowledge to tackle the central question of the field as noted above, and it is not my purpose here to review that history, since I have already done so critically and in detail elsewhere (see Tamdgidi 2002a, 2000b; also 2004/5).

Based on that study, I concluded that the most effective approach to exploring the relation between knowledge and social context is what I have called the *sociology of self-knowledge* (Tamdgidi 1999-2020[1]) which has close affinities with both Karl Mannheim's sociology of knowledge as advanced in his *Ideology and Utopia: An Introduction to the Sociology of Knowledge* (1936) and the sociological imagination tradition as introduced by C. Wright Mills in his book *The Sociological Imagination* (1959). Therefore, it may be regarded as overlapping with these traditions, broadly considered.

However, in important respects the sociology of self-knowledge is also different from them. More specifically, as far as my own approach to defining this field is concerned, I treat the 'sociology of self-knowledge' as a theoretical component field of what I more call the quantum sociological imagination, of which 'human architecture' and 'utopystics' are the methodological and empirico-historical component fields (Tamdgidi 2002, 2020).

Regarding the above overlapping, or superposing, fields of inquiry and how I arrived at their formulation as such, I have already offered some brief notes in the preface to this book. Further details of the same can be found in the preface to my recently published work *Liberating Sociology: From Newtonian Toward Quantum Imaginations: Volume 1: Unriddling the Quantum Enigma* (2020). For now, since in the present series I plan on applying a hermeneutic method of textual analysis that is framed by what I

---

1. For a list of my further writings on this topic see the bibliography at the end of this book.

call the quantum sociological imagination, I find it necessary to elaborate in more detail in this first chapter of the present book on its affinities with the Millsian sociological imagination, and their distinctions from one another.

Having done so, I will then further explain (in the three chapters to follow the present chapter) what a hermeneutic study of Khayyam's texts in a quantum sociological imagination as applied in the present series implies.

In his work, *The Sociological Imagination* (1959), the American sociologist C. Wright Mills strongly advocated for advancing a sociological vision that always, as a matter of continual concern, whatever the research problem at hand may be, studies social reality in terms of exploring how personal troubles and broader public issues relate to one another. According to him, "the sociological imagination enables us to grasp history and biography and the relations between the two within society. ... No social study that does not come back to the problems of biography, of history and of their intersections within a society has completed its intellectual journey" (1959:6).

Were we to apply the sociological imagination to the study of Khayyam's life and works, in other words, we would be keenly interested in how Khayyam's personal troubles in life on one hand, and the public issues of his time on the other hand, related to one another, rendering any study devoid of attention to such a dialectic deficient and incomplete in advancing a true understanding his life and works.

In fact, when we become more familiar with Khayyam's own works—not just in any disputably attributed robai (quatrain) or literary text such as *Nowrooznameh (The Book on Nowrooz)*, but even in his indisputably attributed scientific texts, such as his treatise on algebra—we may find significant indications that Khayyam himself was quite aware of how the troubles he was experiencing in his life as a person, scientist, or thinker were intimately linked to the public issues of his time. Therefore, we can safely consider that, even though Khayyam obviously did not use the term as such, a sociological imagination of interactions between his own personal troubles and the public issues of his time were intimately woven into how he himself tried to understand his own life in the context of his social milieu.

Again, we should recall that for C. Wright Mills adopting an imaginative sociological approach as described was not a matter of choice, but of necessity. At its face value, such an emphatic advocacy for the sociological imagination by Mills may sound quite odd and forceful as it is introduced in his book. But he seemed to mean exactly what he said. That is, he did not regard adopting the sociological imagination to frame research as a matter of scholarly preference—as if one could undertake one sociological investigation using such a vision and another without—but as an *essential* requirement of *any* sociological study, insisting that no sociological study is complete without exploring the link between biography and history, between personal troubles and broader public issues, as its central concern. Significantly, his point throughout his book was to emphasize that the sociological imagination *as he defined it* had become, was, and should be pursued as, the new "common denominator" of his "intellectual age." In his view, therefore, it is not to be treated as merely just another short-term, passing, intellectual fad.

Mills was clear about the elements of his proposed sociological imagination as a whole: 1-An awareness of the structure of the society in which the individual presently lives; 2-A world-historical awareness of the position and peculiarity of the given society in the context of human history as a whole; and 3-the specific kinds of "human nature" (such as role and character types) associated with that society, and the nature of troubles commonly experienced by men and women living in that society, as compared with those in other world-historical contexts (Mills 1959:6-7).

Of interest for our purpose here when considering Mills's formulation in the context of studying Khayyam's life and works is Mills's distinguishing not only the private troubles and public issues from one another, but specifically contrasting on one hand (in the macro fold) the contemporary social awareness with the world-historical contexts in which the person finds herself/himself, and on the other hand (in the micro fold) the "inner life" of the person with the variously stated "external career,"[2] "the range of his immediate relations with others,"[3] or "local environments of the individual."[4]

In other words, there was a secondary breakdown *within* each of the private and public spheres that constitute the dialectical pairs of the sociological imagination as a whole.

For Mills, *all* the four landscapes, and more so their influences on one another, constituted the legitimate subject matter of sociology, such that the serious and committed intellectual could not remain so without grappling

---

2. "The sociological imagination enables its possessors to understand the larger historical scene in terms of its meaning for the inner life and the external career of a variety of individuals" (Mills 1959:5).

3. "Troubles occur within the character of the individual and within the range of his immediate relations with others; they have to do with his self and with those limited areas of social life of which he is directly and personally aware" (Mills 1959:8).

4. "Issues have to do with matters that transcend these local environments of the individual and the range of his inner life" (Mills 1959:8).

with *all the elements* that constitute the sociological imagination as a whole. What made the sociological imagination distinctive, in other words, was not one or another element in isolation from the other(s), but the ability to relate the elements together as aspects of any given sociological inquiry.

If we consider in the context of Khayyami studies the above broad framework that is native to Mills's original definition of the sociological imagination, we would be convinced that the fullest and most truthful understanding of Khayyam's life and works can be achieved when we are able—setting aside at this point, again for the sake of our presentation in this and the next two chapters, the problems of secrecy or availability of resources at hand—to understand Khayyam's reflections on, as well as our knowledge about, four elements: (1) his inner life, (2) his personal relations with others, (3) the contemporary social (cultural, political, economic, and so on) contexts of the times or milieu amid which he lived, as well as (4) how such a contemporary context for him was similar to or different from others (including our own) considered in a broader world-historical context.

For instance, when we find Khayyam lamenting about the attitude of persons around him to science and scientists in his time, he must have been reflecting on his own inner feelings, thoughts, and troubles in relation to how others treated him (such as ridiculing him for one or another reason) and how he reacted to them, and how such a state of affairs was a result of his contemporary conditions which must have been (or was considered by him to be) different from earlier (recent, or distant) times, or times he may have imagined or wished to have been or to be then still possible, in a world-history context. These could be expressed through nostalgic, critical, or creative speculations he may have had about Iran's near or distant mythological past or desired traditions as expressed in the events, for instance, of Nowrooz. The point here is to simply illustrate how the more detailed framework proposed by Mills can be used in Khayyami studies as well.

Before we consider proceeding to apply the Millsian sociological imagination to the study of Khayyam's life and works, however, we need to first ascertain the soundness of the Millsian framework itself in light of our current and preferred understanding of sociology. In my recent work published under the title *Liberating Sociology: From Newtonian Toward Quantum Imaginations: Volume I: Unriddling the Quantum Enigma* (2020), I argued that our basic structures of thinking regarding society and sociology cannot escape the scrutiny of what we have taken for granted in a culture deeply influenced by the Newtonian way of thinking.

Therein, I argued that Mills himself directs our attention to the deeper structures, such as Newtonian or Darwinian ways, of thinking that have not been short-term fads that come and go, but deeply embedded ways of viewing the world that have shaped our views in recent centuries. Therefore, a question that can be plausibly raised (as I did raise in my recent work) is whether Mills's own sociological imagination was shaped by Newtonian ways of thinking as well, and if so, do we and should we find it necessary to revisit such structures of thinking in order to critically reassess whether the Millsian sociological imagination *itself,* as *he framed it,* is still adequate for our sociological research in general, and for the one we wish to conduct in this series regarding the life and works of Omar Khayyam.

To arrive at a plausible answer to the question, therefore, I will devote this and the following three chapters of this book to revisiting the Newtonian way of thinking about the world and society, and how the infusion of new developments in quantum science can challenge and advance those structures in a way that can help us understand and apply the sociological imagination to the study of Khayyam's life and works more fruitfully.

In the rest of this chapter, I will revisit the Millsian sociological imagination, raising eight issues that I believe express the limits the classical Newtonian way of thinking has set on Mills's imaginative framework.

In the second chapter, I will outline the Newtonian way of thinking about reality, society, sociology, the sociological imagination, in order to gain a clearer sense of how the deep structures of the Newtonian way of thinking can limit our Khayyami studies.

In the third chapter, I will contrast the Newtonian with the quantum vision of reality, society, and the sociological imagination, delineating the attributes of the quantum sociological imagination as a framework for advancing Khayyami studies.

Finally, in the fourth and last chapter, I will relax the assumption maintained in earlier chapters regarding the challenges posed by the problems of availability of resources and of secretive writing in the hermeneutic study of Khayyam's life and works.

In my repeated readings of C. Wright Mills's book, *The Sociological Imagination* (1959), and his other writings amid my own research and teaching experience in applied settings, eight sets of questions about the conceptual framework of the sociological imagination as proposed by Mills have often presented themselves.

1. The Problem of Dualism: Can Personal Troubles Be Also Public Issues, and Vice Versa?

The first set of questions that comes to my mind when considering Mills has to do with what determines whether a problem is just a personal trouble or (also) a public issue. Here, the concern is with the *relation* between personal troubles and public issues whose dialectic is supposed to be the subject matter of the sociological imagination.

From many passages in Mills's book, one gains the impression that he believed there are some troubles that are private ones, and others that have become or are expressions also of broader public issues.

For instance, he says that if there are only a handful of unemployed in a community, these persons' problems may be regarded as merely private, personal troubles. However, if hundreds or thousands of folks suddenly become unemployed, the afflicted individuals are not merely confronting isolated personal troubles but a broader public issue that implicates the socio-economic structures prevailing in the community.

Note that the determination of what passes as 'just private' personal troubles and what as troubles that hold public issue significance is quite important for Mills, since his "sociological" (in contrast to "psychological," one may presume) disciplinary research interests hinge upon choosing those research problems that have acquired, or potentially hold, public issue status. Therefore, some personal troubles may just not make it to his proposed "sociological" research agenda-setting table and thus not be imaginatively explored, simply because they are deemed too isolated and private, and not yet manifestations of publicly widespread or recognized issues.

I have found such a dichotomization of personal troubles into those that are 'just private and personal' and those that have become or readily express public issues to be quite problematic and rather self-defeating for advancing the sociological imagination.

Consider the following observations, for instance.

(1) How can we presume a personal trouble to be merely 'personal' and not also a public issue without subjecting all and any personal trouble(s) encountered equally to the *same* sociologically imaginative inquiry (which means not privileging some topics over others, simply because in an *a priori* way we have concluded that a problem "appears" to be merely a "private matter" and not worthy of our "sociological" pursuit)?

In other words, how can we dismiss a personal trouble as being not worthy of sociologically imaginative inquiry, without considering it as seriously as the cases that seem to have become public issues outright? Would this not be like putting the horse before the cart, i.e., not studying a trouble because we have already presumed without prior study that it does not fit a publicly significant personal trouble classification? Should we not instead subject *all* personal troubles to the same imaginative sociological research, which alone may reveal the extent to which the troubles are presumably 'just personal and private' or indicative of the potential of being a public issue?

(2) Let us assume that in the whole world only just one person has a personal trouble, such as feeling unfulfilled, sad, depressed, or alienated. Why should we all not consider *that* a *public* issue?

In other words, does not the kind of society we live in also shape how and whether or not we take the sufferings of even a single person as a matter of common injury? Could we lose significant (especially pedagogical) opportunities of learning about and solving social problems by not exploring how even the most isolated and private expressions of our personal troubles can be linked to other more widely recognized troubles and through them to broader public issues of the social structure? Can one argue that even a single instance of a personal trouble is not related to and not arising from one or another social structural dysfunction that afflicts the public at large?

(3) If indeed personal troubles that may be, on the surface, 'quite private' to and isolated in a person (or, even one or another self in a person), prove to be 'rare' forms of expression of a widely recognized or newly emergent public issue at large, does not a research strategy based on ignoring the 'too personal' troubles lead us to dismiss larger-scale trends in public issues early on simply because what we witnessed happening seemed to be isolated cases of 'private' troubles at the specific time we conducted our study?

Note that, if we follow such an argument ignoring the "too personal" troubles, the earliest expressions of emerging public issues, when a broader trend has not yet set in, would always be overlooked and dismissed, since they do not yet meet the more or less quantitative criteria of widespread manifestation of the same personal trouble across many persons. After all, do not widespread unemployment of hundreds or thousands of folks begin with a few workers in this or that specific workplace or firm?

Does such privileging of personal issues that are obviously also widespread public issues against those that do not seem to be so (yet) at the time of conducting the inquiry inherently bias and limit our sociologically imaginative inquiries in not noticing subtle, still-not-yet-public, emerging trends in social problems?

Would this not lead imaginative sociologists to always fail in proactive and preventive explorations of social problems, to always be late-arrivals in investigating social problems when the latter have already become widely manifested as major (at times perhaps irreversible, such as those in the case of global violence or environmental) public issues?

(4) Could our dismissing some personal troubles as 'just personal, too private' troubles and not worthy of serious exploration, itself contribute, in a prophetically self-fulfilling way, to their becoming public issues over time?

This first set of considerations has significant implication for conducting our Khayyami study in this series.

For instance, in order to understand the public issues of Khayyam's time, we may simply disregard a minute clue offered in a robai or quatrain, or a brief introductory note in a scientific or philosophical treatise, simply because we do not see that even such a minute complaint may be telling of significant public issues affecting Khayyam's life. Even the use of (or lack thereof) a specific word, or expression, may offer a hint that we would otherwise ignore because we want the public issues of his time, as he experienced it, to be offered to us in a silver platter of a completed manuscript.

We may say, well, this feeling expressed in this quatrain is just a personal trouble limited to Khayyam, and not having any broader significance in telling us about the public issues of his time. And yet, especially in a poetic context, we could instead intimately note how a highly personal expression of sadness for a flower's dying, or joy in witnessing a rose blossoming, have not only a wider temporal, but even universal and existential significance in Khayyam's worldview about the human condition.

Conversely, significantly well-known public issues of Khayyam's time may be overlooked among issues that may have precipitated the composition of a particular poem or passage, simply because we have rigidly dualized or compartmentalized the public issues and private troubles of Khayyam's time in our own thinking as observers and researchers.

We may have routinely read in historical accounts about how, for instance, the project of building an astronomical observatory remained incomplete as a result of the untimely death of Soltan Malekshah or the assassination of his vizier, Nezam ol-Molk; and, yet, not consider how Khayyam, deeply involved and vested in the project for years, must have felt hurt, troubled, and sad witnessing a lifetime's wish and labors go to waste in a matter of a few days.

Not paying serious attention to such minute details, in other words, may lead us to fail in making significant discoveries about wider public issues (and vice versa) when reading Khayyam's prose and poetry, and this comes about because we maintain a rigid, dualistic, binary conception of what personal troubles and public issues are and how they relate to one another.

2. The Problem of Atomism: Which Self's Personal Trouble Is It?

The second set of questions that has often entered my mind following from the above about C. Wright Mills's framework has had to do with the unit of analysis on the *micro* side of the sociological imagination dialectic.

Is it the whole person, or particular selves in the person, who is/are supposed to be, or not, afflicted with troubles?

Is it possible that a self in a person associated with a particular social role may experience personal troubles that other selves in him or her, consciously observed/acknowledged or not, do not experience? Can one assume that the whole person afflicted with a given "personal" trouble is actually afflicted across all his or her intrapersonal landscape by that trouble in everyday life? Can the same person be characterized by many, more or less fragmented, selves among whom some selves have troubles that other selves do not, relatively speaking?

May various selves have different crisscrossing troubles, i.e., one has a trouble that another self does not, while the latter has a trouble that the former (or yet other selves) do not? Can a personal trouble be shared by one group of selves in a person associated with specific roles they play in everyday life, but not by another group of selves? A variation of these would be a situation where a "me" self is having a trouble when the person's observing "I" self denies afflicting his or her person altogether, at least for a while. The person, so to speak, is characterized by others (or by a later, or paradoxically even a forgetful former, confessing self in the same person) to be "in denial."

The point of the above second set of questions, in other words, is to ask whether the "person" experiencing the trouble is to be assumed to have monolithically a singular and "individual" (or individuated) self-structure throughout his or her lifetime as a whole, or whether he or she is indeed a multiplicity of selves or personalities, each of which may share, or not, one or another "personal" trouble with other selves in his or her inner subjective landscape at one time or another—and this may vary more or less during different periods of one's life, or during different historical "times" one finds oneself living in?

In short, what is the proper unit of analysis for the entity having, or not, a "personal trouble"—the presumed whole person, or one or another (or group) of his or her selves?

This issue can invite significant considerations when we conduct our study of Khayyam's life and works.

When we encounter different, at times quite opposite, sentiments or feelings in the attributed Robaiyat or quatrains, are we supposed to automatically assume that they must not have been composed by the same person, expressed in different times and places as far as biographical and social contexts are concerned?

Why should we assume that those poems, or other philosophical, scientific, or literary writing, are voices of an impossibly monolithic personality that supposedly remained entirely the same from youth, to mid-life, and into the old age, moving from one social role and status to another, from one success or failure in life to another, from one stage of self-examination to another, and so on?

Should we assume that anyone, including Khayyam, when writing a text is completely and absolutely aware of all the complexity of mixed thoughts or feelings he or she is experiencing when composing a given text?

Conversely, should we assume that composing a diversity of seemingly contradictory meanings across quatrains are accidental, and not deliberate and intentional, in pursuit of certain pedagogical, literary, or spiritual aims?

When considering my earlier (first) point about Mills noted above in terms of the problem of dualism, why do we find that the same quatrain, the same passage in Khayyam's scientific, philosophical, or literary, writings means differently for even ourselves when we are in good or bad moods during a given day, month, year, or period of our lives?

Are we ourselves often not quite surprised to find when reading our past writings, say diaries, how at one point or another we expressed a thought, a feeling, or reported an event, of which we have no recollection whatever, but have no doubt that it was us who wrote it? In other words, are not our own changing moods and fragmentary self-experiences themselves contributive to how we go about understanding a text, a work of art, a poem, a conversation?

How should we then approach, in the process of such reflections, the diversity of often-fragmented thoughts or feelings we witness having had in the past? Do we simply delete some or others as not "fitting" in a monolithic conception of ourselves, or do we try to understand them and perhaps seek to find a way of incorporating or integrating them in favor of perhaps a new and broader sense of self-identity of who we have been, presently are, or could be in the future—eventually arriving at an understanding of our lives not as an entirely good or bad, but as, say, a bittersweet, experience through time.

Let us say Khayyam wrote some quatrains early in life, expressing a depressive mood. Then, he experiences another period in his life that is more uplifting. And yet another period that is most pleasant. It is the same Khayyam who has experienced, in different times, such different selves. To these we may even add another self in Khayyam who is cognizant of such ebbs and flows in his life, reflecting on his life as a whole, considering the entirety of such experiences to express his sense of identity, of what he went through in his life amid the changing conditions of his times. Why should we consider that poems or writings expressing such different personal troubles are not expressive of the flow of life of the same person, instead doubting their attributability to the same author? Even a single poem, when expressing reflections of a self later in life can contain sentiments of a multiplicity of changing personal troubles experienced by the same person, in one line expressing a happy childhood, in another a sad or wasted mid-life, and in yet another the effort of an old poet trying to make sense of his life and times.

Therefore, adopting the *self* as a micro unit of analysis can offer us a much more fruitful lens to explore the richness of (or lack thereof) someone's, including Khayyam's, personal life experience, preventing us from dismissing any multiplicity or fragmentation we may perceive across his writings as being indicative of their being authored by different authors.

3. The Problem of Separability: Whose Public Issues Are These?

The third set of questions I have had regarding Mills's sociological imagination framework has had to do with the unit of analysis on the *macro* end of his central concern with the dialectics of personal troubles and public issues.

If on the micro side one may question the presumed *singularity* of the person having, or not, personal troubles, on the macro side one may question the presumed *multiplicity* of larger social groups in global and world-historical contexts, as if the public issues arising from each could truly be understood apart from the singularity of the human experience they have endured in both a long-term and large-scale world-history context, and in terms of contemporary time and regional scales.

Of course, Mills does have a good point to make when he notes that public issues change over historical time and place, and what may be a public issue now or in one nation may not have been so in the past or in another nation. But, can we even recognize the difference and uniqueness of public issues without adopting a world-historical approach such that we would then be able to compare and contrast the commonality or the distinctiveness of public issues we have or could face? Can we in fact assume that the public issues of one historical spacetime can be understood apart from those of other, including our own, historical spacetimes?

How far do we go in broadening the spatiotemporal framework of our macro unit of analysis when considering what our public issues actually are? The public issue of being situated in the 'external arena,' or colonized in a 'peripheral' or a 'semi-peripheral' part, of the modern world-economy (using terms drawn from world-systems studies, for instance) may be instead a publicly celebrated issue of national pride to another crowd (if not all those) living in the core regions of an imperial world-system.

For instance, what was a proudly symbolic Confederate Flag for a people living in the American South was not only a loathful symbol of slavery for others then, and still to many living in the US today, but a symbol of untold misery, torture, and enslavement to a people horribly chained, kidnapped, abused, shipped, and murdered, en mass like cattle from another continent.

To offer another example, still to this day, even after having acknowledged (reluctantly, by this or that recent US President) the role played by the CIA and the British in toppling the democratic government of Mohammad Mossadegh in Iran in 1953—disrupting and violating a people's historical development through the neocolonization of their economic, political, and cultural resources with enormous costs and implications involved—the US and the British (amid the West as a whole) still seem to find their having committed the coup in Iran in the context of Cold War to have been more or less justifiable, and a cause (outwardly expressed or not) for celebration of their presumed political prowess.

And, moreover, they self-righteously wonder why Iranians treated the US embassy as a den of spies—leading some in the West to expect compensation for damages for a 444-day hostage situation when their own decades-long hostage-taking of a people's land, resources, politics, culture, and history via their imposed local agencies as personified in the late Shah and his Western-installed government is still simply ignored and deemed to be not pursuable in the international courts of law.

The coup in Iran still remains more of a historical 'public issue' for Iranians than for those committing it in 1953 and now conveniently calling for "moving on from the past." Even amid the Iranian political scene today, especially abroad, some in the opposition who are against the status quo in

Iran, laugh off the 1953 coup as if it is a past history, and not one that is being in fact persistently and systematically repeated in new shapes, forms, and tempos, under new excuses and pretensions during the now four-decades-long draconian regimes of sanctions. They are not willing to consider that the 1953 coup having taken place over a few days or weeks is now being repeated, in a much more widely spread-out mode over decades of harshest sanctions imposed on Iran to induce "regime change"—the latter being just another euphemism for "coup," now of a type that is spread-out over decades.

I often cringe when I hear a US President or official speak of supporting democracy in Iran, when he or she has or demonstrates little remorse about what one or another US administration did to Iran in the course of the 1953 coup. They are shocked (reluctantly or not) at a violent mob taking over their Capitol in Washington, D.C., yet regard it as a masterpiece of their CIA intrigues to overthrow a democratically elected government in Iran or Chile by mobs of thugs or military juntas, and then wonder why their people do not trust Western lip-services to the cause of democracy and international norms in consular affairs. Which international laws and norms allow the personnel of an embassy to plot and carry out coups against their host governments? For them, these happening elsewhere are proud public expression of the might of an imperial power interfering in other's lives in the name of "liberty and freedom," when they themselves appear quite shocked or alarmed at their own political lives being intervened by 'the Russians.' For those who suffered the coup, and even for this (now, also) American citizen, such reactions tell of a sad public tale of scientifically verifiable imperial duplicity and shameful double standard that are personally deeply troubling.

Mills clearly distinguished between the "contemporary society" and the "world-historical" context, and indeed included both in the basic conceptual structure of his proposed sociological imagination. After all, we cannot know what is particular in the forms of public issues we face in contemporary society if we are not able to compare them to those arising in other historical and geographical contexts, including our own. The question that comes to mind in this regard, however, is the extent to which Mills considered human society, and its public issues, also as a *singular world-historical process*— any spatiotemporal part of which are regarded as not being adequately understandable without knowing the system as a whole.

Sadi, a Persian poet of the thirteenth century, wrote: "Adam's descendants are in frame from one strand/While in their creation aim as one soul stand. /If a member is in stress from his time's scar, /Others become restless, nearby and afar. /If you're about others' griefs and pains carefree, / You don't deserve the name of humanity." In such a poetic and imaginative conception, the world-historical singularity of humanity as a whole is depicted and simply assumed, and it was considered as such centuries ago in "another" culture. It poetically depicts a sociological imagination in which any person's troubles are universally everyone's public issue. That may sound like a "grand" conceptual proposition, but it indeed has (at least in my mind) quite significant analytical and explanatory implications for understanding the nature and kinds of public issues we choose to study and in relation to them the kind of personal troubles we experience.

To what extent did Mills have in mind the world-history as a *singular unfolding* of the human story when he used the term "world-history"? Or, did he understand by it "contemporary world-history," to which he contrasted the "contemporary society" as a system of presumably independent nation-states that otherwise interacted with one another (and whose comparative study he increasingly advocated toward the end of his life)?

A macro-conception of world-history as a singular unit of analysis does not offer a choice for understanding, say, German, French, or American, "contemporary society" (and thereby sociology) without understanding Iranian, Islamic, Chinese, Indian, Asian, African, or Native American "contemporary society" (and thereby sociology, as embedded in their respected cosmologies). In such a conception, you would not be able to really understand the public issues of the US today without relating them to how they treated the black slaves, or the Native Americans, in the past— and do so today. You would not be able to understand the public issues facing democracy "domestically" without understanding American, British, French, government "regime change" policies and supposed spreading of "democracy" to other parts of the world through inhumane sanctions and coups benevolently camouflaged in intelligence double-talk. However, in a compartmentalized conception of contemporary or world history as a system of presumably independently developing yet interacting nation-states or civilizations, the choice is (in my view, wrongly) assumed to be possible.

To what extent did Mills's notion of "contemporary world-history" encompass non-Western societies, present and past, and is it possible to truly understand the nature of "social structure" then or today and in any of its spatiotemporal nation-state or civilizational parts (hence, the public issues arising from it) without understanding the world-historical (and not just its contemporary, or even modern world-systemic) context? Can one adequately explore public issues of the social structure in "contemporary society" and its "world-history context" within a conceptual framework in which nation-states or civilizations can be regarded as understandable more or less on their own, or is it necessary to adopt a singular world-historical approach in which the public issues are considered to be spatiotemporally local manifestation of the unfolding of a singular human social reality and history as a whole? Whose public issues are we really choosing when we remain Eurocentric compared to when we adopt a truly world-historical lens?

What was the uppermost macro unit of analysis of Mills's "sociological" imagination, in other words? In what way are such observations relevant to Khayyami studies, especially the one we intend to undertake in this series?

The relevance becomes more tangible and evident when we realize that, when we consider Khayyam's time, we need to consider the public issues that he was experiencing or referring to, or the public issues we ourselves may choose to explore, can best be comprehended not in a spatiotemporally local, or contemporary, sense but also in a regional and world-history context.

It would be impossible to understand Khayyam apart from not just the local and contemporary, but also the wider regional/global and world-historical (leading to and including his time) experiences of cultural imperiality and colonialism shaping the medieval period. The appeal of Khayyam's attributed quatrains to a broad humanity has in fact been due to their addressing not specific spatiotemporal public issues afflicting just one person but those experienced by humanity as a whole. Khayyam was very much interested in the universal patterns (in what he called the "kolliyat") of human experience for reasons that call for in-depth investigation. So, for him, world-history and not just those living in the region of his time, seems to be a framing macro unit of analysis.

The intersection of ancient Persian, Arab, Turkic, and other ethnic cultures and politics shaping what Khayyam called his "times" ("zamaneh") involved a complex set of non-binary, intertwining and interpenetrating ways in which social and personal identities were shaped.

The Arab conquest of Iran had originally been not just a simplistic form of cultural and religious imperiality, but arising from a genuine sense of what classical Islam of the Prophet Muhammad offered as a more just alternative to what the latter-day oppressive Persian kings had to offer, while the nostalgic memory of the justice of earlier kings such as Cyrus (in the mythological form of Jamsheed) was still attractive in certain respects (though, not entirely, as even wisely acknowledged in *Nowrooznameh*).

But the emergent Shia resistance, in the form of the Ismaili or other Shia intellectual movements or currents of his time, to Islam's conservative traditional (Sunni) Islamic domination was not simply an ethno-national but also an intra-religious/Islamic affair. What may be regarded as the "public issues" of Khayyam's times, in other words, may have been determined to be quite different depending on whom you asked to list them, or when in their lives, and amid which inner or external-career experiences, they were asked about them. A Khayyam busy constructing his royal-court-sponsored astronomical observatory in the hopes of reforming the Persian calendar as legacy for his posterity, must have had a different assessment of the public issues of his time, than one surviving the Turkic Seljuk king's suspicious death following the assassination of his Persian vizier, Nezam ol-Molk— witnessing the collapse of the public projects in which he had invested so much of his life and talents. It would be a fundamental mistake to disregard the colonial context of the times in which Khayyam himself lived, which may provide us with quite a different historical lens through which we can interpret his reluctance to engage more actively in the political affairs of his time.

The world-historical context is also important from the point of view of *who is studying that past*, that is *we*. What we regard as the public issues of the day also influence how we look back at Khayyam's time to consider the public issues of his day. A FitzGerald living in the mid-nineteenth century Victorian British imperial context would consider Khayyam's public issues from his time's point of view differently than how we do so today, confronting the geopolitics of the Middle East in a global context.

4. The Problem of Objectivity: Can We as Observers Separate Ourselves from Others' Personal Troubles and Public Issues?

My fourth set of questions regarding Mills's sociological imagination has had to do with the question of objectivity and the "person(s)" whose troubles are supposed to be, in relation to their broader public issues, the continual subject matter of the sociological imagination. It is, after all, one thing to study how *other* people's personal troubles and broader public issues interrelate, and another to reflectively study *one's own*, that is, *the investigator's own* personal troubles in relation to others' personal troubles and both to their and our broader public issues.

Should we not include our own personal troubles and their related public issues of our own time and place in the subject matter when studying the personal troubles and public issues reflected in Khayyam's life and works?

Granted, Mills clearly constructed a distinction between "inner life" and "external career" to demarcate the two dimensions of the micro side of his sociological imagination dialectic. So, he was aware that the imaginative sociologist should consider exploring both the inner and the external, the intrapersonal and the interpersonal, dimensions of personal troubles in relation to broader public issues at least as far as the micro dimension of the sociological imagination dialectic is concerned.

However, note here that the imaginative sociologist can still be concerned with studying the inner lives and external careers of *others*, say, those belonging to the "new men of labor," the middle-class folks, or the "power elite," 'out there,' and still not pay attention to or implicate the inner life and the external career of *himself or herself* 'in here,' that is, the sociologist/investigator's *own* biography while advancing the sociological imagination.

In other words, designating "inner life" as a structural element of the micro dimension of the sociological imagination dialectic *does not necessarily* imply including the *investigator's own inner life and external career* in the imaginative sociological investigation. Similarly, note that Mills does not explicate, in the macro fold, a parallel distinction between "own social public issues" and those arising from "external relation" with other societies or nation-states in "contemporary society." We need to also keep in mind that there is a distinction between the public issues affecting the lives of "others" we study and the public issues affecting our own lives as sociologists trying to develop and apply our sociological imaginations.

For instance, let us say you and I are studying the same text or even an attributed robai (quatrain) of Omar Khayyam.

Are we to say that you and I can completely abstract from our own "personal troubles," or the "public issues" of our own time, when trying to interpret what Khayyam is offering in his text?

Say, a writer that is quite depressed and bent on committing suicide reads a poem in Khayyam that paints a dark picture of the world, and then finds another where Khayyam speaks joyfully of pursuing happiness. Would we find that our depressed observer, in finding an echo and confirmation of his own troubles, would brand one quatrain as being more authentic than another among those being attributed to Khayyam?

Or, consider that a scholar, experiencing a bad mood one day studying Khayyam, dismisses or forgets (or, dissociates from) an insight he actually entertained as being significant just a few days before, an insight that may have offered a clue, from a close analysis of Khayyam's writings, about how what public issue or event precipitated the author of a passage or quatrain, presumably Khayyam, to write it.

Or, consider how another Iranian writer, holding a personal grudge against another author who had just published *Nowrooznameh (The Book on Nowrooz)* as a manuscript plausibly attributable to Khayyam, knowingly and intentionally devises a devious strategy (just for the fun of it, of humiliating his opponent at the expense of taking Khayyam's newly discovered book seriously, and admitting later for having done so) of dismissing the accomplishment by knowingly weaving a rather hypothetical theory of how there must have been another person named Khayyam writing the quatrains, later on feeding the curiosities of those who wish to find a way of appropriating the scientific Khayyam as a part of Western or Arab culture, by dissociating all or some of the Robaiyat written in Persian from him.

As another example, a literal interpreter of Islam's holy book would find an attributed quatrain of Khayyam unpleasantly challenging to his own views, so dismisses it as being misattributed to Khayyam, misinterpreted, or just a clever attack on religion, targeting religious beliefs like snake-bites. Or, a reader or British translator, actually bent on drinking wine when depressed, would find lots of quatrains attributed to Khayyam confirming his habit and mood amid his own feeling of loneliness, insisting that Khayyam must have 'undoubtedly' meant the "wine of the grape" in his poems. He then goes out of his way to arrogantly criticize another, say a French, translator who argues instead for the wine standing for a spiritual state of mystical consciousness.

Someone reading Khayyam during the reign of the Shah, and sympathetic to him, feels proud when reading references in the Robaiyat to Iran's distant past, and now, with Shah gone, is nostalgic about the same times needing to be revived. Another, critical of the Shah during his reign, reads Khayyam's references to the ancient kings having come and gone as a sign of their passing nature and impermanence, interpreting the texts, especially after the Iranian Islamic revolution, as a confirmation of the same.

The above are meant to simply illustrate the point that it would be difficult, in a *classical* "objectivist" framework of conventional sociology which pretends its "facts" are present "out there" independent of one's own biases and troubles, to adequately understand the complexity of any study of Khayyam, whether or not the sources for such a study are available or remain secretive—the latter of which, as we shall see, adds even more complexity to this point I am raising regarding Mills's classical framework.

The issue of reflexivity is not limited to micro analyses of personal troubles across the observed-observer domains, however, but also significantly relates to macro analyses of public issues.

If we consider the significance of including ourselves in the subject matter of our Khayyami studies, we become aware of the fact that not only the public issues of Khayyam's times or his past, but also the public issues of his future extending to the public issues of our own recent and contemporary times become integral parts of our Khayyami studies. In other words, paradoxically, both in terms of what preceded and was contemporaneous to Khayyam's time and the world-historical context *since* his time amid which we *ourselves*, as observers and researchers, are seeking to understand our subject matter, become legitimate and inescapable subject matters of our study of Khayyam's life and works.

Recall that the latter issue becomes more tangible when considered in light of the two other issues I raised earlier, both in the sense of the divided nature of the intrapersonal and interpersonal lives and selves in the micro side as well as the singularity of the world-historical context in which our studies of Khayyam are undertaken on the macro pole of the dialectic.

For instance, it would be quite naive to think that what we know about Khayyam, what he did, what he wrote, which quatrains we regard as authentic or not, what book attributed to him we regard as authentic or not, and so on, have little to do with the Western, especially British, colonial context in which much of the modern discourses on and about Khayyam have evolved.

Even the very question of what robais should be regarded as authentic or not, how much credit is to be given to Khayyam's scientific discoveries, whether to take *Nowrooznameh* seriously or not—questions that have been significantly influenced by the controversies even among Iranian writers and researchers over the past century or more regarding the authenticity of Khayyam's writings—cannot be adequately understood apart from the world-historical context in which FitzGerald's reinvented "Khayyam" of the Victorian England era was born amid an Orientalist tradition in the West, the subsequent semi-colonial experience Iran underwent, the 1953 CIA coup in Iran, the rise of Westoxication and Occidentalism under the Shah, and the experience of the Islamic revolution and its aftermath in Iran, including the new imperial policies of sanctions now being spread-out in the guise of duplicitous "regime change" strategies wrapped under the imperial Western guise of "freedom and democracy for Iran" over several decades.

We may even come to realize that decades before a 1953 political coup happened, another, much deeper, cultural coup could have happened in Iran and the East, one which we have to seriously revisit and reconsider in terms of the severity of a misappropriation committed by the hands of a (British) imperial culture against the cultural values and symbolic wealth of a scientifically rich and critically-minded tradition in Islam—one that sought after its own models of spiritually rooted political resistance in innovative art forms in the works of an Omar Khayyam living centuries before.

When reading Khayyam now, some abroad and in the opposition find his critical thinking and skepticisms to be signifying doubts about Islam and the government in Iran, when, to be more correct and plausible, his critical thinking within Islam should be directed against those like the literalist Wahhabi, Al-Qaeda and/or Daesh-type abusive/genocidal practices of pseudo-Islam often associating themselves with the Sunni tradition, to whose rise the US, British, and Western oil-motivated support of a "Saudi" Arabia has significantly contributed, and against which in fact Iran's Shia religious tradition and resistance have offered strong counterweights. No regional power was more instrumental and decisive in fighting ISIS and their barbarism than Iran's predominantly Shia Islamic forces, despite the challenges, shortcomings, set backs, and even domestic corruptions, they have faced in the context of a decades-long Western embargo. Do we really think that our Khayyami studies can be advanced without equal attention to such regional and global contexts in which we ourselves live today?

In any case, how all such "public issues" past and present have shaped the life, works, and legacy of Khayyam and our own lives and studies of him should also be intricate and integral components of any imaginative sociological study we undertake in advancing our Khayyami studies in the present series.

Did Mills consider the study of the observer/investigator's own personal troubles and his own time's public issue to be in and of themselves legitimate subject matters of the imaginative sociological research, as he conceived it? Did he clearly and unambiguously argue that both others' and one's own personal troubles and the public issues of their respective times are to be equally and in tandem, simultaneously—that is, in the one and the same study—subjected to the sociologically imaginative inquiry and thus explicitly reported on in the same research account as such?

Did he consider such personal and broader social self-reflexivity on the part of the investigator himself or herself to be also an indispensable condition and legitimate object of the sociological imagination, whether or not other peoples' personal troubles or their time's public issues were (also) being investigated as a primary focus of the study at hand? Would he have considered the task of an ideal sociological inquiry in his proposed imaginative framework completed, if, for instance, other peoples' personal troubles in relation to broader public issues were studied *without* any explicit or implicit attempt at conscious and intentional interrogation of the observer/investigator/sociologist's own personal troubles and the public issues of his or her time in the one and the very same sociological inquiry?

Can a sociologist in fact conduct sociologically imaginative studies of others' personal troubles and biographies in relation to broader public issues without being—at the same time, and during the same study—continually self-reflective about how one's identifications and explorations of others' personal troubles in light of broader public issues may be influenced by one's own value-judgments, life experiences, biases, biography, and intellectual perspectives and sensitivities, both personal and scholarly?

And if one does recognize and study one's own biography and history, should one be as forthcoming in explicating such self-reflections in the writing process and the scholarly narrative account, published or not, as one reports on the link between other people's biography and history, between others' personal troubles and broader public issues? Should I have, in the name of "academic objectivity" and expediency avoided raising the above political issues regarding the role played by imperiality in my and our own times as a context for conducting our Khayyami studies?

5. The Problem of Determinism: Is It Always the Case that Only Society Shapes the Individual/Self, and That Only Public Issues Shape Personal Troubles, and Not Also the Other Way Around?

Moving on to my fifth set of questions about Mills's proposed model for the sociological imagination, one can see that fundamental *causal* assumptions come along with the adoption of dualistic definitional structures that seek to dichotomize "personal troubles" and "public issues" (and their respective components) in an absolute way.

Only in a dualistic conceptual environment is it possible to say A universally determines non-A—arguing, for instance, that social structural problems manifested in broad public issues are the "causes" of our personal troubles, such that to do away with the latter, we will have to "first" take care of the former.

In an alternative non-dualistic conceptual framework characterized by simultaneity, such causal imputations would be rather impossible to maintain, since the personal trouble experienced may be recognized as the very interactional node in which the broader social structural problem reproduces itself, such that a personal act may have the potential to precipitate, at the same time, an important "butterfly-effect" to bring about calls and actions to address broader public issues resulting from deep-seated problems of the social structure.

Would it not be missing the forest for the trees, so to speak, if we do not recognize the public (including diagnostic, explanatory, and mobilizational) significance of a seemingly personal trouble?

Take, for instance, the case of the self-immolation by the personally troubled street vendor, Tarek el-Tayeb Mohamed Bouazizi, experiencing economic hardship in Tunisia, helping spark widespread protests throughout a region leading to the so-called Arab Spring. Can one readily separate the personal life and unfortunate death of Bouazizi from the broader social structures and public issues of which it is a part? Did not his personal story at the very same time carry structural implications for the nature in this case of prevailing economic and political conditions in a large and volatile region of the world-system?

Or, consider the case of Rosa Parks (and/or others who did the same) amid racial turmoil in the US, refusing in 1955 to give up her seat on a bus so as not to perpetuate racial discriminatory laws. Did she not break the cultural and political chains of a specific social structure by a personal, yet also historic and public, act? Was her act a case of "mere personal trouble" or a significant cause of social structural transformation in the civil rights status quo in the US (or lack thereof), expressed via a public issue?

Amid non-dualistic conceptual structures, it is difficult to presume a particular model of causal linkage to be universally at work across all historical conditions. How can A universally determine non-A, if non-A is conceived to be a part of A? May concrete investigations of specific historical situations in fact indicate that it was the personal troubles of concrete and specific historical individuals that led to the arising of public trends and issues that subsequently brought on the establishment of new, historically specific social structures?

As far as the problem of determinism is concerned, the earlier sets of questions noted above implicate more definitional structures of the Millsian sociological imagination than those associated with the distinction between personal troubles and public issues.

For instance, consider the distinction between "inner life" and "external career." On the surface, this Millsian distinction seems to be a helpful analytical device. But, considered more carefully, it raises exactly the same kind of questions I raised above regarding an either/or conception of personal troubles versus public issues, which in turn makes possible implying a causal model universally operating between them (i.e., public issues 'causing' personal troubles, or social structures 'determining' individual behaviors).

In the commonly presumed "sociology" parlance, it is the *inter*personal relations of individuals that shape or determine their inner, *intra*personal, self-experience. This definitional dichotomy of the "inner" and the "external" is usually operationalized in observations and narrative statements such as "the social origins of self," or "self arises from social context."

While these statements may seem explanatory and just taken for granted, when examined more carefully and phenomenologically problematized, even using deeper sociological insights and theories already at hand, they reveal often tautological definitional structures of thinking to be at work.

George Herbert Mead, from whose work much of the sociological theories of the self are derived, did emphasize that the self arises from social experience. However, he did also note well, paradoxically, that self and society are "twin-born," and he did emphasize that the self, once arisen, can take a life of its own and be itself an initiator of new social realities. This is, in fact, what is most valuable in the distinction he makes between the "I" and the "me" in his sociological insight, arguing that the former represents the creative, the spontaneous, the active sense of self, while the latter represents the self in us that is the result of social upbringing and conditions.

Of course the distinction of I/me for Mead is also situational, in the sense that a "me" that is a result of upbringing and therefore represented an object subjected to socialization, can, in another situation assume the role of an "I" and subject others to the same socialization. In contrast, the same "I" following a socialized prescription order or behavior, may also suddenly act creatively and spontaneously, inventing new identities or values for the same person. In this sense, Mead did allow for the "I" to act creatively and as an emergent agency, even though it itself arose from a "social origin."

While it may seem sufficient just to make a definitional statement about "the self arising from social context," closer study reveals that the "social context" and the act of human social relating are really impossible to exist without self relations already present and at work—which, again, points to

Mead's notion of twin-bornness of self and society.

To elaborate, as far as concrete human experiences are concerned, we cannot "socially relate" to others without having developed a sense of self. I can relate to you interpersonally, in other words, because through a symbolically interactive process of self-development and upbringing especially made possible through learning and using language, I have developed a capacity to have a self in me that symbolically represents you. My relation to you, therefore, is at the very same time, simultaneously, a relating to a self in me that represents you. My conversation with you is at the very same time also a conversation within myself. So, self and society being twin-born implies much more than what can be simplistically captured in a presumed universal causality that "society determines (or shapes) the self."

Here, then, we have a similar conceptual situation where dichotomous definitional structures themselves shape the possibilities that may potentially be generated amid an otherwise creative dialectics of self and broader society,[5] lending the "self" as much creative powers to shape society as we often presumptively consider to be exclusively attributed to society shaping selves. The causal modality of such both/and conceptions of self and society, of "inner life" and "external career," then becomes much more unpredictable, probabilistic, and ambiguous in such a non-dualistic conceptual framework.

So, if, when confronting the conceptual pair "inner life" and "external career," we presume a causal relation to be at work where the interpersonal interactions of the person having trouble is more or less assumed to be causing his inner life troubles, we may be falling into a dualistic conceptual trap, also involving a self-fulfilling prophecy, that may mask the actual reality of how a personal trouble may have actually started.

The same sorts of questions can be raised in a different way regarding the conceptual components of the macro dimension of Mills's sociological imagination dialectic that I discussed above.

For instance, there are two different ways one can consider how "contemporary society" relates to the "world-historical context"—twin distinctions that Mills also makes when elaborating on the macro dimension

---

5. Note here the alternative language I am using in order to avoid a duality of "self and society." In the expression "self and broader society," in other words, I am acknowledging that self is a social reality, and here we are exploring a relation of a part to its broader whole. The same can be expressed in reverse, i.e., that all social relations are self-relations of intra-, inter-, and extra-personal kind in terms of how we relate to ourselves, to others, and to our environment/nature, all conceived as expressions of a reality of which is ultimate that constitutes us as our own make-up.

of his sociological imagination dialectic.

In one conception, the world is comprised of presumably separately standing or developing nation-states or civilizations, present or past, that otherwise interact with one another to shape contemporary or past world-history. In an alternative conception, however, each of those presumably separate units are regarded as organic parts of a singular whole, such that an understanding of the uniqueness of each part could not be arrived at without a consideration of the working of the whole human story in a long-term, large-scale, world-historical framework.

So, while it may appear plausible to argue that a "Western" contemporary society is different from and is influencing developments in an "Eastern" society, i.e., similar to an A determines a non-A logical and causal framework, closer examination reveals that over a larger-scale and longer-term world-historical development Western and Eastern attributes (as actual as they may have become) are themselves products of their interactions, and not reducible to the presumed insular developments in each of the sides of the dialectic.

Problematizing dualistic definitional structures may therefore render the presumed causal significations carried by the terms "personal" versus "public," "inner life" versus "external career," "contemporary society" versus "world-history," meaningless in abstraction from concrete and specific biographical and historical investigations.

Did Mills's proposed sociological imagination imply a presumed causal model governing the "personal" and the broader "public" in terms of the latter universally shaping the former? Did he imply, as it is considered usually in conventional sociology, that "external career" has a generative and causal primacy in relation to the "inner lives" of the persons reporting personal troubles? Can one readily understand what is distinctive about the West without understanding the East, including their sociologies, philosophies, and cosmologies? Did an academic interest in legitimating the "disciplinarity" of his proposed imagination as a Western "sociological" endeavor underlie Mills's causal emphasis on the publicly manifested social problems at the expense of investigating the 'merely private' expressions of the same in 'isolated' individual cases? Consideration of further questions below may shed further light on the issues I wish to raise regarding the Millsian sociologically imaginative conceptual framework.

The implications of this, fifth, issue for our Khayyami studies in this series are vital. The reader may simply ask himself or herself, why is it that a simple robai (or quatrain) attributed to Khayyam, about the passing of a moment, of a green drying, a paradise experienced here and now, the beauty of the Moon—feelings expressed by someone amid the experience of personal troubles of his own amid the public issues of his time nearly a thousand years ago—became so world-historically publicized to render his poetry to be nearly as popular as the Christian Bible?

Can we really say that the power of a Khayyami quatrain is simply a reflection of its author's personal troubles, or is it or has it been (also), simultaneously, a force shaping whole cultures and their public issues? Where or how do we draw a causal line between how a text reflects a reality and how it shapes it? Is reading a passage in Khayyam where he complains about the lack of support for genuine scientific work in his time simply a matter of affirming what happened to him in the past, or is it also a reflection on what we ourselves, academics or not, have ourselves experienced at times absurdly organized and at times even personally abusive university institutions, and does it, or should it, not motivate us to do something about it?

When Khayyam tells us in one of his quatrains to run away from formal schools and instead caress the Beloved's Hair, is he just offering an amusing insight of a personal or private nature about his own time, or is he also offering a significant, a universal, advice of deep epistemological and methodological import regarding abandoning wasteful inquiries undertaken in formal schools in favor of basic questions about the wonder of existence? Is he pointing to a significant difference between mental rote-learning, and a holistic learning that involves not just intellectual, but also emotional as well as sensual modes of learning motivated by a passion for learning or teaching than one enforced today by panoptic regimes of higher education surveillance fed to us in the name of "science," "peer review," and "objectivity"?

Are not our personal troubles as academics, at times mocked for pursuing stigmatized intellectual projects, not similar to what Khayyam was experiencing centuries ago, when he complained about others duplicitously pursuing science for extrinsic gains while mocking others who are genuinely motivated to seek truths? Which is a symptom, and which a cause?

6. The Problem of Continuity: Are We Supposed to Find Causal Relations Amid Easily Locatable and Traceable Causal Chains?

My sixth set of questions related to C. Wright Mills may be considered in terms of the apparent *continuities* we may perceive to exist in the causal relations influencing the dialectics of personal troubles and public issues.

We have become used to considering causal relations in terms of continuities of causal chains. A causes B, B causes C, C causes D, and so on. The assumption is that there is a causal chain at work that takes place through the intermediation of each local cause. A deeper structure of thinking guiding such a view, if you may notice, is that objects are atomistic and separable, where one, like a crudely conceived billiard balls game, causes the next, and the next causes another, and so on, motion.

Were we adopting such a 'classical' point of view, we would expect that what is happening to us locally now is somehow limited to that here-and-now and not itself caused by a seemingly "separate" cause elsewhere, be it someone else's personal trouble on the other side of the Earth, or in a different culture or historical period. In other words, we are not used to, in our classical worldviews, including the same in our sociologies, seeing how seemingly "separate" local personal troubles in different times and places, or seemingly "separate" local public issues in different times and places, are causally related and display apparently enigmatic discontinuities—or what I prefer to call instead 'transcontinuities' (see Tamdgidi 2020).

This perception may arise both in terms of finding ourselves, personally, afflicted with personal troubles that someone else experiences or experienced continents or centuries away, or to public issues a people, society, or even civilization has experienced, or is experiencing "discontinuously" across seemingly unrelated historical time and space.

Consider for instance how we ourselves relate to, and are inspired by, what we find in certain quatrains attributed to Khayyam. It may appear as if he is from a completely different culture, and time, and yet, we find him intimate and close, when we appreciate what he was trying to do, and failed in doing, given the difficulties of his time. We therefore feel personally troubled by public issues that seemingly existed centuries ago, or find that amid our public issues of today, we find reasons to relate to the personal troubles of someone whom we never met and who lived nearly a thousand years ago.

In a classical worldview where causalities are deemed to be continuous through apparently localized and locally traceable causal chains, if we are looking for an explanation of an event, we would be looking for seemingly obvious clues where we "should" be able to find an answer. It may not even occur to us that an explanation on a problem in domain B could be found in a seemingly "separate" domain Y, leaping over all the seemingly "unrelated" links in between. So, we become disappointed when we do not find any passages in our extant manuscripts dealing with topic B, because we are looking only at B, or at best A or C, and not the seemingly discontinuously located Y. So, we become despaired and resigned to a puzzle or enigma that we think will remain unsolved forever.

We may not even consider that it could be possible to find causes or explanations of a topic while exploring seemingly separate "other" topics, by way of strangely "unrelated" and "short-cut" exploratory wormholes. Since we see the realities we explore in fragmented and "discontinuous" ways, we do not suspect that topics in them could be related in deeper ways than how they appear. So, when even exploring a personal trouble and its causes, we look for causes in "obvious" places, and do not realize that the seemingly unrelated personal troubles or public issues may in fact be deeply "trans-related" in a different reference frame.

But the above does not annul the fact that still there are causal forces at play. What they point out, rather, is a distinction between a classical, straightforward chain of continuous local causal factors that are easily traceable, and a different way of considering causation that allows for experiencing leaps of creative insight that we could not predict coming to us beforehand, and yet happen, because the objects we study are not simply localized and separate objects, but are spread-out in different frames of reference in which we study them, such that they are transcontinuously related in fact in other ways not immediately perceptible to our common senses.

7. The Problem of Disciplinarity: Are We Always Better Off Dividing and Specializing Our Knowledges Into Fragmented Disciplines?

The seventh set of questions arising from my considerations of Mills's sociological imagination framework, one that follows the previous sets outlined logically, is regarding the broader intellectual "social structures" embedded in Mills's own notion of "sociology," and thereby his "sociological imagination," both considered in their academic disciplinary contexts.

In what way may Mills's notion of sociology be regarded as one that is, both in its broader world-historical and its more specifically academic disciplinary senses, situated, particular, and provincial? Can one regard his drawing on American Pragmatism or Western (particularly German) sociological theories and concepts as "objective" and "scientifically" neutral and unbiased, or did his "sociological imagination" also have a particular disciplinary taste or aim, identity and location? Is Mills's sociological imagination a particularly *Western* sociological imagination?

Is there only one way of cultivating a sociological imagination or many— again in terms of the broader meaning of the term, and the specific academic and disciplinary, or even sociological, cultures prevalent during his time, or today? What was Mills's attitude toward academic disciplinarity, consciously or not, in words and deeds? He clearly was uncomfortable with being "boxed in" sociology as a rigid field. Still, was his maintaining a "sociological" identity for his imagination telling of a subtle adherence to modern academic "scientific" disciplinarity despite the obvious and at times severe criticisms he launched against the prevailing academic sociological traditions of his time?

A significant implication of the above observation for our Khayyami studies in this series has to do with the lens with which we study other lenses in the past. In other words, are we aware of how our own "scientific" and "sociological" efforts—so intricately and organically shaped, consciously or not, by the compartmentalized and "disciplined" models of disciplinarity still prevalent in the Westernized university world-system today amid which we have ourselves been trained—can shape how we understand Khayyam's intellectual project? Are we to judge his writings on science, philosophy, religion, poetry, astronomy, and so on, with the same fragmented disciplinary lenses we have become accustomed to using in our universities?

As noted above, we find in the Khayyami Robaiyat at times a strong critique of traditional schooling, learning by rote, depending too much on the verbal and the intellectual in contrast to the intuitive and the emotional capacities of the heart. How are we to understand and judge such sentiments?

Can we in fact understand, only intellectually, what Khayyam had to offer, when at times he in fact explicitly notes that others cannot come to know him or the truth through pure intellection and conventional learning, without engaging what he calls *tazkiyeh-ye nafs*, or "self-purification," which is a reference to meditative practices he must have seriously engaged in, ones that may have even (as reported) "physical exercises"? Was Khayyam's practice of poetry indeed *a part* of his scientific endeavors, and simultaneously also a meditative practice? Can our modern day visions conditioned by the separation of the natural sciences, the social sciences, and the humanities, lead to an understanding of how for Khayyam the pursuit of poetry could at once be philosophical, spiritual, scientific, and aesthetic/artistic endeavors?

Amid technical commentaries on the purpose of algebra or geometry, for instance, Khayyam suddenly states that a given insight will lead to a better understanding of God or existence. How can we truly understand this odd utterance, using our fragmented lenses of our academic disciplinarity today? Or, he uses the notion of "nothing" preceding "A" (or Alef) in the alphabet, as an expression of how God is a Necessary Being, uncaused by anything preceding him. Number 1 is not a number, according to him, because a number is preceded and followed by an integer (zero not being considered one); the analogy is significant in terms of a spiritual principle it helps to demonstrate. For Khayyam, pursuits of mathematics and geometry are at once searches for understanding God, quite unlike how, in my view, the still-at-heart Newtonian science today is conceived—itself, ironically, quite unlike even how Newton himself made his discoveries, deeply immersed behind the scenes in alchemy and a passionately mystical pursuit of knowledge of God.

Are the procedural and institutional structures of our universities and "scientific" pursuits today—characterized by separations of natural science, social science, and humanities cultures—conducive to, or preventive of, our effort in going about understanding Khayyam's life, works, and legacy?

8. The Problem of Scientism: Is Science Always Western, and Still Newtonian?

My eighth and perhaps most fundamental and all-encompassing set of questions (including those listed in the previous seven sets above) regarding C. Wright Mills's proposed model for the sociological imagination has to do with a seemingly odd anomaly that grips the broader strokes of the whole argument that runs throughout his book.

In *The Sociological Imagination* (1959), Mills wrote:

> In every intellectual age some one style of reflection tends to become a common denominator of cultural life. Nowadays, it is true, many intellectual fads are widely taken up before they are dropped for new ones in the course of a year or two. Such enthusiasms may add spice to cultural play, but leave little or no intellectual trace. That is not true of such ways of thinking as 'Newtonian physics' or 'Darwinian biology.' Each of these intellectual universes became an influence that reached far beyond any special sphere of idea and imagery. In terms of them, or in terms derived from them, unknown scholars as well as fashionable commentators came to re-focus their observations and re-formulate their concerns. (1959:13-14)

As expressed clearly in the above passage, Mills believed that in contrast to short-term intellectual and cultural fads or fashions that come and go and leave brief traces in scholarly and scientific cultures of any period, broader worldviews, "intellectual universes," and "ways of thinking" such as Newtonianism (and Darwinism) leave lasting traces in all cultural and scientific fields and "styles of reflection" in a given era.

Yet, time and again, we find Mills himself repeatedly and continually, albeit at times (but not always) critically, advocating in his book a "return" to the "classical tradition" in sociology, a tradition that in fact arose in the context of, and was deeply inspired by, such paradigmatic scientific revolutions as Newtonianism. These 'social scientific' worldviews, in their efforts to establish sociology as an academic and 'scientific' discipline, went to great lengths to identify 'objective' laws of motion of society or history, or at least 'dominant' historical trends in them, seeking to 'discover' root causal forces shaping history and society as 'foundational' 'social' explanations for secondary, individual acts and behaviors. These "classical" sociologists were also quite busy, more or less, trying to establish the foundations and boundaries of sociology as a "scientific" academic "discipline" distinctly and clearly demarcated from others.

Were Mills's comments on Newtonianism and the Newtonian "way of thinking" in his book meant to acknowledge that he himself was gripped by and embraced Newtonianism in his proposed critical return to "classical" pursuit of the sociological imagination, or did he instead mean to question such fundamental structures of thinking, seeking ways to move beyond them in favor of newer scientific, cultural, and sociological, imaginations?

Or, are we confronting here a seemingly odd and paradoxical case that we have not one, but two, if not more, Mills selves writing his book, one hand being unaware at times of what the other hand was writing, so to speak?

Did one self in Mills practice, in pursuit of cultivating sociological imaginations, the very "classical" Newtonian sociological disciplinary and conceptual environments that another self in Mills sought to interrogate as the limiting public structures of knowledge and cultures of an earlier intellectual age, "mechanical," "bureaucratic," "grand theorizing," and "trivializing" ones that needed to be transcended in order to foster his proposed "sociological imagination" as another expression of a "new common denominator" of cultural life in the (then) twentieth century?

It may seem paradoxical to argue that a Newtonian worldview, a way of seeing the world that came to dominate the scientific spirit long after the time when Khayyam lived and worked may be deficient in fostering a sociological framework to understand his work. However, if we consider historical trajectory of time not as linear, but dialectical, where long past trends can reappear again in new forms, and what appears to be an advance in ways of knowing may also contain, despite its contributions, also shortcomings and limitations in understanding reality, then we may find that ways of knowing Khayyam seemed to pursue and advocate may have less to do with what we call today Newtonian ways of going about science and more affinities with quantum ways of imagining reality that have become increasingly paramount since the beginning of twentieth century, to which I tried to extensively draw readers' attention in my recent work *Liberating Sociology* (volume 1, 2020).

When considering the above in relation to our Khayyami studies, would we be surprised, in a leap of insight, to realize that in fact Omar Khayyam himself was an inventor of a sociological imagination of his own time, besides being a philosopher, mathematician, astronomer, writer, physician, and poet? May we find that the attributed Robaiyat represent in a poetic form, what his philosophical writings did in the abstract, or his geometry or algebra did in technical forms, a highly and deeply creative sociological imagination at play, through which he conveyed the dialectic of his own personal troubles and the public issues of his time in the most concise, lucid, and beautiful, form, in the hopes of finding a happier way for humanity to live his or her life ridden of incidentally avoidable personal troubles and public issues?

May we find that Khayyam's way of imagining the world through his Robaiyat itself had more affinities with a quantum sociological imagination founded on nondualistic, nonreductive, creatively dialectical ways of thinking—and for that reason such an approach would be a better way of understanding his life and works?

In this book I will further use the above eight sets of question and observations of the seeming anomaly in Mills's manner of framing his proposed sociological imagination as a pathway for advocating a quantum sociological imagination, one that preserves the best and the most useful elements of the analytical framework Mills offered for the sociological imagination, but reframes and transcends them in favor of a quantum sociological imagination that I will argue offers a more fruitful methodological framework for conducting hermeneutic studies of Khayyam's life and works.

However, before coming back to delineating what my proposed quantum sociological imagination consists of, and how it may implicate Khayyami studies in general and the one conducted in the present series in particular, we need to more clearly understand of what the quantum way of imagining reality consists and how it overlaps or contrasts with the Newtonian worldview. And to do this, we should first start by understanding what the Newtonian way of imagining reality is.

In the next two chapters I will draw on my studies of the Newtonian and quantum ways of thinking about reality as shared in my recently work

Liberating Sociology: From Newtonian Toward Quantum Imaginations: Volume 1: Unriddling the Quantum Enigma (2020). My purpose here will be to both report in summary and then illustrate in an applied way, by way of commenting on the implications of the discussion in the context of Khayyami studies, how the Newtonian and quantum ways of imagining reality, society, and sociology, differ from one another and how such a contrast allows us to foster quantum sociological imaginations that can more fruitfully frame our new Khayyami studies.

Abstract

This essay, titled "The Promise and the Classical Limits of C. Wright Mills's Sociological Imagination," is the first chapter of the first book, subtitled *New Khayyami Studies: Quantumizing the Newtonian Structures of C. Wright Mills's Sociological Imagination for A New Hermeneutic Method,* of the twelve-book series, *Omar Khayyam's Secret: Hermeneutics of the Robaiyat in Quantum Sociological Imagination,* authored by Mohammad H. Tamdgidi. The study of texts to understand their meanings in social context falls in the subdisciplinary field of the sociology of knowledge, broadly defined as a branch of social scientific inquiry concerned with understanding how knowledge and social reality relate to one another. Studying Khayyam's attributed works and those of others about him in order to understand his views and life in historical context, therefore, can be framed as a study in the sociology of knowledge, broadly speaking.

In this chapter, using Khayyami studies as an applied exploratory setting, Tamdgidi revisits the Millsian sociological imagination, raising eight issues that he believes express the limits imposed by the classical Newtonian way of thinking on Mills's imaginative framework. He explores the eight issues in terms of the following questions. 1. The problem of dualism: can personal troubles be also public issues, and vice versa? 2. The problem of atomism: which self's personal trouble is it? 3. The problem of separability: whose public issues are these? 4. The problem of objectivity: can we as observers separate ourselves from others' personal troubles and public issues? 5. The problem of determinism: is it always the case that society shapes the individual/self, and that public issues always shape personal troubles? 6. The problem of continuity: are we supposed to find causal relations amid easily locatable and traceable causal chains? 7. The problem of disciplinarity: are we always better off dividing and specializing our knowledges into fragmented disciplines? And 8. The problem of scientism: is science always Western, and still Newtonian?

The author asks and explores whether Mills's comments on Newtonianism and the Newtonian "way of thinking" in his book were meant to acknowledge that he himself was gripped by and embraced Newtonianism in his proposed critical return to "classical" pursuit of the sociological imagination, or did he instead mean to question such fundamental structures of thinking, seeking ways to move beyond them in favor of newer scientific, cultural, and sociological imaginations?

CHAPTER II—The Newtonian Way of Imagining Reality, Society, Sociology, and Khayyami Studies

In order to understand how C. Wright Mills's sociological imagination may be, advertently or not, practiced in a Newtonian way to frame our Khayyami studies, and to evaluate the usefulness and inner consistency of such a Newtonian way of imagining reality as a framework on its own, we do not need initially to leap into an alternative quantum way of imagining reality, although we will do so in due course in the next chapter.

To offer a heuristic model of the Newtonian way of imagining reality, society, sociology, and the sociological imagination, and demonstrate (later in the next chapter) how such a perspective is different from the quantum way of imagining them, I will use in this chapter the "billiard balls game" metaphor that has been widely used (in my view wrongly) to characterize the Newtonian way of imagining the world.

As far as the relevance of what follows to our Khayyami studies is concerned, let us imagine the various sources, textual or otherwise, of information we have about Omar Khayyam to be fragments, like the billiard balls in our metaphor, that we will generally use to elucidate the Newtonian way of imagining reality.

To elaborate, while still continuing to assume for now (as in the previous chapter) that we are not confronted with challenges such as secrecy or unavailability of resources about Khayyam's life and works, let us still assume and imagine that we have a set of data items such as, say, some quatrains, several passages of prose in philosophy, religion, science, or literature authentically attributed to Khayyam, plus several other verifiable passages from his contemporaries or beyond about him or his works as well. We can even throw into the mix other physical data such as the various graves built for Khayyam over the centuries and the writings (if any) on them. Let us say all these fragmentary data from and about Khayyam are available to us like billiard balls of data studying which offers us the best chance we have of reliably learning about him, especially regarding the existence, nature, and purpose of the Robaiyat in his life and works.

In my recent book *Liberating Sociology: From Newtonian Toward Quantum Imagination: Volume 1: Unriddling the Quantum Enigma* (2020), I have explored more extensively and in much more depth, in the context of understanding the so-called "quantum enigma," the Newtonian and quantum ways of imagining reality that I will now also share below in summary form, with new applied insights added in relation to Khayyami studies. Some of the material below are borrowed from that work because it is important that a broad understanding of the Newtonian and quantum ways of imagining reality is held when applying the same in pursuit of the Khayyami studies before us in this book and series. Therefore, when sharing the material, I will do so while illustrating how what I presented before in *Unriddling the Quantum Enigma* (2020) can help us build a new methodological framework for Khayyami studies.

From the late seventeenth century onwards following the publication of the works of the English physicist and mathematician Sir Isaac Newton (1642-1726)—especially his two books *Philosophiæ Naturalis Principia Mathematica* ("Mathematical Principles of Natural Philosophy"), first published in Latin in 1687, and *Opticks; or, A Treatise of the Reflections, Refractions, Inflections & Colours of Light*, first published in English in 1704—a new way of thinking about the world emerged which became associated with his name.

Newtonianism became in time one of the defining and dominant features of modern culture and the so-called 'scientific' revolution because it substituted for the preceding speculative and mysterious conceptions of the universe governed by unknown or unknowable supernatural forces a mechanical conception of it as a law-governed universe.

At the heart of Newton's major contribution that made such a law-governed view of the universe possible was the formulation of a new universal theory of gravitation to explain not only the motions of planets in the solar system, but also the motion of any object in the universe, terrestrial or cosmic, very large or very small.

To gain a basic sense of Newtonianism as a distinct way of thinking about the universe as a law-governed reality, we should begin with how Newton characterized the three fundamental laws of motion of bodies. In *Principia Mathematica*, in his own words as translated later on from Latin into English by Andrew Motte (1846), Newton stated his three laws of motion as follows[1]:

> LAW I. Every body perseveres in its state of rest, or of uniform motion in a right line, unless it is compelled to change that state by forces impressed thereon. ...

> LAW II. The alteration of motion is ever proportional to the motive force impressed; and is made in the direction of the right line in which that force is impressed. ...

> LAW III. To every action there is always opposed an equal reaction: or the mutual actions of two bodies upon each other are always equal, and directed to contrary parts. ...

To compare, let me quote here in passing two popularized versions of the first law, randomly drawn from two different educational websites on the Internet:

> When viewed in an inertial reference frame, an object either remains at rest or continues to move at a constant velocity, unless acted upon by an external force.[2]

> [or ...]

> Newton's first law states that every object will remain at rest or in uniform motion in a straight line unless compelled to change its state by the action of an external force.[3]

The reason I am quoting these two other renderings of the first law is to highlight a chief characteristic of the Newtonian worldview as conveyed more explicitly in them, namely, the so-called 'billiard balls game' conception of the universe, in which bodies, very large to very small, act upon one another

---

1. See: https://en.wikisource.org/wiki/The_Mathematical_Principles_of_Natural_Philosophy_(1846)/Axioms,_or_Laws_of_Motion (accessed on 9/14/2015).

2. See: https://en.wikipedia.org/wiki/Newton%27s_laws_of_motion#cite_note-first-law-shaums-2 (accessed on 9/14/2015).

3. See: https://www.grc.nasa.gov/www/K-12/airplane/newton.html (accessed on 9/14/2015).

from outside, externally. For this way of thinking about the universe to be at all possible, in other words, two conditions are essential and mutually necessary. One is that units of matter are presumed to exist as bodies, from the very small to the very large, clearly separated from one another, in a "chunky" way, so to speak; second, that these bodies interact and exert forces on one another from *without, externally.*

Interesting to note here—and that is why I quoted the other two renderings of the first law for comparison—is that in Newton's own words and as expressed in his own particular language, the *externality* of the impression of force is not necessarily implied. The notion "impressed thereon," in other words, leaves it open to consider whether the object (or any part or parts thereof) could impress a force upon *itself*, for instance, as one of a wide range of possibilities.

However, that is not what Newton obviously had in mind given his focus on inanimate objects in the works written, and that is why (or, more important perhaps is, how) he was interpreted in the scientific and broader public imaginations later as conveying the notion of force being externally impressed on the object as in the imagery of a billiard balls interaction.

It is one thing to say one is elucidating the laws of motion of inanimate objects, and another to claim, or be (mis)interpreted to be claiming, that one is expressing the "universal" laws of motion of all bodies, presumably including animate, in particular human, "objects." Whether Newton meant it as such, or not, is besides the point here, since the subsequent conscious or subconscious entanglement in the scholarly and public imaginations of the sciences of society and of human actors with a Newtonian paradigm claiming to be advancing knowledges about the "universal" laws of motion of all bodies in general was bound to have significant implications for how social and human reality came to be subsequently understood, let alone transformed.

The imagery of a "billiard balls" game cannot capture the possibility of a ball being self-motivating and impressing forces upon *itself*, nor that of initiating a force *sui generis* that can creatively move the whole set of balls of which it is a part. Of course, we should consider the god-like figure of the billiard balls game player initiating the first strike, but then, here we are left with the imagery of a mechanical system subsequently interacting on its own based on a set of presumably objective laws following the first strike, but not as a result of the balls impressing their own creative powers upon themselves, on one another, or on their table environment.

Attributing such self-motivating, creative powers to the balls themselves, of course, would undermine the notion of an objectively law-governed and predictable reality and would have to accommodate the "odd" notion of the possibility of artfully creative and unpredictable bodies amid an emerging scientific paradigm bent on advocating a predeterministic and predictable way of thinking hard at work at distinguishing itself from philosophy, religion, and the arts.

The assumption of externality of objects interacting with one another is vital to the Newtonian 'scientific' imagination that was emerging because in order for two objects to exert forces on one another (or others), it is logically imperative that they are presumed to exist external to one another. For, otherwise, it would be tautological to suggest that A, or even a part of A, exerts a force upon A. Parts of A can be regarded as exerting forces upon one another, to be sure, helping to constitute the totality of what makes A what it is in addition to the interactions A itself (along with its parts) has with other objects (and their parts) outside it. However, to suggest that a part (or parts) of A exerts a force on A as a whole would undermine the logical consistency of what the Newtonian laws were presumed to universally explain. That is, it would make it logically ambiguous to claim that something is exerting a force on A when that "something" is A, or a part of it.

It is for this reason that in the metaphorical expression of the Newtonian way of thinking, we confront an imagery of separate balls exerting forces on one another from without, and not an imagination that seeks to illustrate the forces of a part and its parent whole interacting with one another.

The Newtonian way of thinking, therefore, implied a universe structured as bodies, from the cosmic large to the atomic small, whose motions are law-governed by the forces they externally exert on one another. This view, we should note in passing, still accommodated Newton's and his time's prevailing religious worldviews generally speaking (despite considerable disputes that also emerged regarding the religious significance and implications of Newton's scientific discoveries), since the ultimate "external" force may still be regarded as one exerted by God as the ultimate cause. God, through His Will, in other words, can still be regarded as imposing itself as an externality on matter in such a cosmology. After all, Newton also was and remained a deeply religious man and a strong monotheistic believer in God throughout his life. In fact, recent studies of his papers have clearly established that his search for understanding the cosmic order and its laws was deeply motivated and inspired by occultist passions for knowing God's secrets.

Nevertheless, it is also crucial to point out that the Newtonian way of thinking, as it emerged from the late seventeenth century without an adequate knowledge then of the Newton's secretive religious and occult motivations for his work, was registered in the scientific and broader public imagination as a largely secular revelation about the nature of the universe and its laws of motion. As such, therefore, the conception of the universe he ushered made it possible for those not believing in any god to also argue using Newtonianism that the universe is a self-moving, self-contained, law-governed reality that does not need a prime mover to continue to exist. God in the Newtonian imagination was a possibility, but not a necessity.

From an epistemological standpoint, further assumption here was that even though we may not know exactly at a given time or place the forces exerted by bodies on one another in very large or very small scales, and may therefore have to resort to various 'scientific' tools for measuring their outcomes—allowing there even for the possibility that we may not, practically speaking, know everything about the universe—the forces are considered in and of themselves determinable and predictable. Newtonianism in the public imagination thus became identified as a belief in the notion that the order of the universe from the motions of the largest to those of the smallest bodies of matter is precise, determined/determinable, and potentially knowable.

The power of the Newtonian science was so immense that later on, in the early decades of the twentieth century, even Albert Einstein, despite his own newfound conception of the universe and spacetime based on his theories of general and special relativity (overturning the way Newton conceived the gravitational force at the heart of his cosmology), could not abandon Newton's ultimate vision of universe as an ordered medium. "God does not play dice," Einstein said when dismissing new arguments that were being advanced by the emerging quantum physicists in favor of a vision advocating a less determinable and less predictable universe. Or, countering quantum physics' finding that the nature of subatomic "reality" is dependent on human observation of it, Einstein once quipped, "I like to think the Moon is there even if I am not looking at it." He, like Newton, was intensely eager to discover and read "the mind of God," so to speak, in order to provide the ultimate explanation for the nature of the universe, and by extension, of human existence.

The rise of the Newtonian worldview marked a revolution in the prescientific cosmologies preceding Newton, because it made it possible to move beyond mysteries and speculations about Nature, and to motivate generations of scientists to seek the truth in actual facts of existence. The 'billiard balls game' imagination of objective reality thereby legitimated a 'billiard balls game' conception of science itself, both in terms of the legitimacy of its divisibility into separate/separable disciplines internally (which explains the subsequent splitting of the preceding "philosophical sciences" into increasingly specialized disciplines and the rise and division of separate academic cultures into the natural and the social sciences and the humanities), and the legitimacy of the external separability of science itself from other religious, philosophical, and artistic cosmologies (which explains the continuing and subsequent division of the all-encompassing pre-modern and integrative Renaissance spirits of inquiry into separable and specialized traditions of inquiry now dominated by an authoritative scientific paradigm).

Most important for our consideration here of Mills's sociological imagination are the explicit or implicit, conscious or subconscious, assumptions that come along with the Newtonian 'billiard balls game' imagination of, or way of thinking about, the universe. The entanglement of the rising social sciences in the subsequent centuries with the broad strokes of the Newtonian imagination—later called "classical," when the quantum revolution emerged as a contrasting worldview beginning from the early years of the twentieth century—was an historical development that left its deep imprints on the very fabric of the sciences of social phenomena, including sociology, that gradually emerged.

In Mills's own words the impact of the "ways of thinking" such as Newtonianism (and Darwinism) on the prevailing public and intellectual cultures were deep and enduring, and not simply a passing fad. The entanglements were deep, and because of their "imagined" quality, penetrated beyond the conscious verbal modes of knowing (or not) into the deepest non-verbal subconscious mental realms and were thereby not (self-) consciously apparent to those holding onto such views. The complexity of the entanglement, therefore, could be such that when acknowledging and appreciating, even when applying, the insights of quantum revolution, we could be doing so using linguistic and conceptual habits that are still deeply entangled with classical Newtonianism.

In fact, an important point advanced in my research on the so-called "quantum enigma"—the results of which were released on January 20, 2020, and for which this series on Khayyam serves as both a motivation and an applied site of empirical exploration—is that what has made quantum science and its findings enigmatic and puzzling has much to do with our own conceptual instruments as observers, instruments that are still deeply and subconsciously embedded in Newtonian language and imagination, even when we conduct quantum scientific research, while trying (or not) to interpret the physical meaning of its abstract formulations and equations.

To unpack further the above broad strokes of the Newtonian way of thinking about or imagining reality, I proceed below to elaborate further on what exactly, in my view, constitutes the playerless and ideologically distorted "billiard balls game" nature of the Newtonian imagination of, or way of thinking about, the universe, including society and ourselves.

In the exposition that follows, I will try to introduce the details parallel to the order in which I shared in the previous chapter the eight sets of questions about the Millsian sociological imagination. I will later on return more explicitly to this point, but the purpose of proceeding as such is to help the reader establish parallel links between the Newtonian way of thinking as described here and the eight sets of questions about Mills's sociological imagination I raised in the last chapter.

In the process, I will also try to elucidate by specific examples what implications such a discussion can have on framing our Khayyami studies in general, and as conducted in this series in particular.

The Newtonian way of imagining, or thinking about, the universe may be broadly characterized as having eight notional attributes—namely, its notions of (1) dualism, (2) atomism, (3) separability, (4) (subjectless) objectivity, (5) determinism (including its associated notion of predictability), (6) continuity, (7) disciplinarity, and (8) scientism—which can be illustrated by using a (what I will argue is an ideologically distorted) metaphorical "billiard balls game" way of imagining reality as commonly used for the purpose.

I will use such a framework later on to show how such parameters also have shaped our Newtonian conceptions of society, sociology, and the sociological imagination, and may also continue to frame our Khayyami studies if we fail in bringing them to conscious awareness as a precondition for reframing our sociological and Khayyami studies in more fruitful, quantum ways.

1. Dualism: Can An Object Be A And Non-A at the Same Time?

The Newtonian way of thinking is fundamentally dependent on a vision of reality as a system in which bodies are divisible (infinitely or not) as systems of *separate* wholes, without considering the broader wholes to which those wholes belong as parts.

This means that the Newtonian vision is fundamentally dependent on elements that must stand, and be conceived to stand, separately from one another in a "chunky way" in order for the causal laws said to be presumably governing their interactions to make any sense. The logical architecture of such a vision, in other words, is formal, since only in a formal logical environment where A is separate from non-A can one claim that A causes non-A, exerts forces on non-A, non-A is impressed upon by A, and so on. An alternative, nonreductively dialectical, logical environment which would allow for A and non-A to be one another at the same time while also being distinct from one another—that is, to simultaneously have a relation of identity and difference—cannot accommodate a Newtonian vision of reality, for it would be meaningless to argue that A impresses a force on non-A while acknowledging that non-A is or can also be A, at the same time.

Note that what contributes to such a "chunky" way of imagining reality is not something built into reality itself, but results from a *notional* attribute of the way we ourselves, as observers, go about imagining that reality.

To illustrate this, let us say someone claims that there are more or less intelligent creatures living in the Sun, insisting that he has absolutely no doubts about it, such that he could offer practical examples of it right now, as you are reading these words. Anyone hearing this would certainly regard the claimant to be either joking, as having gone mad, or as having made quite a strange and obviously fantastic statement.

To make this more interesting, let me just say that I myself confidently believe in such a claim.

The key here is to consider the language one is using to make such a claim. In a conception that regards the Sun as a rather large billiard ball separately existing 'out there' exerting its gravitational force on these other billiard ball-like planets at a distance, certainly the notion that there are intelligent creatures living in it would be absurd, a joke, or clearly an enigmatic utterance. However, if one suggested that the Sun is actually not the corpuscular, detached ball of fire out there, but a broader reality constituting the entire Solar System, any part of which, not just other planets but even all the presumed "void" in between, are intricately parts of the system as a whole, then it becomes obvious that this Sun being defined now as the entire Solar System as a whole is comprised of a Solar center and planetary parts, in one of which exist more or less thinking creatures, a practical proof of which is the process before your eyes on Earth, your reading words written by me just now being a proof of it.

So, you and I, in this alternative conception and way of thinking, are citizens of the Sun (considered in the broader sense of the Solar System).

Similarly, the Earth is not just this ball over here as distinct from the Moon as that ball out there, but a sphere that includes both the Earth, the Moon, and all that in between, all being one of numerous planetary subsystems of the Solar System as a whole. One can of course extend this way of thinking regarding the Sun (i.e., the Solar System) as part of the Milky Way galaxy, and the latter as part of its galaxy cluster, and so on.

If I were to claim moreover that by changing myself, I change society, the Earth, the Moon, the Sun, the Solar System, and the entire universe, in the context of such an alternative language used, I would not be making an entirely senseless claim, but one that it is entirely truthful.

The point here is that in this alternative conception, changes in you and me are by definition and simultaneously changes in society, in the Earth, in the Sun, in the Milky Way, and as such, changes in the interactions these presumed bodies have with other bodies as parts of the universe. Granted, the changes can be miniscule and small, but this is subject to historical variance, for it is certainly the case that changes in the thinking of specific individuals in past history have had more or less significant and consequential "butterfly effects" on the lives of others in society, on human technologies, and on their built and natural environments. After all, the world, including that of science, we know of today would be quite different if an unknown inventions clerk in the early twentieth century had not daydreamed in his spare time about how a beam of light would look like if he was chasing it.

The corpuscular conception of things in a "chunky" way as billiard balls forces us to think of reality as chunks where something in one chunk cannot be at the same time in another. A conception of reality in terms of part-whole dialectics, however, allows us to conceive of the possibility that something in a part is at the same time in a whole to which that part belongs, while also considering that the two positions are not entirely the same. In other words, we can visualize the dialectical notion of the identity of difference in the dialectics of part and whole.

Note that we have not had, yet, a need to consult quantum science to observe and to question the dualistic way of thinking as described above as being a foundational attribute of the Newtonian way of imagining reality.

In the context of our Khayyami studies, the implication of our Newtonian way of framing it is enormously significant.

For instance, when we consider whether Khayyam composed a quatrain, we habitually think of a quatrain conveying certain thoughts, feelings, or sensibilities, in a corpuscular way, that is, in its congealed form comprised of four lines of poetry, three or all of which rhyme. So, we end up considering several quatrains attributed to Khayyam as if they are separate chunks, themselves separated from other chunks of philosophical, religious, scientific, or literary prose that may also be attributed to Khayyam.

But, note how we do not apply that fragmentary view of things consistently to other things. For instance, Khayyam himself is imagined as a solid entity, divided or not within, imagined as unchanging biographically from time to time and place to place in an historical context, one that itself is also seen as "objectively" standing separately from his life events and works. Consequently, in our studies of his life and works, we end up imagining our task as a way of linking these chunks, already presumed to be separated and separable from one another.

In such a Newtonian way of treating the quatrains attributed to Khayyam, we would then find ourselves having to decide, in an absolutely "yes or no," dualistic way, whether a quatrain belongs to him or not. Is it "authentic," or not? Is it his, or not? If we regard it as authentic, we study it, if not, we simply disregard it. We would find a FitzGerald composing a systematized collection of self-admittedly "free translations" of Khayyam's poems to be an invention by FitzGerald and imposed on his originals from without and not necessarily one already present internally, explicated or not, in Khayyam from which FitzGerald may have, consciously or not, drawn inspiration. So, we simply assume that the quatrains must have been completely separate chunks of poems that required a FitzGerald to come along and give it some order as a story line of a day/night in a poet's life.

Adopting a Newtonian approach, we would similarly compartmentalize Khayyam's writings into the scientific here, the philosophical there, the literary elsewhere, and the poetic yet somewhere else, our study and project becoming simply that of understanding how such separate chunks of Khayyam's life and works can be juggled with and related to one another from without.

But, we could alternatively imagine a quatrain to have a "two-fold" reality in terms of simultaneity, one congealed/corpuscular and one spread-out throughout all of Khayyam's works. We could see even a single quatrain, not simply as a work of art, but also a philosophical reflection, a spiritual statement, a scientific observation or experimentation, a sociological proposition and innovation, a literary innovation, an exercise in social activism, a reflection on his personal trouble at a given moment of his life, an expression of a specific public issue of his times, a poetry of personal troubles that becomes, itself, a public issue for those considering it, out of ignorance or not, like snake-bites threatening a frozen and dogmatized orthodox religious point of view, in favor of an open-ended, critical, creative mindset. Is this quatrain then a chunk, a thing, a particle, or a spread-out object, a wave?

This is similar to the point I was raising above regarding how we ourselves conceptualize, or imagine, our subject matter. It is *we* who choose to observe reality, and the language we construct and use to do so, and it is because of *our* choice that we end up pursuing different strategies in our Khayyami studies, one of which may prove fruitful, while another may lead us to an impasse. The impasse would then not be necessarily a result of our lack of adequate information about the subject matter at hand, but because of the dualistic, Newtonian way we ourselves chose to imagine those data objects.

2. Atomism: What Is the Micro Unit of Analysis of the Object?

"Atomism" (from Greek roots meaning 'indivisible') has historically been associated with the notion that what exists is composed of particles that cannot be further divided, and through whose combinations/attractions or collisions/deflections all material forms in the universe are made or distinguished from one another.

Those adhering to this way of thinking have variously held this view across centuries, ranging from those strictly adhering to the notion of indivisibility of matter beyond a certain point altogether, to those who reinterpreted the notion as referring to the smallest unit of any object that still retains the properties of that object.

Scientific investigations in time established that even though what was once regarded as an indivisible atom is found to be composed of subatomic particles which are themselves further divisible, it is as a result of specific combinations or interactions of subatomic particles that definite atoms of the elements as basic building blocks of matter are formed—blocks which, if further divided or differently combined, lose the qualities associated with the specific elements formed by them.

Atomism and the scientific interest in identifying the smallest unit of analysis of any object as a way of exploring its nature have thus historically been associated with the view that one can better understand the nature of a more complex object by identifying its simplest "cell-form," so to speak. This can lead one to better understand what its building blocks are, how they interact to constitute the nature of the object, and how the variations of their interactions account for the variations in which the object is manifested.

The Newtonian way of imagining reality has also been characterized by the atomistic way of thinking, one that may be more specifically called corpuscularism. In order to further explore how atomism/corpuscularism characterizes the Newtonian way of thinking, let us again use the billiard balls analogy to make some conceptual clarifications.

What is the unit of analysis of a billiard balls game? In what may seem at first to be a rather straightforward way of answering the question, the unit of analysis of a billiard balls game may appear to be the ball, the solid body, the corpuscule, in the process of interaction of a set of which the billiard balls game as a whole may be readily conceived.

By adopting a corpuscular way of thinking to identify the ball as the 'atom' of the billiard balls game, however, we learn little about the reasons for the balls' existence, their particular nature, and the history of their development and use. In that way of thinking, the balls are presumed to be standing detached, on their own, and interacting through forces they impose on one another from without. However, if we adopt a 'relational' or 'dialectical' approach to identifying the "cell-form" of the billiard balls game, we can do much better in establishing the simpler grounds for understanding the history of the billiard balls games in their full complexity.

For instance, let us alternatively say that the unit of analysis, the 'cell-form,' of the billiard balls game is not a physical ball, but *the strike*—that is, of a human being striking a ball with a cue stick over a table. From this relational imagery, one can extrapolate much more about the billiard balls game, what they are for, why it originated, who originated it, in what small or larger settings, and further explain the diversity of balls and games played.

In the narrower view of our unit of analysis as the ball, we end up thinking that by just studying physics, we can understand the game. In the broader view of our unit of analysis as the strike, we cannot really understand what is going on in the game without adopting a transdisciplinary approach. We have to gather and integrate all of our knowledges of the natural/built environment, of our social reality, and our minds, including not just rational but even irrational, not just scientific but also belief systems, not just conscious but also subconscious minds, not just our physical skills but also our emotions, and sensibilities, our moods, and so on, to truly understand what makes a billiard balls game what it is.

We ask what is it that allows for such a different, more fruitful identification of the "atom" of the billiard balls game?

This involves the use of a different language, a different conceptual framework, by the observer who is trying to understand that object. So, the observer's willful role in the shift in perspective cannot itself be ignored here. Our alternative unit of analysis does allow for the inclusion of the role played by human beings in their creative social construction of the game. But how that reality is understood "objectively" has a lot do with the natures of the observer and the observations made of that presumed reality.

The role of the observer may seem to be at first merely extraneous, i.e., external to the "objective reality" of the billiard balls game, and thus readily dismissed by our scientists who wish to understand the 'billiard balls' game "on its own," so to speak. However, in doing so, they end up missing a large part of the story of how the game came into being and how its nature, in all its physical, emotional, and mental, complexity, has evolved in time.

This is because the human player, even in our alternative relational unit of analysis, is not just an observer, but a player as well, and in the course of multiple games has come up with new ideas about the game, about how to make its equipment, about how to create the game rules, about how to act and behave while playing the game, and how to choose and set up the physical and social settings in which the game is played.

These new ideas of the observing game player have thus contributed not just to the efforts in understanding the game, but toward the constitution, the construction, of the reality of the game itself as it is now played. By including the human actor in our alternative unit of analysis, we have thus also made it possible to allow for the inclusion of human beings' roles in the process not only as practical actors, but also as practical observers. So, even here, our alternative, relational unit of analysis yields more insight about the game as compared to adopting a crudely corpuscular way of thinking about the 'atom' of the billiard balls game.

But the human player involved in the game is himself or herself comprised of parts, of various ways of interacting with an object, with various selves representing the various social roles, or not, he is involved in. In this characterization of the multiplicity of roles the human aspect plays in the unit of analysis of the billiard balls game, therefore, a further insight emerges that would otherwise be lost in the corpuscular way of thinking about the atoms of our object. Somehow, for some reason that can be in fact historically and ideologically explained, the chunkiness of things is seen in everything but not, as well, in the presumed "individual." But the human aspect itself is also not a singular whole, but a multiplicity of selves performing a multiplicity of roles in the process of making and playing the game.

Again, in other words, we confront a difference between a corpuscular way of thinking about the human actor that somehow attributes the will, intentionality, and action to the "individual" actor as if he or she is an indivisible whole, than a relational way of thinking that considers the human being a multiplicity of relational parts or selves, within and without. Without such a relational way of thinking about our unit of analysis, we will not be able to understand the particular behavior of our player, who at one point is highly focused on striking the ball, and in another is distracted by an attraction or repulsion he or she feels toward others in the environment, or due to an anger he or she may have brought in from home before leaving for the game that evening. He strikes the ball at times feeling sad, at other times, when he is joyful, and in other times when "in the zone," so to speak.

All such minute insights would be lost in a corpuscular way of thinking about our player as a solid 'individual' presumed to be unified in character and in self-structure, and fully attentive to the requirements of his game.

The 'language' and the conceptual framework the observer uses when trying to understand the "objective" reality of the billiard balls game is consequential in not only understanding the game, but even the constitution and the socio-historical development and transformations of the game itself. The language in the mind of the observer, in other words, is a part and parcel of the totality of relations that constitute the unit of analysis of our object. A corpuscular way of thinking about the 'atoms' of objects, is one that imagines reality as being a resultant of apparently solid bodies exerting forces on one another from without—an imagination that arose from the particular reflections on the forces of presumably inanimate objects in Newton's writings but later became entangled, intended as such or not, with the imaginations of all objects.

Since it took such a way of imagining reality to be a universal pattern, it presumes that individuals are also solid objects, somehow ignoring that they may be comprised of a multiplicity of selves playing a multiplicity of roles and thus not being simply solid objects. So, it would be incapable of understanding how the same individual could change and initiate creative impulses and actions; the individual is regarded as a solid object, also shaped by external forces. The Newtonian way of imagining him, and the society in which he or she lives, cannot readily take into account forces other than those assumed to be exerted by objects on one another from without.

One may counter argue here, noting that our object, a billiard balls game, is one that is human made, and thus its very nature and cause of being is intertwined with the subjectivity of human observers and actors. How about objects that have existed in nature without any mediations of human action, one may ask? In what way can we identify a unit of analysis in them that includes human agencies, when they were or are there without any participation of human influence in the constitution of their nature?

In answer to this, we may simply note that to the extent the object comes inside the horizon of human consideration and attention, to that extent the object of study becomes one in which the so-called "thing in itself" and the human observers *both* participate. It is impossible to *consider* any thing-in-itself, without including that '*consideration*' and the '*considerer*' in the process of its cognition, and any knowledge that is gained of the "thing-in-itself" is inevitably tinged by the elements of the process of knowing to which the observer also contributes.

It is this relational conception of any micro unit of analysis that is lost in a crudely corpuscular approach to understanding an 'object' on its own, for it is presumed that the unit of analysis of an object resides somehow physically inside or around the object, and not, relationally, in a wider whole process that now includes the observer. A Newtonian way of thinking that is corpuscular and sees objects in relations they have with one another from without is fundamentally limited in considering situations when objects relate to one another as whole and parts.

Consider the Newtonian laws of motion once again. Obviously, in considering any "billiard balls" game, the first assumption is the apparent corpuscular solidity of the billiard balls. For a body to exert an external force on another, in other words, we tend to assume that there are more or less unified, solid, bodies standing on their own, exerting forces on one another from without. For a given whole, since one may also have to consider the law-governed nature of the universe as imagined by Newton to be applicable, we should logically end up with a system in which each whole is "impressed upon" not only by other wholes (and their respective parts) standing outside it, but also by parts standing within and constituting the given whole itself.

However, the need for logical consistency of the laws as expressed and intended by Newton comes into conflict with such an alternative way of thinking that allows for part-whole relations and interaction of bodies where parts can exert equal or even more forces *sui generis* upon the wholes constituting them. To restore consistency to the Newtonian way of thinking about this, one needs then to consider that the interactions of any part with the broader whole of which it is a part is necessarily always mediated by the interactions of the parts themselves constituting that whole. It is for this reason that we find use at times for notions such as "a whole is greater than the sum of its parts."

Whether or not such an observation can be attributed to Newtonianism (rooted in atomism) or appropriated by it, it is helpful to consider the implications of such a point of view, since it can shed light on the distinctiveness of the Newtonian way of thinking about the units of analysis of reality on the micro side.

There are two ways one can interpret the notion that "a whole is greater than the sum of its parts." One is that any given whole is constituted not only by its own parts, but also by other wholes in their environmental context (and their respective parts) interacting with it, such that one cannot assume one can understand the whole by just simply looking at one or another or even the total sum of its own parts; one has to also consider the broader context of reality in which that whole itself (as a part of a greater context) interacts with other wholes. As in the example given above, we cannot really understand why there are these round balls in specific sets and sizes out there without understanding the human social and cultural contexts, among many others, in which they have been created. This interpretation seems plausible, but in my view is not usually what is implied by the notion to which I referred.

In the other, second, interpretation, setting aside the question of the broader context in which the whole interacts with other wholes and/through their respective parts, the implication of "a whole is greater than the sum of its parts" is that a whole has an "objective" reality that stands "structurally" apart from and outside the reality or motions of not only any but also even the entirety of its own parts, resulting in an imagination that necessarily presumes as a universal imperative the systemic unitary status of any whole independent of any forces that one or even all of its parts may exert on the whole to transform its overall structure.

Note that the implications of such a Newtonian way of thinking about the part-whole dialectics is highly consequential particularly in the context of the interactions of, say, selves comprising a presumably 'whole' singular individual (who appears to have a solid, identifiable body, always assumed to have a unified self-structure guiding its actions, that presumably remains the same in everyday/night, here-and-there, spacetime), as well as, more broadly, in the context of the dialectics of a presumed "individual" and society.

In such a way of thinking where a whole is regarded as having a reality separate from even the sum of its parts, we confront an imagination in which the billiard ball player is also regarded as having a separate reality from the reality of any of his selves playing, or not, the game. This, by implication, would lead to the necessity of regarding the whole as, ultimately, the only legitimate unit of analysis of its reality, since, no matter how we "sum up" the interaction of even all its parts, we are told that we will not arrive at an "objective" understanding of the whole without studying the whole on its own. In such an "intellectual universe" or way of thinking, therefore, the whole, and not its parts, are deemed to be the basic and proper interacting units of analysis. The presumed "individual"—and not the selves, that is, social relations within and without that together, as an ensemble, constitute the apparently corpuscular body—comes to be regarded as the proper unit of our social analysis.

Also note the implications this way of thinking has for any efforts brought on by presumably "objective" observers in trying to change the observers themselves (say in learning new rules of the game themselves, or teaching them to others). Since their own part selves, in part or even as their sum efforts, are not ultimately contributing to determining the reality of the whole, and wholes remain stationary or at best moving in constant speeds unless "impressed upon" by other external forces, it necessarily follows that these observing bodies are not in their efforts at knowing and changing themselves ultimately self-determining, but have to subject themselves or allow themselves to be subjected to the study, review, and transformation by other objects. It then necessarily follows that such a way of thinking leads to the recognition of the power of 'other' experts and elite billiard ball players who, paradoxically only when reviewing others, say in the academic context, are regarded as being objective, but when being themselves peer reviewed are not treated as also being possibly "biased" and "subjective" thinkers.

The key here, then, is to understand and question what micro unit of analysis is legitimately considered a viable one in the Newtonian way of thinking. The atomic nature of such an attribution arises not necessarily from the selection of "atoms" as alleged basic interacting blocks of matter, but from the notion that any whole to be considered downward has a reality of its own, apart from even the sum of all its parts—and here, we are not even considering the broader contexts shaping and being shaped by that object.

In such a way of thinking, then, the whole is bound to be presumed somehow more superior and primary in shaping reality than any of its parts.

This way of thinking, then, is necessarily bound to maintain the conception of matter as being constituted of separate billiard ball masses, and not as subatomic relational units that defy categorization and localization in one or another presumed billiard ball spacetimes. "The whole is greater than a sum of its parts," in other words, when misunderstood in a one-sided way as described above, is a notion (whatever its historical roots may be) that serves well the Newtonian way of thinking, maintaining its small or large "corpuscular" structure, no matter what new discoveries are made downward or upward in the microscopic or macroscopic spacetimes.

To put all this in a different way, whether the Newtonian imagination considers the downward, micro divisibility of the bodies in the relational system of bodies in the universe to be infinite or finite, wherever in the range of the scale of bodies one focuses on, one is confronted with a presumed "objective" and laws-governed "logical" imperative that parts have less force or value in reality creation and maintenance than the whole comprising them and that there is a "wholeness" of a body apart from the forces of the parts that constitute that presumed whole. It should not come as a surprise, then, that in the Newtonian way of thinking the resultant sum forces exerted on a whole-body by its own part-bodies must comply with the broader law-governed system of interaction of wider bodies in the universe as a whole. The small is powerless in such a grand Newtonian way of imagining reality.

For instance, it would be inconceivable in such a Newtonian imagination—where wholes themselves are not relationally conceived as parts-made-whole—for a part to exert on its parent whole a force that would be *sui generis* or at least defy the force that the part has received with new additional force of its own. If so, the Newtonian vision would become self-contradictory and inconsistent. A part cannot in such a system suddenly think of, generate, and exert a completely new "creative" force out of the blue, so to speak, that can transform the whole comprising it altogether. It is inconceivable in a Newtonian way of thinking to consider that a part can defy and undermine, against all odds, the "law-governed," "objective" realities of the series of wholes comprising it—challenging the presumably "objective" laws externally perpetuated in the whole presumably apart from one or another, or at best by all the parts comprising that whole. It would be inconceivable that a part would be able to creatively engender sufficient and new creative forces, in fact new laws of motion, for the whole of which it was previously a part, leading to the establishment of alternatively new orders and laws of motion constituting new whole forms in reality.

The presumed corpuscular solidity and wholeness of the billiard balls in the Newtonian way of thinking would be undermined if the balls themselves are regarded or seen as being interacting units of forces arising from within and without their apparently solid boundaries. Yet, the Newtonian imagination is logically bound to regard matter as comprised of corpuscles of solid bodies (excluding the observers themselves) that act as if they are singular actors on the table of reality rather than there being smaller, subatomic part actors whose interactions within and without the presumed atomic ball surfaces are what give them the appearance and semblance of atomic solidity in particular spacetime coordinates.

Wearing the Newtonian lens, the observers see a set of separate balls interacting with one another from without. Wearing an alternative relational lens, however, the observers see a complex system of interaction within and across the apparent surfaces of presumed billiard balls, such that the local interactions in one ball is what constitutes in fact the local spacetime boundaries of other balls, revealing not one, but a series of interacting smaller billiard balls within and across the game whose forces are continually recreating, maintaining, and at times undermining the spacetime solidities of apparently larger billiard balls. The color solidness of one set of the billiard balls, after all, has to do with the distinction they must have from the banded ones, and this knowledge cannot be achieved by the study of each ball on its own, but in relation to other balls in the set.

Also note that in the above consideration of the atomistic nature of the Newtonian way of thinking and the limits such an intellectual universe may pose for our cognition of the universe, again we did not have to resort to any new findings in quantum science in order to convey the notion that a corpuscular-atomic way of thinking about an object limits a truthful understanding of its causes, nature, and development. The difference here was to apply an alternative, relational approach that regards corpuscular manifestations of wholes or parts as being themselves by-products of the relational processes existing among the diverse nodes of a system of intertwined wholes and parts, within and without. Each node is what it is in relation to other nodes of the system, such that a change in one node necessarily implies a change in the wholes of which that node is a part. And the system *being studied* must always be conceived as *including* the observer(s) studying them.

In the context of our Khayyami studies, for instance, let us consider this interesting story, for now simply as a matter of illustration.

When studying the quatrains attributed to Khayyam, when thinking of various criteria to use as a measure to sift authentic quatrains from the rest, scholars stumbled upon an interesting pattern.

To preface the story, we should recall that the Persian robai (quatrain) is defined as a four-lined poem, where the first, second, and last lines rhyme, but the third does not have to.

It happens that some of the quatrains readily attributed to Khayyam in the more reliable secondary sources were found to be of the type in which all four lines rhyme. Looking back to preceding traditions of composing robais, the scholars found that poets coming before Khayyam tended to compose also in the four-rhyme style. So, in search for establishing a "scientific" criterion for sifting the authentic Khayyami quatrains from the rest, some proposed that those that are four-lines-rhymed are the authentic ones, the rest being unreliable.

But, when doing so, they ended up also finding manuscripts, also old, where the three-rhymed types have also been attributed to Khayyam. So, they had to simply dismiss a whole large set as being not authentic.

The point here, by way of this brief illustration, is to note how in our Khayyami studies we may disregard the possibility that the three-rhymed quatrains may have been an innovation contributed by Khayyam *himself*—that he, *sui generis*, in fact ushered a new tradition.

At this point, of course, my point here is simply to illustrate merely a possibility that would be missed among many possibilities one can consider, if we adopted a Newtonian way of framing our Khayyami studies whereby presumed "established" traditions are used as a measuring rod to determine what quatrain is authentic or not. So, the scholar who comes along and says, based on the "whole" tradition of robais composition preceding Khayyam, or even as evident in those reliably quoted by others from him, the "atomic" unit of quatrains is of the four-rhymed type, and that the three-rhymed robais found (quite in abundance, by the way), in other collections are to be readily disregarded as inauthentic, would completely miss the point if we, even speculatively, consider the possibility that in fact Khayyam may have been *the* person who began, for reasons to be explained, the tradition of three-rhymed quatrains.

Therefore, the proper micro-unit of analysis in our Khayyami study is not the billiard ball quatrain, but the poet striking innovative new hits on the board of poetic creativity, changing the very nature of the game as had been previously played. The real subject matter, the proper unit of analysis, to study, then, is how Khayyam seemed to be pursuing projects which involve creating new patterns, new terms, new traditions, which also manifest themselves, in part, in composing three-rhymed quatrains.

Another example may be noted here regarding the "odd" way in which Khayyam, in one of his most important philosophical writings in Persian, *Resaleh dar Kolliyat-e Vojood (Treatise on the Universals of Existence)*, locates the "Active Intellect" not in its "usual" place among the various spheres of existence emanating from God, that is, in the bottom of the hierarchy as it influences human intellect and actions on Earth, but alongside and as an expression of the very First Intellect, emanating directly from God.

Again, the point here not being that of going into substantive detail is that scholars may be judging Khayyam based on what is "usually" the philosophical practice "as a whole," even as found in his mentor Avicenna (Ibn Sina), and not consider the possibility that here, also, perhaps Khayyam, the creative scientist and intellect, may be pointing us toward a novelty he has introduced to the theory or universals of existence for a reason to be understood, an anomaly he wishes us to become curious about and study further, in the way the "universal" elements of his view regarding the nature of existence may be imagined.

The unit of analysis of research here, then, is not the presumed atomic elements of a philosophical system as a whole, but, relationally, how elements of the system are transformed in the course of the playful and creative *strikes* of the master billiards or polo game player who despite reporting the game as a matter of fate in one quatrain, finds a way or hope, elsewhere, in another quatrain, of suggesting that if, like God, he had a hand in his own fate's wheel, he would shatter it to pieces in order to create a new world where humanity could be happily fulfilled.

3. Separability: What Is the Macro Unit of Analysis of the Object?

The Newtonian corpuscular way of thinking is not limited to studying the micro dimensions of the object, but can also influence our efforts in understanding how the object is constituted in its broader, macro contexts.

In considering wholes and parts, we may note that in each case, a part itself can be considered from another vantage point to be a whole constituted of its own parts, and, likewise, each whole is a part of one or more, other larger wholes. In other words, whether the bodies constituting the universe are presumed to be infinitely divisible or not, it is safe to assume that each part also interacts with and influences other parts of a given whole considered, while the latter itself interacts with and is influenced as a whole by other wholes. In this consideration, however, it is often convenient to assume that we can separate a chunk of the object and by understanding it we could understand all that we need to know about it.

However, consider the following way of imagining the object instead, drawing again on our critically reimaginable billiard balls game metaphor.

Each billiard ball is a part of a set of (say, 16) billiard balls. But this general or abstract (partial) characterization does not help us understand what the set of billiard balls is and what it is for. We may also have a set of billiard balls that are smaller or larger than another set of billiard balls; why billiard balls in one set are smaller than billiard balls in another set? Further, in each set, depending on their pattern (solid or banded in color), the collection itself may be divisible into two whole groups of (solid or banded) balls. Yet, each ball has its own (in that set) unique number and color while belonging to one of those (solid or banded) whole sets, one white ball not having any numbers or patterns. Why these differently typed or colored balls?

Looking back in time, further, we learn that older balls were made of ox-bone, then of ivory tusks, now of composite materials, comprised of different material substances and structures that evolved over time. Why the change in the material composing the balls over time? And, then, these balls, in and of themselves, cannot be played with without a table with certain number of receptor exits on its corners or edges, without cue sticks and related equipment and supplies, without a room or place, heated and lighted properly for comfort and protected from the elements, and, most importantly of course, without the human beings playing them, and so on.

Then, there are different types of games (that may explain the different sized ball sets?) and different cultural systems in which the games were and are made up by humans according to whose made-up rules the balls can be played, game rules that may vary from culture to culture, small group to small group, age to age, even from one time of day to another, fulfilling different emotional, mental, or physical needs for one or another player depending on his or her background, biography, and needs, etc. Here, the ball game serves the function of a tournament involving money and ranking; there, it is just a recreational pastime; and yet, elsewhere, a chance to impress and befriend someone by showing off one's skills.

Can the billiard balls game be simply a different way of playing, say, basketball, football, baseball, soccer, or marbles, and so on? And of course, none of these could be possible without specific forms of social organization of work and leisure among those human beings, of built and natural environmental conditions on a planet supporting life forms, itself made possible in a moving Solar System gravitationally organized in a particular way and located in a specific part of a galaxy moving in a cluster amid broader cosmic settings that due to a still unknown cause resulted from a Big Bang billions of years ago; and what was there "before" then, if there was a "before."

The point of such a seemingly extreme stretch in our imagination of the billiard balls game is that in order to understand the true nature of billiard balls and the reasons for their existence and the motions of their parts, we need to understand much more than the balls themselves in both micro and macro directions. And there, it is not simply a matter of making a choice, but it is a matter of necessity; that is, we should understand, if we are good researchers and are curious enough, the broad totality of contextual relations that have made the creation, existence, and playing of the game possible. The very fact of changing physical materials of which the balls are made may have a lot to do with the particular social systems in which they are made and played, the human laws made for their making, materials available in the environment, restrictions established on hunting, and so on. Each part may belong as a part to different parallel whole systems (i.e., physical, social, cultural, game rules), each system being itself a part of a broader whole.

The question that arises here is whether amid the plethora of part-whole structures that together make possible a billiard balls game, should we still identify a basic *macro* unit of analysis, so that through considering it we can arrive at a more 'objective' understanding of what the billiard balls are and what they are for? Can we identify a particular macro unit of analysis, so that by analyzing that unit, we can grasp an image or sense of what the nature of an object under investigation is, what it is for, how it is maintained, how it can change?

The point here is to note the inherent *inseparability* of different aspects and folds of consideration of part-whole dialectics that constitute the reality of the object, while recognizing that for research purposes, one may need to focus on one or another aspect of the organic totality in which the object is situated. But this is very different from assuming that, adopting a Newtonian way of thinking, one can radically detach a part of the object from the rest of its reality, and expect to arrive at an adequate understanding of it altogether.

In conceiving the macro unit of analysis of the universe, it is important to distinguish between a conception which regards all its parts integrated with one another as parts of a singular reality such that each part can be understood in relation to the whole reality, and a conception in which each part is considered to have an existence of its own, and merely contributing via more or less external interaction with the reality of its environment. The point here is that the chunky, Newtonian way of imagining reality of our macro units of analysis prevents us from integrating various spheres of information that altogether constitute the complex reality of the object of our study.

Note, again, that we have not consulted any books in quantum science to arrive at the above conception of the macro unit of analysis of our object of study. The purpose is to show how our Newtonian, "chunky" way of imagining reality, presuming that reality is comprised of separable and separately knowable chunks, may in fact lead us astray on its own in finding more fruitful results in our Khayyami studies.

One of the unfortunate habits in Khayyami studies in search of the so-called "authentic" quatrains has been the effort to decide on the question by simply studying the chunks of the quatrains themselves, trying to somehow draw magical formula rabbits out of the hat of the quatrains to decide on their authenticity. Even when scholars point to the need to find more substantive criteria, such as philosophical or religious worldview, to determine which quatrain is authentic or which not, they ironically use the quatrains (or at best, a few more "reliable" ones) to define those worldview parameters using which the authentic quatrains can be sifted away from the inauthentic ones. They rarely take Khayyam's philosophical, religious, and scientific texts themselves as contextual grounds for exploring the nature and authenticity of Khayyami quatrains, dismissing altogether, without examining forthwith, even attributed literary sources such as *Nowrooznameh (The Book on Nowrooz)* for the purpose. Exploring the authenticity of quatrains by means of quatrains may be one way to go about it, if done amid a variety of approaches in context, but to do so as the sole or a single criteria would be problematic, especially in light of the fact that the initial "authentic" group has not been itself reliably determined.

In other words, there is something that prevents some scholars from seriously expanding their units of analysis to broader spheres of Khayyam's works, including his philosophical and scientific writings; at best they are relegated to 'separate' appendices, themselves rendered in such obscure translations and languages that substantively do not offer significant inroads into the main exploration carried out in their works.

Others choose some of the older and earliest quoted quatrains, that happen to be also to their own liking at times, and say they are the basis to choose the authentic ones from the rest. It does not occur to them that even this list may represent as a sample only one aspect of Khayyam's views, and not his views in general as found in the more dedicated philosophical writings.

Even, the disciplinary dissociations of our times play a part in these efforts, by categorically not finding it relevant to study how Khayyam's scientific writings may also offer clues regarding his practice of poetry. After all, these are seen as "chunks" of separate activities, and not relevant to each other. So, we find a scholar of mathematics, for instance, who conveniently sets aside Khayyam's philosophical writings, not even entertaining that Khayyam's literary or poetic writings may even be relevant to his or her mathematics "specialty" in understanding Khayyam, and, yet, finds it "scientific" to offer an opinion about "another" person named Khayyam having composed the famed Robaiyat.

In the Newtonian way of imagining Khayyami studies, excuses become conveniently abundant in separating various writings of Khayyam from one another, aided by doubts about their authenticity, chunkily separating them from one another, from questions about his biography (including the dates of his birth and death, more or less uncritically following what others have claimed to be such dates), from questions about his times, and in particular in separating the subject matter from one's own biases as conditioned by a series of personal, social, cultural, political, economic, and global cultural (including imperial and colonial) factors that influence one's own supposedly "objective" attitude toward research.

Khayyam's critical spirit of healthy skepticism is celebrated; yet, amid the habitual ways of going about learning about Khayyam, including his dates of birth and passing, such critical thinking and skepticisms are abandoned.

4. Objectivity: Does the Object, While Being Observed, Have An Independent Reality?

Atomism from the standpoint of corpuscular micro unit of analysis (attribute 2) and *separability* of chunks of reality from one another in the macro analysis (attribute 3) all rely on a *dualistic* worldview according to which bodies exist separately from one another (attribute 1). In such a way of imagining reality, it is impossible to consider that something A is at the same time non-A.

Objectivity from the standpoint of a separately standing observer is a consequence of such a dualistic worldview as well. I already have commented on how a narrow notion of objectivity is a hallmark of Newtonian way of thinking, since the germ of such an approach is already seeded from earlier propositions. But further observations in this regard can be made.

The Newtonian way of thinking presumes a "law-governed" universe, including human society and us as its parts, that exists independently of observers who seek to know and change it. Whether the original "force" initiating its reality was presumably exerted by a creator, or not, the reality of the resulting/existing universe is assumed to be an objective, relational system of bodies, large or small, that exert law-governed forces upon one another from without, existing independently from observers trying to know and influence/change them.

It is such an imagination, involving interacting bodies or 'objects' exerting forces upon one another from without, that makes it possible to argue that there are "objective" laws governing the universe, since each body in the relational system of bodies constituting the universe is conceived as resulting from the sum of influences coming from outside its being, to which it can lawfully react only with equal, but never additional—that is, newly initiated, own—force.

So, an observer also, in order to exert any influences on the relational system of bodies, or any parts thereof, has to presumably first come to know the "reality" of what it confronts objectively "outside" itself, so that it can exert whatever influences it can within the law-governed context of the reality facing it. Not only does the observer's knowledge of reality have to be "objective," in other words, its actions on reality is also limited by the law-governed, "objective," nature of that reality which confronts the observer from outside. In such a Newtonian imagination or way of thinking, then, the "objective" reality of a body under study in the universe or any parts thereof must be presumed to stand clearly apart from the "subjective" reality of the observer who tries to know and change it.

It follows, then, that the "objective reality" of what exists "out there" along with the "objective truth" of it as reflected in any observer's mind are assumed to have an attribute of "facticity" regardless of the "subjective" realities of the observers reflecting on that reality. In other words, it is assumed that not only the object itself is constituted by objective forces standing apart from the observer, but also the presumably truthful, "objective knowledge" about it, once discovered, stands apart from any subjective interpretations that one or another observer may have of that "objective truth." The "objective truth" of the reality of the relational system of bodies, thereby, presumably stands regardless of any "subjective" interpretations any observers who seek to know and change that objective reality may have of that "objective truth."

Note that the very notion of "objectivity," both in terms of something being an attribute of an existing reality and in terms of its truthful reflection in an "objective-minded" observer, is derived from and dependent on the assumption of externality of objects comprising the universe (including the observer). In other words, the Newtonian way of thinking about the universe necessarily implies not only the separateness of objects that otherwise interact with one another from without in a law-governed way, but also, as a special case and manifestation of such separateness, the externality and separation of the "object" from the "observer" facing and studying it, the "objective" understanding and change of the former by the latter notwithstanding.

So, here, a playerless, spectator-less, subject-exiling, 'billiard balls game' imagination is again found to be at the heart of the Newtonian way of thinking about objectivity and any role the observer may play in constituting, knowing and influencing/changing the object. Not only is the reality of the object assumed to be constituted independently from an observer standing separately from it, but also that any 'objective' knowledge arrived at by that observer is itself regarded as having a separate reality of its own, as an 'objective knowledge' that somehow takes a life of its own in the arsenal of a presumed 'scientific body' of knowledge, a body of knowledge that now is assumed to exist (and even used in, say, a 'scientific' peer review process of so-called "experts" who otherwise, in their own submissions elsewhere, are acknowledged to be just other scholars needing 'peer review' in turn and thus cannot necessarily be presumed to be 'objective-minded') over and above the interpretive or applicative uses of it in the minds of specific observers.

Again, we do not need to make a "quantum leap" into quantum science to observe the inconsistent and contradictory logic guiding the Newtonian way of thinking about objectivity. The issue here is not that of questioning the notion of objectivity per se, but that of the Newtonian way of thinking about and practicing objectivity. This can and should be done with a mixture of some common sense and some critical thinking, to expose the inherent inconsistency of the Newtonian way of thinking about objectivity.

Here is how it can be done, and to aid the inquiry, we can indeed again draw on the "billiard balls game" metaphor for illustration purposes.

Let us assume that according to the Newtonian way of thinking— whether or not we consider the scenario where a God or a god-like prime mover struck the first cause to set the game in motion—the resulting/existing system is now considered to be an objectively law-governed system of balls whose interactions presumably take place independent of any observer.

The question that arises here is, where are these observers in relation to the system just portrayed as such? Either (a) they are thought to be floating somewhere over and above and beyond/outside the system of interacting balls, or, (b) they are also like balls participating in the reality of the "billiard balls" game, and hence a part of the reality whose objective knowledge is being sought.

If we choose option (a), we would then have to believe that there indeed is a world over and above and beyond/outside the objective reality being studied. However, this would mean that the objective world whose universal laws of motion we sought to elucidate is not as universally encompassing as we originally claimed, since now there is a realm standing outside it. Option (a), therefore, would contradict the premise of the Newtonian way of thinking and would therefore be rendered invalid as a possible argument on the way of thinking's own grounds. If we do include a God in the picture, then we would not have a Newtonianism as portrayed in terms of a worldview of a clockwork universe.

If we choose option (b) as a mode of argument, however, we would then have to accept, by definition (without having to even consult and consider any discoveries made in quantum science), that the observer is an organic part and thereby *constitutive of the reality that is being observed* and whose objective knowledge is being sought. To know and influence/change the objective reality of the billiard balls game, therefore, we have no choice but to know and influence/change ourselves as its observers.

Note that here we have not really abandoned the notion of objectivity and its necessity as a part of any genuinely scientific inquiry, but have corrected/expanded it to *include* the insight that the observer is by definition an organic or constitutive part of the reality *he or she studies*, and thereby his or her knowledge of the object of the study cannot avoid the knowledge of him/herself as a constituting part of that reality, a standpoint which necessarily affects his or her knowledge of reality, the acknowledgment and realization of which is a necessary part of the process of constituting, knowing and influencing/changing the object.

Also note here that this self-including conception and practice of objectivity in understanding the objective world has also transformed the very manner in which we conceive of the life of the object we study and its presumably "law-governed" nature. This alternative way of thinking allows us to observe that we are a part of the interactive process that makes the objective reality what it is and thereby a participant in what may be the structure (or laws) of its development—the conception of "law" here being transformed into one toward whose constitution, potentially, the observer as a participating interactive agency can willfully contribute.

The reality of the billiard balls game, in other words, does not exist without our own participation in it as observers, *once we partake in the act of observation*. A notion of "science" as standing apart from "art" thereby ends, the two becoming inseparable from one another, while also maintaining their distinctiveness—a relation of difference in identity.

Note that in a Newtonian way of thinking about objectivity, where reality is primarily considered in its 'outer' aspect in other objects, and not also in the 'inner' reality of the observer, the task of research necessarily leads to the marginalization of the need for self-reflexivity on the part of the observer—seeking self-knowledge being relegated at best to a back-staged, and at worst an ignored or even purposely and proudly avoided (in the name of 'science'), arena of research conduct. But, if alternatively viewed, the separation of "science" from "philosophy" and both from the "arts" would also necessarily end.

So, the "billiard balls game" imagery illustrating the Newtonian way of thinking leads either to the omission of the observing/observer body from the game altogether, or, at best, to the purely scholastic and "academic" inclusion of the observing/observer body as one of the balls, standing passively and separately from other balls in the name of so-called "science"—implying that to know (and change) the other's realities, one does not also *have to* know (and change) oneself, but instead has to subtract oneself from the overall game so as to make the "objective" knowing of those outer objects possible and scientifically worthy.

In such situations where the observing object seeks to know aspects of observing objects just like oneself, the pretension of 'objectivity' must then be still maintained, i.e., a pretension has to be made to be studying *other* persons, *others'* personal troubles, *others'* public issues, *others'* realities. To practice the same upon one's own reality would thus be eschewed, stigmatized, and marginalized for not being a "scientific" thing to do; practicing such self-reflexivity would then be considered at best as somewhat worthy (relegated to the humanities) but still not a serious, "scientific" academic endeavor.

So, from such a chunky, disciplinary point of view, when Khayyam wrote poetry, he must have been doing it in "spare time," as a marginal practice, nothing serious, nothing related to his interest in algebra, to his interest in Nowrooz and Persian calendar reform, to his astronomical observations, to his birth horoscope, to his science. An "astronomer-mathematician poet" then becomes an exotic thing to be—odd and rare. He was just talking about his personal troubles, we would think—nothing about "serious," "objective" matters, of major public issues set in a world-history context. We would approach our Khayyami studies that way today because we celebrate our disciplinary way of looking at knowledge, thanks to Newtonianism.

Amid such a modern academic context, to be "scholarly" thus becomes defined as one in which the role observers and persons, say, reviewers, are playing in the process are (and have to be, in the name of 'science') "blinded," rather than the very opposite, of making the process optimally transparent, open, and inclusive of any personal views and opinions all participants are offering in the development of genuinely objective knowledge about the object of study. The pretension, therefore, is that any biases observers may hold are somehow magically avoided and evaporated into thin air by simply "blinding" the process (and the more, for instance, double-blinded, presumably the better), rather than through conscious and intentional inclusion of transparent review procedures whereby knowledge of oneself and of any other observers and where each come from in social and historical contexts contribute to the knowledge production process as a whole.

And all this, because the observer's own reality is not regarded a part of the billiard balls game *being observed and studied*. The game players are exiled from the game itself, in the name of science; so are its scientific spectators.

We would be completely missing the point and misguiding ourselves if we presume that our Khayyami studies are supposedly of a Newtonian "objective" reality (of a person, of a historical period, of ancient manuscripts, and so on) "out there," being not inclusive of the selves involved in the sources we study, and of our own selves, our own times, and our own habitual ways of approaching our research and "science." It would then become impossible to understand Khayyam, for whom philosophy, religion, science, creative literary writing, poetry, were unified aspects of the same search for understanding his Creator and reason for existence, through our fragmentary disciplinary lenses deeply conditioned, still, by Newtonian worldview.

Khayyam himself, in his writings, demonstrates an intimate sensitivity to how knowledge and context (both local, regional, world-historical, mythological, spiritual, as well as, interestingly and uniquely, cosmic) relate to one another. Even when he refrains from writing, which are misunderstood (by those unfamiliar with the depth of his intellect) as being supposedly a sign of being miserly in writing and teaching, the silence itself is significant and may speak volumes regarding the challenges he faced in remaining true to his calling as a scientist in light of the superficial ways folks treated him, and in the socio-political context of the times he lived in, characterized by pre-modern forms of coloniality, under the Seljuk rulers and their orthodox and literalist religious associates.

Likewise, in our own Khayyami studies, we should be intimately aware of how any knowledge or opinion we claim to attribute to Khayyam based on supposed "objective" knowledge borrowed from others are socially constructed and rooted artifacts that should always and continually invite critical review and reevaluation through an inquiry that is simultaneously self-reflective and aware of how world-historical and contemporary forces have shaped our own thinking, feeling, and sensibilities. Objectivity is best and only achieved not by impossibly sculpting ourselves out of our Khayyami studies, as if we could jump over our own knees (as a Persian saying goes), but in seriously seeking to become aware of the social-rootedness, interests and biases of our own thinking as we engage in our Khayyami studies.

The presumption of a subjectless "objectivity" in the Newtonian imagination of reality was not an inevitable, "scientific" necessity. We did not have to "discover" it as a result of quantum revolutions. It just happened that quantum science simply demonstrated in an undeniable way, despite the reluctance of some nuclear scientists who still try to avoid the so-called "quantum enigma" by asking us to "shut up and calculate," the absurdity, the limitation, the narrow-mindedness, of our prior, Newtonian way of thinking.

Newtonianism was a socially and historically constructed model of science that by its omission of the observer from its pursuit preconditioned itself for becoming puzzled when the "enigmatic" findings of quantum science presented themselves due to advances in scientific technology and in the accuracy of the means of microscopic observation and measurement.

5. Determinism: Are Causes and Consequences In Objects Certain and Predictable?

The Newtonian way of imagining reality insists upon the precise, "objective," determinability and predictability of reality. Even if we cannot make such causal determinations, the presumption is that such a limitation is a result of our own lack of knowledge, yet, about the reality under examination. The billiard balls are precisely locatable in time and space, at rest, and in their motion, measured in the context of a universally absolute spacetime frame of reference. If you can know one move, you can know all the motions that result from it or even preceded it.

What also follows from the above formal-logically conceived architecture (where a middle state between A and non-A is always excluded) of the Newtonian universe as a relational system of whole-bodies (and part-bodies) is a vision in which the larger bodies necessarily impress more forces on smaller bodies than the reverse.

The predictability of causal forces raises the question of what determines what in terms of a perceived scale, so far as parts and wholes are concerned. The higher the relative speed of a body in relation to another, the more force it impresses on the other body. The spatiotemporal presumptions embedded in the Newtonian vision of the universe are thereby significant. In the Newtonian worldview, the relatively larger and faster moving bodies are supposed to dictate the causal and/or dominant trends in the reality of which they are a part. The relatively smaller and slower moving bodies or part-bodies are thus deemed to be passive recipients or resultants of forces exerted upon them from without. The relatively larger and faster bodies rule in the Newtonian imagination of, or way of thinking about, the universe.

As far as the presumably predictable causal linkages of "objective" phenomena are concerned, of course, the lesser extent to which we interfere in the object, the less of a changed object (as a result of our own lack of interference) it would be that we study. However, even if we do not interfere at all and simply observe the object, even what we include or not in our observation, what we omit or not in our conception of what goes on in the game, will determine the outcome of how we explain the reality at hand. A billiard balls game without the players would certainly appear quite a magical scene and enigmatic compared to one in which we include the players and ourselves (as agencies who make such a conceptual inclusion or exclusion).

The relatively larger and faster bodies rule in the classical Newtonian imagination of the universe. The reason for such a presumably "objective" and "predictable" way of imagining reality is that we are assuming that the parts do not have any force of their own to add, to resist, to change, to influence, the outcome of the interaction. In such a vision, the visibly big and forceful are presumed to have more predictable and causal power in external their interactions with other things than the tiny, bumpy, imperfections, say, in the cloth covering the game table. In such a view, the reaction is always equal to the action, and it would be inconceivable, given the "laws of motion" claimed, to see that a tiny part could offer an effective and energetic "asymmetrical" reaction to a large ball delusionally proud of its mass.

In considering the deterministic way of thinking attributed to Newtonianism, its elements as inherited from Newton must be kept in mind.

For Newton, the motions of bodies take place in a spatiotemporally uniform frame of reference that stands the same for all bodies and observers. Besides, there is an assumption of vacuity characterizing the spacetime between bodies other than the forces (visibly or not) they exert on one another, such as in the case of gravity as Newton conceived the force acting (a view that later on was radically overthrown by Einstein). In the spatiotemporally uniform frame of reference, then, bodies move (or not) per laws of motion identified by Newton in ways that can be measured with more or less certitude, depending at most on the power and measuring abilities of the observers. Technically, the speed and location of bodies can be determined with certitude in the Newtonian universe, and if there is any limitation in this regard, it is due to the subjective limitations of the scientists than to any incertitude being built into the motion of bodies themselves. For this reason, the motions of bodies in the Newtonian universe are determinable in the past, at the present, and into the future, and such a universe is predictable.

The Newtonian way of imagining reality, when guiding our research such as that in our Khayyami studies, leads us to pursue deterministic, predictable, dualistic modes of analysis. We become uncreative researchers.

Thinking, in a predetermined way, what is supposed to have caused something else, we end up recycling our research projects. We end up often recycling the same findings and approaches, and exercising the same habitual ways of reading our sources, analyzing their details, and relating their parts. Give me the beginning of a Khayyami study, I will tell you how it will end.

We draw on the same sources and references, repeating the quotes again and again to demonstrate our "scientific" endeavor, without considering that in drawing on such sources as "objective" authorities we may be simply repeating the same errors they have made in pursuing their inquiries. So, we end up with the same dilemmas, enigmas, puzzles, and impasses, as those preceding us. And another thousand years pass.

Another way in which Newtonian thinking can shape our Khayyami studies is the predictable and predeterministic ways in which we study our subject matter. Just because Khayyam claimed Avicenna as a mentor does not mean he followed him blindly; so we may not understand the same concepts and terms Khayyam uses in his writings, or the same metaphors or tropes we have become accustomed to finding in the poetry that were composed a century before or after him, when trying to understand Khayyam absent specific efforts to understand how *he himself uniquely* used and applied those concepts in his writings. Understanding Avicenna does not automatically determine and predict our understanding of Khayyam, even if we find him reportedly reading Avicenna's chapter on "the One and the Many." He may have been pointing as much to a problem in Avicenna, as to a solution; otherwise, why would he still be reading him, we could ask? After all, we know Khayyam was a thinker who raised questions.

Take for instance *Nowrooznameh (The Book on Nowrooz)* attributed to Omar Khayyam. Scholars doubting the attribution of this work to him have passed such a judgment based on the assumption that what the author says is the purpose of the book, to find the truths about the tradition of Nowrooz, to be only that. So, finding that the way its author interprets, say, the meaning of the names of the months in the ancient Persian calendar, to be different than how "objective science" of Iranian history has established—that is, in terms of their association with the Zoroastrian worldview—they come to the conclusion that the author has gone astray, the book not becoming of such a careful "scientist" as was Khayyam; so, the book must not be his.

So, "predictably," such scholars have readily dismissed and disregarded the tract as being not worthy of attention in their Khayyami studies. Instead of studying the book to decide and determine for themselves whether or not it belongs to Khayyam, they dismiss it in an *a priori* way, since their starting point is that the book is either his or not from the outset, in a predetermined way. As a result, they end up not having any parts of their study devoted to the book. The causal linkages are already assumed, and not resulting from the actual study of his text. Afraid of losing their academic reputations, perhaps, they simply dismiss a book by Khayyam because "other scholars have said so." This was not supposed to be a scientific way of proceeding with our studies, one that instead requires questioning the taken for granted.

The same predictable attitude may be adopted with regards to the study of the Robaiyat. They regard a quatrain to be either Khayyam's or not, and since they cannot tell, it is judged as not being worth further study. Even when studied, predeterministic causal models are applied when evaluating the significance of a piece of writing. A scientist must not have taken poetry seriously, they say; so, even if Khayyam wrote poetry, it must have been a marginal hobby on the side. If an observer says Khayyam was miserly in writing or teaching, he must have been so, their reasoning goes, and we should predictably accept that view for another thousand years, even though at its face value, we can see that the biographer reporting such a claim is not aware of some of the most significant writings of Khayyam already discovered, or even already known in his own time.

If Khayyam is said to have had a temper, he must have had it, no questions asked about whether, why, when, and how. It must have been his philosophical writings that shaped his poetry, and not the other way around. His philosophy is present in the quatrains, not the other way around. We can never find a way of discovering whether he wrote robais or not, so, why bother. Studying his scientific writings offers no clues to his poetry. Poetry is here, science is there. How can one cause another with nothing in between, without any trace of any chain of "local causations"? His birth horoscope has little significance for his poetic, scientific, or philosophical interests. Any ways, it has already been studied and "determined" to point toward his "true" birth date. Indians discovered it, Russians confirmed it; case closed. The British interpreted the quatrains, job done, "wine" is just wine, they condescendingly keep on reminding the "mystical" interpreters. The French revealed why Khayyam avoided higher than third-degree equations in his algebraic classifications, ignoring negative numbers, and so on. All done. Case closed.

These are all statements that become habitually frozen as dicta. So, we end up reproducing the results of our findings century after century, in inevitable, predictable, and predetermined ways—ways that have led us to the present impasse in our Khayyami studies.

6. Continuity: Is Influence Exerted Through Chains of Local-Causations?

The motions of bodies in the Newtonian universe are determined through chains of local causations in time (from past to the present and into the future) and space (interacting things in direct local ways), in a way that is predictable. A causes B, B causes C, C causes D, and so on. The effects also in turn reciprocally interact with their causes, but there is a continuity in the chain of causation such that one would not expect A to cause D directly in an apparent "leap" or discontinuity, but only through the mediation of successive local causations in time and space.

Causal determinations in such a universe, therefore, are *continuous* in the Newtonian way of thinking, in the sense that there can never be a local causality that cannot be traced in terms of its immediate causes and effects in an apparent chain of causation into the past and the future, or from one thing to another locally. For this reason, the predictable determinism characterizing the Newtonian universe cannot accommodate non-local causality in time and space, in the sense of causes being exerted from one body to another, or from one time to another, without the apparent continuity of causal chain and forces mediating the process as *sui generis*, emergent, self-motivating and self-moving bodies that do not follow the apparent laws of motion and dicta of bodies are also not accommodated in a Newtonian way of thinking.

Since the Newtonian worldview sees reality as being characterized by atomism and separability, the continuity of causal interactions are assumed to be what glues reality to each other, so to speak. If you wish to find C, you will look for either C, or for B and D predictably assumed to be preceding and following it. This is the case both in terms of space and time. You will not find a clue to a chunk of reality to be non-locally elsewhere in time and place.

When applied to Khayyami studies, such a Newtonian approach to continuity will seek answers to questions about his life and works by trying to directly study the "local" regions in his or others texts, or "local" time periods and age-related questions, where the answers are predictably expected to be found. So, if you read a text by or about Khayyam on a seemingly "unrelated" subject, you would not expect to find an answer about a "completely separate" question. When you study his algebra or his solutions to the equations of the third degree, you would not be expecting to find his philosophy or the Robaiyat there. If you study a comment about why he "predicted" his grave's location, you would not be able to find a clue there about a completely different subject matter such as astronomy, astrology, or mathematics.

Khayyam himself makes comments that at times seem out of place. As noted previously, in the middle of a sentence about numbers, he makes an association to God, stating that numbers do not begin with 1, but 2 (ignoring negative numbers), since number, for him, signifies an integer that has a cause before and after. The number 1, therefore, cannot be considered a number, since all numbers proceed from it, but it does not itself proceed from anything. So, it represents the One, God. He symbolically associates A (or Alef) in the alphabet with God. So, here, with our present educational upbringing, you read numbers as, well, numbers. You do not expect that such a disciplinary chunk can be linked to God through a leap of imagination.

One could say the same thing about other aspects of Khayyam's texts, but also about any text about him, actually, as far as expectation of continuity is concerned. You would not expect to find a cause for solving a problem, say, about his date of birth, by examining a completely non-local, 'seemingly irrelevant' topic. You would not expect to find a clue about his authorship of the Robaiyat in a 'completely separate' information about his life and works.

This is because the Newtonian way of thinking about and imagining reality has conditioned us to seek answers to our questions in predictable ways in areas, topics, and subjects that we have habitually regarded as the "first place to look into." And if we do not find any ready-made answers there, we become despaired, our Khayyami studies reaching an impasse.

7. Disciplinarity: Fragmenting Our Knowledge of Reality?

Since according to the Newtonian worldview reality is perceived as being compartmentalized into separate parts that interact with one another from without, then presumably we would be better off developing ways of organizing scientific work by splitting knowledge and research into separable parts called disciplines, or more broadly in separating the natural from the social sciences and both from the humanities.

Of course, as interacting billiard balls influence each other, the academic disciplinary works can and should interact with one another, as we would have it even in various so-called inter- and cross-disciplinary programs. But, even so, the disciplines must be regarded as self-sufficient and self-organizing in understanding their domains and as such protective of their own disciplinary or academic culture islands.

Only in such a disciplinary architecture could one discipline or another claim to be more important than the other, as if the knowledge gained in, say, the humanities, does not have any direct bearing on what goes on in the lives and minds of the nuclear physicist busy crashing particles into other subatomic particles, or making it possible to do the same, actually or in threats, on the heads of millions across cities; and vice versa.

Even despite the advent of quantum revolution, most of our universities are still organized along Newtonian ways of imagining reality. So, when it comes to our Khayyami studies also, we fear breaking out of the disciplinary boundaries, experimenting with new and creative ways of going about knowing our subject matter, in ways that transgress disciplinary boundaries.

Some fear losing academic reputations by disrupting established disciplinary borders. "Why should I study Khayyam's horoscope? I will leave it to the astrologers, if not the astronomers. I am an economist." "Robaiyat is not my domain, I am a serious mathematician and cannot waste my time studying his marginal hobbies." "What? Philosophy? Nothing there relevant to studying his algebra, or his *Nowrooznameh*." Khayyam's Arabic poems? Nothing is there related to his philosophy, or science.

We thus use our already outdated Newtonian "disciplined" lenses to study an intellect for whom seeking truth had no rigid intellectual borders.

8. Scientism: Presuming the Superiority of Western, Newtonian Way of Thinking?

The Newtonian vision of the universe as a relational system of objects (whole-bodies or part-bodies) in which the relatively larger and faster moving objects determine the relatively smaller and slower moving objects (whole-bodies or part-bodies) is also inherently inclined to "impress" itself more forcefully upon any alternative, often smaller and more slowly emerging, visions of the universe arising from its midst or margins.

The Newtonian imagination presumes itself to be a culturally neutral, objective, perspective on how the universe works. But it is not. Its own ontological ("what is reality") stand makes possible and legitimizes its epistemological ("what knowledge of reality is") and methodological ("how knowledge of reality can be acquired") conclusions in such a way that is presumed to be "natural" and hence devoid of cultural particularity or diverse subjective interpretations. But, it is not. "We are the scientists, and you, 'others,' are not." Arbitrarily omitting the mystical side of our own Newtons, and Khayyams, "we regard your interpretations to be mystical, utopian, pseudoscientific," and so on, while "what we say is fine even though nonsensical and outrageous too, because we consider our ideas such as 'parallel universes' to be subject to 'objective' verification, even though we cannot do it (yet) or will never be able to."

In such a view, where subjects are either omitted or reduced to willless objects, other ways of imagining reality become irrelevant. "We in the West know the world better than you in the East. It is how *we* define science that is correct and there is no other way of going about knowing reality, since objective knowledge must be devoid of any cultural or personal coloring." "Khayyam was great because it seems he was like us Westerners, not like you Muslims." "His 'wine' is definitely that of the grape; we know better than you how to interpret his poems since you are not able to understand even your own culture, like we do ours, and yours." "You cannot know yourselves, we have to tell you who you are and why you wrote your poems."

Conversely, we find Iranian and Eastern scholars who, having failed on their own in understanding Khayyam, simply seek to emulate the Western scholars, and their findings, as standard-bearers of Khayyami studies. They continue looking up to them, as if they owe the West for making Omar Khayyam who he was, repeating the tales about how FitzGerald discovered Khayyam and others discovered FitzGeralds, and so on, sidestepping or ignoring altogether the Orientalist mischaracterizations and distortions that may have also crept into his "translations" of Khayyam's poetry for the world.

"If they tell us all these 'Rubaiyat' must be doubted as being attributable to Khayyam, they must be right, and we must be wrong, since they are more scientific and advanced than us." "Western scholars are correct. Only a handful of the Robaiyat are Khayyam's, nobody knows who composed the rest." "We should let the West judge who Khayyam is, for, after all, they are the ones who made Khayyam famous. We did not care much about him before, beyond some stories here or there about his greatness, or his having composed those poems that 'bite like snake.'" "Khayyam was great, Westerners say, because he was not 'as' religious. If he said he was a Muslim, it must have been said in fear." "If we find Khayyam referring to Jesus or Moses in his poems, that is fine, nice, in fact exotic, refreshing and cosmopolitan; but you must flatly ignore the ones in which a Muhammad or an Ali is mentioned, they must have definitively been added by others."

It may seem interesting that in delineating the eight attributes of the Newtonian way of imagining reality as done above, I have at the same time found it possible to offer hints at what the quantum way of imagining reality may be without having yet drawn on any findings in quantum science.

Although limitations of space here does not allow me to go into further detail—having already done so in *Unriddling the Quantum Enigma* (2020)—it suffices to suggest here that what quantum science and its findings have done have been to demonstrate, though in enigmatic ways, how we have ourselves erred, as scientific observers, in interpreting and understanding reality in Newtonian ways.

Such a thesis in fact is consistent with one of the most central findings of quantum science—that *observed* reality does not have a reality of its own, in itself, but must always be understood as a broader reality in which the observers studying it co-participate. A necessary result of such a view, from the point of view of our particular interest as social scientists and sociologists, is that our pursuit of knowledge about reality and its transformation is always also a human, social, and therefore sociological endeavor.

Following the attributes I outlined above for the Newtonian way of imagining reality, I offer below the broad parameters of what in my view the Newtonian sociology consists, since only with a clear perception of the Newtonian vision of the universe (in contrast to a quantum vision) can we have a yardstick with which we can evaluate whether a particular sociological perspective, in this case the Millsian sociological imagination, falls into or deviates from and transcends one vision in favor of the other.

For this reason, in the next few closing pages this chapter, I will briefly summarize a vision of "classical," "Newtonian sociology"—that will hopefully clarify further the implications the broader Newtonian vision I outlined above has for framing the "classical" sociological imagination.

Parallel to the eight attributes I outlined above regarding the Newtonian way of imagining reality, what could we say about the elements that typically define what we may call "Newtonian sociology"?

(1) The classical Newtonian sociological vision always makes and maintains a *dualistic* distinction between the presumed "facticity" of the *structural* conditions of society broadly speaking, on one hand, and, on the other, the individual, and his or her *agency*. We thereby presume society to be comprised of structures in whose confines individuals act, within and across smaller or larger groups.

Therefore, society (in small-groups or larger settings) as a whole is always regarded as being larger than its parts, having a reality that cannot be reduced to, or be interactively subjected to, the will of one or another (or a whole group of) persons. Society and the individual are not treated in terms of differences in identity, as being twin-born, but as separate realities in which the larger "social" predetermine "individual" natures and behaviors.

In other words, an inherent dualism informs the Newtonian conception of society, and therefore sociology, and the society and the individual, such that it makes it possible to stress more the social over the individual in advancing what is conventionally regarded as a "sociological" discipline.

(2) On the *micro* side, the "individual" is assumed to be the primary unit of analysis of social groups and treated as the basic "atom" of society embedded in a relational system of interacting small-group or large-group atoms which live, think, feel, and act as singular, "individual," entities. If any contradictions are observed in the behavior of such a presumed unitary, atomic, seemingly solid entity called "individual," they are regarded as (perhaps clinically deviant) exceptions to the rule of what is expected from the behavior of the individual "as a whole" in relation to other individuals, in groups, small or large. The micro unit of analysis is not the subatomic selves

but the presumably considered 'solid' and atomistic individuals.

(3) Even when the *macro* unit of analysis is considered to be human history as a whole, Newtonian sociology is usually studied within the context of particular civilizational, differently world-systemic, or nation-state units thereof, the separate civilizational, world-systemic and/or national trajectories presumed to have more or less dynamic of their own, which brings them into otherwise often more or less acknowledged reciprocal interactions with one another in definite historical contexts. The macro unit of analysis is not considered to be world-history itself, beyond any of its historically presumed separated nations, civilizations, world-systems, and so on.

(4) Newtonian sociology is concerned first and foremost with discovering and/or delineating the *"objective"* laws of motion of society and history or, stated in a different way, the broadest objective patterns dominant in social and historical development. Self-reflexivity is eschewed in such an "objective" endeavor to know social reality, presuming that one can really go about understanding the "facticities" of social life without being always, inescapably, self-reflective about how one co-participates in the way such knowledges as well as the realities they study are socially constructed.

The presumption here is that social laws or patterns have been shaped independently of human will, by nature and/or during earlier periods arising from the "systemic" nature of human social reality (which cannot be reduced to the will of human individual parts), and are thereby not readily changeable through human agency except within the spatiotemporal confines of what is "objectively" possible, to the extent in which they are considered "objectively" knowable by those actors through applying scientific methods and theories.

In such a vision, it is possible to achieve a subjectlessly "objective" understanding of social reality over and above any personal biases and interests the observing investigator may hold—hence, for instance, legitimating "blinded" procedures of knowledge production, review, and evaluation about the reality presumed to be objectively existing "out there" and representable.

(5) Newtonian sociology presumes a *predictably causal* primacy of the social structure in relation to individual's life and behavior, seeking to explain the latter by discovering the more or less predictable objective laws or 'determining' the broad developmental patterns that objectively hold sway over the historical process. The larger structures, social forces, and groups are often presumed to be more powerful and determinant in shaping everyday life than individual personal actions—dynamic and fast changing social realities generally presumed to be necessarily preferable to relatively

more slowly evolving, traditional social arrangements.

(6) When considering social causes, the *continuities* of local causations in a chain are presumed. In other words, it is assumed that, say, if an event occurs culturally, it must be caused by a politics, that has its roots in an economy, and so on, in a causal chain. The possibility of emergent, or *sui generis*, creative causality that involves no observable or immediate precedent is not seriously entertained. If it happens, it must be a result of a causal chain in a locally predictable and determinable way.

The chains of causations are assumed to be continuous in both space and time as well. Local causes are assumed to be results of immediately adjacent factors. What happens now must have always a cause in the past, and will result in predictable futures. If an event happens in one place, it must be the same way it happened in other places.

(7) Newtonian sociology adheres to its own disciplinary boundaries, even though, even as a discipline, it is transdisciplinary to the extent that it "allows" for the study of a variety of social relations, economic, political, cultural, artistic, and so on. However, even so, it is defensive of its own disciplinary boundaries, eschewing transgressing and erasing them. At best, if favors cross/multi/disciplinarities that still maintain traditional boundaries.

(8) Newtonian, Western sociology presumes to hold a superior "objective" "scientific" self-identity in contrast to other cultural traditions or perspective, as if its own tradition is not civilizationally, culturally, or structurally located—offering what is otherwise a provincially Western perspective on the nature of human society. It regards itself as a universal model for pursuing sociological knowledge, even though it is not, that is, when it is also a *particular* way of going about seeking knowledge.

Newtonian, Western sociology, considering itself as *the* only authoritative, scientific approach to the study of human society and behavior, tends to disregard (often using labels such as "utopian" or "mystical" in the derogatory senses of the terms) other cultural viewpoints as non-scientific traditions inherited from the past or emerging in the present.

How can the basic attributes of the Newtonian vision of the universe and of Newtonian sociology as rendered above help us evaluate whether the Millsian sociological imagination is confined to, or breaks away from and beyond, such Newtonian visions of the universe and society? In other words, what is a Newtonian way of framing the sociological imagination?

(1) The Newtonian sociological imagination adopts a *dualistic* conception of personal troubles versus public issues; it treats some personal troubles

as being worthy of its imaginative sociological attention while dismissing others as not relevant to the public issues at hand.

(2) The Newtonian sociological imagination, in the *micro* sphere, treats the personal troubles as attributable to solid individual units, rather than the subatomic selves constituting those individuals. It does not ask whether it is the whole person (others and/or the investigator him/herself) or one or another self (having troubles or not) constituting his or her person that is to be regarded as the proper micro unit of analysis.

(3) The Newtonian sociological imagination, in the *macro* sphere, treats society in terms of national, civilizational, and at best world-systemic (modern, premodern, ancient, and so on) separately knowable units of analysis. It does not adopt *human world-history* as a whole as a singular unit of analysis. It asks whether it is the contemporary society of one or more "nation-state(s)" amid the contemporary world-history context, which needs to be the proper macro unit of analysis rather than adopting world-history as a singular unit of analysis as a whole.

(4) The Newtonian sociological imagination does not directly and inescapably problematize and study how the investigator *himself/herself* should be personally implicated in that analysis as part of its practice of social scientific *objectivity*, in terms of how one's own personal troubles, or the public issues of one's times, influence one's research.

(5) The Newtonian sociological imagination presumes predictable modes of *causality* and "patterns" shaping social life, the individual/selves being more or less causally dependent on the workings of the social structure. The creative power of selves and individuals to question and transcend inherited intrapersonal and broader social structures, even when studied, are made dependent and perceived to be conditional on the extent to which "objective" conditions allow for such creative outcomes.

(6) The Newtonian sociological imagination seeks to explore the interaction of personal troubles and public issues by studying continuities in causal chains of factors, ignoring the possibility of unexpected, *sui generic*, creative interactions and insights that may implicate such micro-macro interactions. This way the underlying interconnectedness of seeming discontinuities across personal troubles and/or public issues across historical spacetimes are ignored.

(7) The Newtonian sociological imagination still regards itself as being "sociological" in the narrow, *disciplinary*, meaning of the term. As such, it still sees itself as part of a university world-system and academic context,

to whose boundaries, modes of organization, recruitment, and discipline it, more or less willingly, submits.

(8) The Newtonian sociological imagination carries along the arrogance of its self-identity as the superior Western "scientific" *cultural* endeavor, distinguishing itself from other, subaltern sociological modes of knowing in deeds if not in words. It sees itself as the sole, the only, way of conducting the sociological imagination, such that even when recognizing the Newtonian ways of knowing the world in others, it forgets that it could itself be a conduit of the same, advertently or not.

Note that what makes the sociological imagination Newtonian is not simply that it avoids studying linkages between its elements. What makes it Newtonian is its treating those elements in a "chunky" way, in presuming that the elements are separate billiard balls to begin with, that they do not overlap with one another, instead simply needing to be linked with another, to interact with one another from "without," in order to make the imagination work. It does not imagine those elements as already embedded in dialectical part-whole relations of identity in difference, of difference in identity.

Personal troubles are here, public issues there. Some personal troubles are not public issues, some public issues not relating to personal troubles. The "inner life" of the individual is separate from her "external career"; social contexts of nation-states, civilizations, world-systems, are separate from one another. What goes on in the East is separate from that in the West. Our national public issues are separate from your public issues. What happened a thousand years ago, or will happen a thousand years from now, is separate from what goes on today, here-and-now, and vice versa.

It is amid such a "chunky" way of imagining society that it becomes possible to speak of an "objectivity" by impossibly omitting the researcher from his or her research, of arguing that there are "objective" laws of motion of history independent from our, including the researcher's, will. It is such a chunky way of imagining society that leads to the chunky way of separating an American sociology from a German sociology from an Iranian sociology, regarding one as superior to another, of separating sociology from other disciplines, of separating academic cultures from one another, and then trying to make them cross-this or cross-that—as if they are not already existing in overlapping ways with one another.

It is such a chunky way of imagining sociology that leads one to think one can readily separate "science" from spirituality and philosophy, and presume the superiority of one over the other, rather than recognize that what one considers one's own insular cultural identity is in fact a result of a whole series of cultural and intellectual discourses in a world-history context to which all have diversely contributed.

Figure 2.1 illustrates how a Newtonian sociological imagination treats the various conceptual elements defining it as separate billiard balls to be juggled and linked from without.

It follows from the above, then, that our Khayyami studies adopting imaginative sociological approaches may still remain Newtonian, when the various elements of its framework are conceptualized in a chunky (and playerless) billiard balls game way.

We would study Khayyam's personal troubles and his time's public issues and try to relate them to one another from without, as if a personal trouble expressed in a quatrain or a public issue addressed in a passage in a scientific text do not signify or inform us about, at the same time respectively also, public issues and personal troubles. Accounts of those calling him miserly in writing are taken at face value as "facts," not problematized as examples of the same manner in which he reports elsewhere he was mistreated and misunderstood, and ridiculed, for being different. His time's religious attitudes are taken out of context, and approached from a Victorian English cultural lens deemed superior by default, and what has been passed on as the "facticities" of his life, including his birth and death dates, are simply taken for granted as "objectively" settled and not influenced by the biases, errors, and misreading of specific researchers who, advertently or not, became too proud of their findings to see where they have obviously erred.

Our studies of Khayyam would be allowed, in a Newtonian framework, to be pursued in a fragmentary way following the disciplinary divisions of our lenses, leading us to think that it would be of no value to seek answers about his poetry in his scientific tracts, of his sociological innovations in his literary creative writings, the clues to his life's secret work in a cryptic statement about his birth horoscope, or even in the architecture of a seemingly lost or "left incomplete" monument in Isfahan.

To know Khayyam, it would be presumed that what the West has had to say is of more superior worth than the findings of scholars from his own cultural and spiritual tradition, adopting different lenses and ways of seeing, imagining, and studying reality.

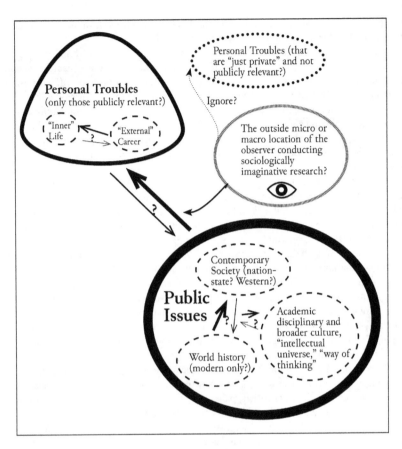

Figure 2.1

Visual Expression of the Newtonian Sociological Imagination

Abstract

This essay, titled "The Newtonian Imagination of Reality, Society, Sociology, and Khayyami Studies," is the second chapter of the first book, subtitled *New Khayyami Studies: Quantumizing the Newtonian Structures of C. Wright Mills's Sociological Imagination for A New Hermeneutic Method*, of the twelve-book series, *Omar Khayyam's Secret: Hermeneutics of the Robaiyat in Quantum Sociological Imagination*, authored by Mohammad H. Tamdgidi.

To offer a heuristic model of the Newtonian way of imagining reality, society, sociology and the sociological imagination and demonstrate (in a following chapter) how such a perspective is different from the quantum way of imagining them, the author uses in this chapter the "billiard balls game" metaphor that has been widely used (in his view wrongly) to characterize the Newtonian way of imagining the world.

According to Tamdgidi, the Newtonian way of imagining, or thinking about, the universe may be broadly characterized as having eight notional attributes—namely, its notions of (1) dualism, (2) atomism, (3) separability, (4) (subjectless) objectivity, (5) determinism (including its associated notion of predictability), (6) continuity, (7) disciplinarity, and (8) scientism—which can be illustrated by using a (what he argues is an ideologically distorted) metaphorical "billiard balls game" way of imagining reality as commonly used for the purpose.

More specifically the attributes of Newtonian imagination Tamdgidi explores are in terms of the following questions: 1. Dualism: can an object be A and non-A at the same time? 2. Atomism: what is the micro unit of analysis of the object? 3. Separability: what is the macro unit of analysis of the object? 4. Objectivity: does the object being observed have an independent reality? 5. Determinism: are causes and consequences in objects certain and predictable? 6. Continuity: is influence exerted through chains of local-causations? 7. Disciplinarity: fragmenting our knowledge of reality? And 8. Scientism: presuming the superiority of Western, Newtonian way of thinking?

The author uses the above framework to show how such parameters also have shaped our Newtonian conceptions of society, sociology, and the sociological imagination, and may also continue to frame our Khayyami studies if we fail in bringing them to conscious awareness as a precondition for reframing our sociological and Khayyami studies in more fruitful, quantum ways. Tamdgidi concludes by summarizing a vision of "classical," "Newtonian sociology" that can clarify further the implications the broader Newtonian vision he outlined above has for shaping the "classical" sociological vision, and the sociological imagination as a framework for conducting Khayyami studies.

Introducing a diagram for the Newtonian sociological imagination, Tamdgidi notes that what makes the sociological imagination Newtonian is not simply that it avoids studying linkages between its elements. What makes it Newtonian is its treating those elements in a "chunky" way, in presuming that the elements are separate billiard balls to begin with, that they do not overlap with one another, instead simply needing to be linked with another, to interact with one another from "without," in order to make the imagination work. It does not imagine those elements as already embedded in dialectical part-whole relations of identity in difference, of difference in identity.

CHAPTER III—Quantum Sociological Imagination as a Framework for New Khayyami Studies

Classical Newtonianism, as a model for science, was a product of an historical compromise between a receding religiosity and an emerging secularism in the West. In such a model, willful and creative subjects, observers, and scientists are to be consciously and intentionally omitted as such from the object of research (unless themselves treated as willless subjects) in the name of "objectivity"—even though such a requirement is essentially impossible to fulfill. This arbitrary approach to scientific research modeling was made possible by the dualistic architecture of a longstanding (inherited from ancient times) formal logic that was also adopted by classical Newtonianism, one that allowed for a universally 'chunky' view of reality comprised of separable parts in all realms of reality, from the atomic to the cosmic.

Such a logic and resulting atomistic and chunky view of reality absent of willful subjects, then, made it possible to legitimize the search for predictable causes and deterministic laws of motion operating in reality. The fact that even the most inanimate objects of research had to be explored through the participation of the subjective worlds of observers and scientists conducting research—and that, therefore, the separation of the object from the subject was impossible to make in order to arrive at a presumably "objective" research absent of the researcher's consciousness—was simply ignored.

A self-fulfilling prophetic attitude built into the classical Newtonianism, therefore, in effect deleted its own role and the roles of willful subjects (ranging from curiosities about God or gods down to Earthly subjects, observers and scientists) from the object of its study, resulting in a "scientific" model of reality that was devoid of any role creative agencies played, or could play, in setting its "laws" in motion.

The presumably deterministic model of classical Newtonianism devoid of creative subjects thus constructed in the West was especially consequential for the sciences of society, mind, and human behavior. A scientific culture gripped by the classical Newtonian spell was writing, in the name of science, its own academic narrative of what a deterministic science of society and mind should be like and found itself quite unenigmatically pleased with its imperial self-regard. It was so proud of itself that it even claimed at times that the basic task of (classical Newtonian) science was over and that there is not much left to be known, except for some detail here or there.

And it was the same imaginary presumptions of a universally atomistic and chunky macroscopic reality (and in fact to perpetuate such an imagination) that led to and legitimized the construction of the modern academic organization of knowledge production, fragmenting it internally into the organizational sub-cultures of the natural sciences, the social sciences, and the humanities, each with its own further separately imagined and institutionalized disciplinary and subdisciplinary fields and departments which were then treated hierarchically as some having less or more importance and value than others. It was assumed that each can arrive at its domain's truth on its own, and collide with other academic disciplines and cultures if needed, in the spirit of playing a reified interdisciplinary billiard balls game.

In a similar way, the academic organization could then separate itself in time from other religious, mystical, utopian, artistic, and non-Western ways of imagining reality, also implying a hierarchically superior self-regard in relation to other Eastern ways of knowing considered now to be of lesser scientific value in relation to those presumably belonging to Western culture and science. Such a view would of course find it exotic that a Persian "astronomer-mathematician," Omar Khayyam, would also write poetry (even if at all, heatedly arguing about those "wandering quatrains")—since the presumably separable chunks of philosophy here, religion there, science elsewhere, and poetry in "spare time" (if at all) seemed to fit better the Western disciplinary expectations of what pursuing chunky philosophical, spiritual, scientific, and literary pursuits would entail.

This model of science was an historical compromise emergent in the West in the sense that its logical and conceptual architecture allowed for two things: 1) it still accommodated a religious point of view that was becoming increasingly marginalized, keeping it in line institutionally and conceptually amid a secularizing Western context (pertaining to a God who struck the first creative strike, but then sat aside in favor of watching the autonomously operating creation go on existing, subject to its own "laws"); and 2) it pursued an "objective" science that presumably did not have to concern itself with any enigmatic questions regarding spiritual meanings of existence; and if anyone dared to cross the line, he or she would be deemed and labeled a "pseudoscientist."

The fact that such a dichotomy actually had not been present in Isaac Newton himself and his own scientific spirit as a scientist, theologian, and alchemist—that he was indeed deeply enigmatized by the puzzles of existence in his own way behind the scenes—did not matter. The mystical side was dualistically set aside in time in favor of a disenchanted, historically compromised, secular classical Newtonian model that came to be taken for granted as a "theory of everything" of its time. Consequently, such a Western compromise under the secular ideology of scientism found it easier to marginalize and decenter "other" ways of knowing that it had itself benefited from in its arising while drawing on sources of knowledge from other cultures. It could now relegate them to a secondary intellectual and cultural status serving well its expanding capitalist, Orientalist, and imperial/colonial conquests involving incorporations of other lands, peoples, and cultures.

Even though we have used the billiard balls game metaphor to illustrate the Newtonian way of imagining reality, on closer examination we realize that it was not the game as such, but *a particular way of imagining it* that played such a heuristic role in elucidating the Newtonian way of imagining reality. In other words, as I tried to elaborate in the previous chapter— and have done so more extensively in my recent work (Tamdgidi 2020)— by constructing alternative imaginations of the same game by redefining its micro or macro units of analyses, for instance, the billiard balls game does not have to be imagined only in a Newtonian way, but could in fact also be alternatively imagined in a quantum way, if we succeed in changing our habitual lenses. It is *we* who imagined the game in a Newtonian way and then raised it to the status of a singular metaphor for Newtonianism.

So, it is misleading to metaphorize such an ideologically compromised classical Newtonianism as a billiard balls game, to which it was certainly *not* similar were we to imagine and consider in a different way. In order to fit such a Newtonian model, the billiard balls game had to rid itself of its more or less creative players and observers (unless they are also treated as willless and passive bodies) and the very unpredictable, playful nature of its game—whose particularly human constructed nature in contrast to other natural events was not essential to considering the basic incompatibility of the model with the metaphor to be valid.

But the likening had its functional benefits for the emerging and hegemonic scientific model. It somehow naturalized and reified the Newtonian scientific model in order to claim a universally valid and "lawful" status for itself on one hand, and, on the other, to suggest that reality is not essentially a malleable, creative, unpredictable, entity that could be sooner or later subjected to human will as a part of that reality in order to realize its dreams for a better world, but one that had to abide by the "objective" constraints dictated by an "objectively existing" matter or motion of history. This of course served the interests, both religious and secular, of those wishing to maintain the status quo in society in general and in its Newtonian academic organization and disciplinary regimes in particular.

The scientists emergent from such Newtonian institutional structures would then of course have to be quite enigmatized when confronting new scientific events and experiments in their own laboratories inside and out when the model reached its cognitive limits and fell into deep crisis. They could deny things in the past because it could not be readily observed and verified; but now the increasing findings were undeniable.

How to respond? Either (1) take the new findings to their logical conclusion and thereby undermine the whole structure and edifice of science and its academic disciplinary and university architecture, and risk their own status and tenures along the way (or at least fear losing them and thus be kept in line and disciplined); or (2) deny the applicability of the microscopic world knowledge to the macro world via ever newer Copenhagen-type, "shut up and calculate," compromises; or (3) come up with theories and celebrations of a decades-long, perhaps forever unresolvable and at times quite entertainingly exoticized, "quantum enigma."

It is this overall classical Newtonian model of science—presumably applicable universally to all realms of matter from the atomic to the cosmic and within which scientists in recent centuries had more or less operated, one which they had taken for granted as the "only correct" way of going about conducting "scientific" investigation—that became shattered, at first gradually, and then in sudden leaps amid unprecedented new discoveries.

It thus became increasingly apparent that Newtonianism at best (even when radically rethought by new theories of relativity) could claim to be only an approximating paradigm for understanding macroscopic realms of reality and not be actually suitable for understanding what goes on in the sub/atomic world—a world that paradoxically constitutes the macroscopic realm but seems to be operating in a radically different way. It seemed different, because we had already habitually accustomed ourselves to a narrow vision of the universe along Newtonian lines and supposed that such a narrower vision applied to everything, known or yet unknown. So, the aftershocks of the twin revolutions of relativity and quantum science have still not left the scene because the enigmas that ensued remained unresolved for more than a century since the time the first signs of anomalies began to manifest in scientific experiments.

Certain problems, left on their own as seemingly subjectless or willless "objective" realities, happen due to a series of chained causes. It is possible to determine and predict certain trajectories of motion, certain social, cultural, or political processes, certain technical or economic trends—especially when such realities have themselves been socially constructed by humans in a mechanistic and habitual way using classical Newtonian models—so as to understand how to intervene in them to pursue preconceived aims.

A social system in which economic life is institutionalized separately and is regarded to be primary, for instance, is not necessarily so because of natural causes, but because it was socially and historically constructed as such by humans applying definite causal models which, in their view, would bring about more profit for some, even if not prosperity for all because profit for some necessarily implies loss for others relatively. However, it was this mechanical and habitual way of going about conducting social organizing and engineering and scientific investigation and practice that the findings of quantum science seemed to increasingly challenge, leading to a dichotomous and discordant cognitive dilemma that recognized macroscopic realities to be constituted by microscopic realities while having to reckon with the fact that each "level" seemed now to have a different life or set of "laws" of its own such that both could no longer be explained by the old or even the relativity-corrected Newtonian model.

The point here is to problematize a perspective that has become habitually and subconsciously a taken-for-granted building block of the so-called quantum enigma narrative leading to two major assumptions: one, the assumption that somehow the Newtonian model (when corrected for relativity) still explains "well" the macroscopic reality, an assumption I problematized above; and, two, the assumption that our macroscopic view of reality was somehow not enigmatic to begin with, a lack of enigma that is itself a socially constructed perspective to which we have become anesthetized in recent centuries.

The West had already stripped Newton's scientific spirit from its enigmatic, mystical, elements in favor of a "common sense," secular and "objectivist" Newtonianism, one that excluded spiritual curiosity, the participatory role of willful and creative subjects and investigators, and the resulting unpredictable and creative nature of reality as studied by human subjects. If those elements had been retained, the macroscopic reality's wonder and enigmas would have remained intact as part of the scientific spirit. That's how Newton himself, Einstein later on, or, say, Khayyam or Avicenna before them, going back to many other examples one could cite in Middle Eastern, ancient East Asian, Greek, Mesopotamian and Egyptian thinkers as well, had approached the pursuit of truth about reality.

Wonder and enigma were inescapable parts of Khayyam's scientific work. Not even the most abstract mathematical, geometrical, philosophical, or literary problems were addressed or explored in his scientific texts without starting and ending the report with expressions of greetings to his God, the prophet(s), and to his spiritual awe, wonder, and curiosity. The circle was not just that, but represented the wonder of coming and going into existence. The first letter of alphabet represented a "One" and the number 1 was not to be counted as a number because it represented the source of existence, not being preceded by another number—negative numbers not considered by him as such. The pursuit of solving algebraic equations was made in the hopes of shedding light on God's secrets and understanding the secret pearl of the order hidden beneath the surface of the ocean of creation.

And of course none of these early scientists were directly involved or could be involved in subatomic research to feel so perplexed or enigmatized by what they confronted in their research. The awe and wonder were expressed about a deeply enigmatic *macroscopic*, cosmic world. The wonder and magic of what they saw around them in the macroscopic world had not been lost to a model of science that exiled the search for the source(s) of existence or doubts about its orders of fate and chance in favor of not only a mechanistic view of the universe but also a natural and social world that were intended to be made and run mechanically, as classical Newtonianism later on promised.

It was only by way of a more or less arbitrary, though historically and socially constructed, ideological stripping of Newtonianism from the enigmatic elements of its namesake, Isaac Newton, that a model of science had been socially constructed that beginning in the twentieth century found itself deeply shocked and enigmatized by what it discovered in the course of scientific experiments on light and the subatomic world. Deeply habituated by the "common sense" lens of enigma-stripped Newtonianism, it could not really fathom how microscopic reality can seem so contradictory to what it had taken for granted as its long-cherished classical "theory of everything."

The new discoveries of course offered new insights and new ways of seeing reality, but the enigma experienced had also much to do with the observer's own classical Newtonian ways of seeing that had been simply taken for granted as a way to describe and imagine reality. And this consideration of the role played by the observer's own previously held points of view in experiencing what it regarded as enigmatic was, paradoxically, an essential contribution that quantum science was now making and had to be reckoned with in its research pursuits.

Albert Einstein's theories of special and general relativity leading to the odd view of the sameness or identity of mass and energy and offering a new theory of gravity radically challenged the propositions of separability and observer-omitted objectivity in the classical Newtonian model of science and its way of imagining reality in its macroscopic realms. In that sense, one may argue that the first major revolutionary shock to the classical Newtonian model—one that was later on also affirmed by the microscopic findings of quantum science—was exerted in relation to what was perceived to be the macroscopic world. Einstein's notion that spacetime is relative, and not absolute and separable, deeply disturbed the prevailing classical Newtonian model of science in two ways.

First, by offering a spacetime-relative notion of reality and theory of gravity, it challenged the notion of separability of bodies "externally" exerting forces on one another from without. Here, we now have an imagination of reality that treats the "spacetime" in between the seemingly separate bodies to be itself implicated as wave-like attribute of the seemingly "corpuscular" and "particle" presences of the "objects." The Sun is not just out there as a mass, but also here in the spatiotemporally curved presence of an "included middle," relating the planets (including the Earth) with it as parts of a singular whole that includes the Sun's and the planets' gravitational spacetime curvatures interpenetrating one another.

Second, at the heart of the explanation that made the inseparability of seemingly "separate" bodies evident was the notion of observational relativity built into the theory of relativity—that is, the notion that space and time are not separate from one another as absolute realities "out there" but ones whose realities are dependent on the observational reference frame we choose to study them. The observer could no longer be regarded as separate from the object of observation. This was a massive revolutionary blow to the classical Newtonian model of science, even without invoking yet any of the findings of quantum science. Or, rather, one may also interpret this, that is, the theories of relativity, as expressive of the quantum revolution in our understanding of the macroscopic reality—because, the notions of inseparability in the universe, and the dependence of its knowledge on the position of the observer, are at the heart of the quantum way of imagining reality as well.

The theories of relativity, in other words, had already challenged in the macroscopic world, without even considering the advent of the quantum revolution in the microscopic realm, the notion that anything observed could be readily explained without including the observer in the investigative research model and design. Einstein's general relativity theory of gravity had also challenged the notion of "separability" of bodies from one another, since their gravitational forces on one another "at a distance" could not be explained without considering the in-between spacetime reference frame acting as an included-middle element in their interactions.

However, while the theories of relativity undermined some of the most basic assumptions of classical Newtonianism in relation to macroscopic reality, it was the advent of the quantum revolution that fundamentally challenged Newtonianism in relation to the microscopic, sub/atomic reality.

I have traced in much more detail, in my recent work *Liberating Sociology: From Newtonian Toward Quantum Imaginations: Volume 1: Unriddling the Quantum Enigma* (2020, hereafter referred to by the first volume subtitle), the way the quantum revolution undermined the basic attributes of the classical Newtonian way of imagining reality, leading to an enigmatic shock that lasted for decades, and has still not gone away. In the book, however, I have also offered a new relativistic interpretation for understanding and unriddling the quantum enigma and its expressions across various experiments.

Therein, I have argued that the notion of "wave-particle duality of light" constituting the skeleton of the quantum enigma, so to speak, embodies in itself the whole diverse set of experimental expressions of the quantum enigma fleshing out the elephant in the room that the quantum enigma's Schrödinger's cat has morphed into over the decades. I have shown how that notion is inherently flawed and is responsible for the cognitive impasse that has come to be known through the decades as the quantum enigma. In the process, I have also identified specific new interpretive errors that were additionally introduced to the enigma's cat gone elephant in order to account for a riddle that had its roots in the "wave-particle duality of light" false narrative. By reinterpreting the notion of "wave-particle duality" in a new relativistic way, and correcting the additional interpretive errors arising over the decades, I have argued that we can unriddle the enigma and its expressions across various associated actual and/or thought experiments.

In the book, I have demonstrated that the notion "wave-particle duality of light" is a false narrative, an interpretive blunder, not just because of the reference to a duality that needs to be itself problematized, but because it poses the duality in terms of a false contrast. The notion presumes that the distinction, the so-called "duality," is between two things, A and non-A, wave and particle, when the distinction in actual experiments has nothing to do with a choice of something being wave and a non-wave. In all conditions, light is a wave. What we are confronting is not a choice between two wave and non-wave behaviors, but of two different ways in which the wave behavior is manifested or is to be observed or visualized. The problem is not to interpret how an object can be a wave and a non-wave at the same time, but how the *same wave* can be at once spread-out and localized.

The basic idea of the relativistic reinterpretation of the false narrative "wave-particle duality of light" as introduced in my recent work is that motions of objects relative to one another bring about relativistic distortions of spacetime such that an object observed as a localized object in an observer's reference frame is regarded also, at once, as a spread-out object in the moving object's own reference frame. For low relative speeds of motion the effect is negligible and unnoticeable, but for speeds approaching that of light, the relativistic effect is significant.

What is at once localized and spread-out, and how, depends on the object's nature. An electromagnetic wave such as a photon at once flashes by and spreads-out as a wave. That is, the photon as an electromagnetic wave flashing by as a localized object in our macroscopic reference frame, while being subjected to the relativistic effect also spreads out as a wave in its own reference frame. The photon that appears as a tiny, localized object to us in our observers' reference frame spreads-out as a wave in the photon's own reference frame displaying wave behaviors such as interference. As odd as it may sound, but not so in the world accurately portrayed from a relativistic point of view, we live inside the universally spread-out wavy photons we otherwise observe to be tiny, localized "particles" flashing by.

From our point of view, from the point of view of the young, 16-year-old Einstein imagining chasing light during a time when still it was considered to be only a wave, or from the point of the 1905 Einstein writing and publishing his first miracle-year paper on the nature of light arguing that light has (also) a particle-like behavior as far as the photoelectric experiment proves, a photon is something "out there" separate from us "here." It is tiny, because it is contracted, seemingly massless, given it is moving at the highest possible speed. Like the Earth-bound scientists' explaining muons' behavior from their own point of view, saying that in their own frame of reference, given its very short life span, its time is dilated just enough to reach the surface of the Earth, we say the photon is a flashing ray or beam of light. It is a contracted object that represents a quantum lump of energy of one or another electromagnetic wave frequency. It is a flash moving (being considered nearly massless) at the speed of light that it alone can claim; and for the same reason, it is tiny and contracted, as if it does not have any mass, even if it does, were it at rest (which it can never be, physicists tell us, since massless particles are deemed, by definition, to travel at the speed of light).

However, there is another side to this plot that is also important to keep in mind—if only we could put ourselves in the shoes of the photon instead.

As I have explained in more detail in *Unriddling the Quantum Enigma* (2020), pointing to a previously unnoticed historical anomaly in 1905 Einstein's reporting of his youthful 1895 "light-chasing" thought experiment, for the photon traveling at the highest relativistic speed at which it alone can move, not only the Earth, but indeed the solar system, the Milky Way galaxy, and indeed the universe contract to a tiny size, and relative to its own, the universal time slows down to a near halt. From this point of view, photon is no longer a tiny particle but is a giant wave spreading in all directions, one that embraces in principle the whole universe, and certainly the whole Earth, even though in concrete contexts and lower speeds, it may take a while for such an embracing of the universe to happen, moving at the speed of light, but with the corresponding distance/length contraction of the universe relative to it withstanding.

As the fish in the tank does not notice the water because it is in it and the water in the fish, we do not see the photon *because we are in it*. We would have to consider (from the photon's standpoint) that we are indeed living inside photons, their energy encompassing us, and not the other way around—that is, from the standpoint of the photon, of course. From our vantage point, it is the opposite. The photon is a tiny, flashing object. From our point of view in our reference frame, the photon seems like a particle (but it remains a wave throughout), a seemingly localized object that is propagated as a tiny electromagnetic wave; from the photon's own point of view and spacetime reference frame, it is a widely spread-out wave.

For the young, 16-year-old Einstein, the wave, and for the 26-year-old Einstein in the patent clerk's office, the photon, is a tiny particle to be chased; that is still a valid point of view, a "proper" point of view, but only from the standpoint of Einstein and us human observers. From the standpoint and reference frame of the light photon wave deemed otherwise to be a tiny localized particle by us, however, it is a giant object spreading-out with every second of our time in light-speed to encompass, in principle, the whole universe. This is why I problematized in *Unriddling the Quantum Enigma* (2020) the famous light-chasing thought experiment by Einstein, finding the anomaly and error that has escaped our attention (and escaped his) for decades. It was because of Einstein's assuming light to be a tiny particle moving in a beam that he could have imagined "chasing" it. If the 1905 Einstein writing his first miracle year paper acknowledging the "dual" nature of light across the optical and photoelectric experiments had asked the question about which behavior of light was manifested when he was chasing it, he would have raised to himself the question of the possibility that the light he was chasing could have (also) been chasing him as well. In no (photon's) time, he would be inside it any ways, if the light photon spread in all directions. I argue that it was this blind spot, or imaginal blunder, that laid the ground for the subsequent dichotomizations of the nature of light, resulting in a cognitive enigma lasting and expanding for decades.

It is the classical, Newtonian, playerless billiard-ball-game playing, mentalities of our own, of the 16-year-old, and also of the blundering 1905 not-yet-published, special relativist June-1905-author Einstein self writing his first paper on the heuristic of light first, that have habitually and subconsciously reproduced a dualistic landscape which has then necessitated being explained away by all kinds of dualistic and spooky interpretations. Ironically, the incompleteness of the quantum theory Einstein lamented about his whole life was caused by an imaginal blunder in the same light-chasing thought experiment that led to his theorizations of relativity. And, more ironically, it was the genius of his relativity theories in the conceptual fold of his vision that can ultimately explain and help unriddle, via a relativistic interpretation, the quantum enigma.

As I have argued in *Unriddling the Quantum Enigma* (2020), from the point of view of a consistently relativistic Einstein, were he to complete his imaginal oversight *spatially*, the very same light photon possessing wave characteristics as a tiny object, is, from the localized wave's own frame of reference, embracing us and our double-slit experiment or other experiment setups, across vast distances.

It is not that light is at times a particle and at other times a wave, a view falsely advanced according to the so-called "Complementarity Principle." First of all, it is throughout a wave. Second, it is at once localized moving in a straight path as a ray or beam in any direction we look or experiment with, and spread-out across like a ripple in the universal pond. It is a flash in time for us; we are flash in time for it. It is tiny for us; we are tiny for it. It is, relativistically, at once a flashing tiny and a spreading-out giant wave.

The "wave-particle duality of light" is a misnomer for what should more properly be called the "localized/spread-out simultaneity of light wave" because the two attributes are two "folds" of the *same* photon *wave* light relativistically manifesting itself in its own and in our spacetime reference frames. We are not encountering here two separate objects in reality. It is one object that is observed differently from two different reference frame folds.

Since I have previously offered in detail my alternative interpretive solutions to the quantum enigma (2020), I will not repeat the same here in this chapter, and encourage readers to consult that work directly to read my account of how the so-called quantum enigma arose and evolved over the decades, and how I solved it. Instead, in this chapter my aim is to try and share the basic findings of that study in an applied way, in terms of what exactly the notional attributes of the quantum way of imagining reality consists, and how they can altogether offer a new framework for reimagining society, sociology, and Khayyami studies.

In the previous chapter I summed up the classical Newtonian way of imagining reality by identifying its following eight characteristics: 1-dualism; 2-atomism; 3-separability; 4- (subjectless) objectivity; 5-determinism; 6-continuity; 7-disciplinarity; and 8-scientism. The quantum way of imagining reality can also be characterized as having eight sets of attributes: 1- simultaneity (not "duality," nor "complementarity"); 2-superpositionality;

3-inseparability; 4-relativity (subject-included objectivity); 5-probability; 6-transcontinuity (which is a term I prefer to call what is commonly referred to as "discontinuity"); 7-transdisciplinarity; and (8) transculturalism.

Note again that in listing and describing above the eight attributes of the quantum way of imagining reality, to be further detailed in the rest of this chapter, I have basically followed a pattern of listing the eight attributes in a way that is parallel to the eight defining attributes of classical Newtonianism. Note also how in the first chapter I delineated the eight sets of questions raised in my mind over the years about the classical limits of C. Wright Mills's sociological imagination as proposed in his work in 1959. I have introduced the eight questions about the sociological imagination and the eight attributes identified for each of the classical Newtonian and the quantum ways of imagining reality as such in order to help us see how they parallel one another in terms of how their integrated understanding can contribute to a quantum sociological imagination which can also serve as a framework for our Khayyami studies to be conducted in the present series.

Here again to be noted is the logical interdependence among the attributes offered for the quantum way of imagining reality, one leading to the next and others. The basic thrust of describing the eight attributes below is to understand how the overall universally chunky imagination of reality as found in classical Newtonianism is radically challenged by a holistic and nonreductively dialectical vision of reality as advanced in the quantum imaginative framework.

In considering the eight notional attributes of the quantum way of imagining reality as further described below, we have to keep in mind the distinction between the classical Newtonianism that was socially constructed over the centuries involving ideological attributes and constraints, one that did not necessarily correspond with Newton's own spiritually-motivated worldview as I explained in the previous chapter, on one hand, and what one may call the relativistic Newtonianism of Albert Einstein, on the other.

In Einstein's special and general theorizations of relativity important elements of classical Newtonianism were radically undermined, and they do correspond to the quantum ways of imagining reality (in the macroscopic world). More specifically, his theory of gravity emerging from his relativistic theories undermined the notion of separability of objects even in the macroscopic realm given its overturning the notion of an absolute spacetime frame of reference, showing that the universe is comprised of inseparable events. His relativistic theories also radically and irreversibly undermined the notion of observer-omitted objectivity.

These contributions by Einstein overlap significantly with the contributions of quantum science to how reality can be differently imagined. In a way, Einstein's relativistic Newtonianism may be regarded as providing the hidden third, the included-middle, logical element that unites what may still be found useful (reinterpreted in a quantum way, of course) in the old classical Newtonianism and the new quantum ways of imagining reality.

Therefore, we have to always distinguish between *three* kinds of Newtonianism: *classical, incompletely relativistic,* and *completely relativistic*. The *classical* Newtonianism universalizes the eight attributes as listed earlier. The *incompletely* relativistic Newtonianism is the kind prevalent today, confused, enigmatized, still not freed from the classical bounds but not yet fully embracing attributes that it could have independently discovered for itself, ones that it would have found to be "completely" resonating with the quantum science findings (itself stripped of elements contributive to the quantum enigma, such as the "wave-particle duality," "Complementarity Principle," and so on). For the *completely* relativistic Newtonianism I have coined (2020) the seemingly paradoxical term *Quantum Newtonianism*. It is a Newtonianism that treats the reality from the standpoint of any observer's reference frame to be a local reference frame or fold of the broader quantum reality as a whole.

So long as the classical and incomplete Newtonian attributes are universalized and absolutized to all times and spaces within a presumably common universal reference frame, we would be enigmatized by what we find in our quantum science findings. However, once we consider *Quantum Newtonianism* as a local reference frame/fold of the broader quantum reality, we will find that the list of quantum reality attributes I listed earlier (and will be explored further in the rest of this chapter) to be applicable *to all reality*.

The way to go about unifying the two attribute lists of the classical Newtonian and the quantum reality is by discarding the assumed universal character of the attributes in the classical Newtonian list in favor of a relativity-corrected, quantum-theory accommodating Newtonianism—one I call *Quantum Newtonianism*—one that would always insist on correcting and problematizing in a completely relativistic spirit the classical attributes as cross-sectional manifestations in the observer's own reference frame in favor of what is more fully described by the attributes in the list for the quantum way of imagining reality. The quantum attributes describe what goes on in all reference frames in a relativistic way, but appear to do so at a longer- or shorter-term, larger- or smaller-scale way depending on how an observer observes the world in his or her own reference frame in contrast and relative to how he or she observes the world in other reference frames.

. Note that I am not saying in the above that the quantum way of imagining reality only applies to the microscopic world, and the supposed relativistic Newtonian way only on the macroscopic world. The quantum way of imagining reality applies to all reference frames, to reality as a whole, while the *Quantum Newtonian* way is an expression of how the quantum world manifests in an observer's own reference frame. *The quantum world encompassing all frames of reference subsumes Quantum Newtonianism as the way an observer would experience the quantum world in his or her own frame of reference.* Here, we should note that when we speak of an observer in any reference frame, we are not limiting it to our present, human, macroscopic reference frame. If you put yourself in the shoes of the electron, and in its reference frame, for you that would be the macroscopic reference frame, and conversely what we now regard as our macroscopic reference frame would be, for it, a microscopic reference frame.

What takes places in all frames of reference is quantum, according to the list of attributes described in its respective list above, which I will further elaborated on in this chapter. It only appears to happen in relatively slower and larger way in the observer's reference way. To observers, their home reference frame appears as slower-larger home spheres (the differences in spheres in this case refer not to "levels," but to the speeds of motion of objects involved in one or another sphere relative to one another across the spheres). So, it happens that in the reference frame in which observers are located, the quantum attributes of that sphere appear, cross-sectionally, like the attributes listed in the completely relativistic, *Quantum Newtonian* list. These attributes are cross-sectional manifestations in a limited way of the overall quantum process that reality undergoes in that sphere of reality.

By studying what happens in the microscopic world, we are able to gaze more accurately into a total, holistic, picture of reality, because, there we can see the whole process underway, as if from a bird's eye point of view. But, we should also not lose sight of the fact that what we experience and observe in our own reference frame is a more detailed, magnified, close-up manifestation of the same quantum process as experienced in our observations here and now. We may try to use huge particle accelerators to see what goes on in their world by smashing them in high-speed collisions. But, strangely, we are ourselves living in what would be to those particles, *their* particle accelerators amid our lived experiences. When we observe, or speculate about, very short-term, very tiny, elementary particles that disappear as soon as they appear on our collider screens or in our theoretical observations of them, from the standpoint of those particles, we are like "god particles" that come and go in flashes of lifetimes lived in nanoseconds of the particle's time.

When we study our own physical, natural, built, social, and inner worlds in a quantum way, not in a classical Newtonian, nor incompletely relativist Newtonian, but in a completed, *Quantum Newtonian* way, we are also studying the world of those particles from within. In our macroscopic frame we experience in a slowed-down larger-scale way what happens in much more rapid and smaller scale way in the microscopic world, relative to us.

The *Quantum Newtonian* attributes as experienced in the observer's home reference frame are cross-sectional, not frozen or universal, but still dynamic, expressions of what are described more fully by the holistically conceived attributes described in the quantum way of imagining reality; if observers were around long enough and spread-out widely enough, they would see the same patterns and attributes they assign to their microscopic spheres undergoing in their own reference frame as well. Depending on where we locate ourselves in various spheres of reality, in *that* sphere we confront reality in a way that *appears, not fictionally but in a real way,* to be governed by the seemingly classical Newtonian list of attributes, where those attributes are simply cross-sectional momentary expressions of a fuller *Quantum Newtonian* process that is described by the attributes describing the quantum world. Unfortunately, they appear to be going on according to the classical Newtonian list of attributes, but those are false, ideological, blundered, ways of looking at the world. Our purpose will have to be always to problematize what appears to be like the classical or incomplete Newtonian list, in favor of bringing them in resonance with the complete Newtonian, the *Quantum Newtonian*, list of attributes.

What appears to us dualistically as atomistic, separable, subjectlessly "objective," deterministic, locally continuous, and knowable only through disciplinarity and ethnocentric scientism are so manifested falsely because they are frozen, falsely universalized, cross-sectional expressions in longer-term, larger-scale manner in our own reference frame of a fuller process that is much more rapidly enacted in microscopic world—characterized by simultaneity, superpositionality, inseparability, relativity (subject-included objectivity), probability, and transcontinuity, understandable through transdisciplinary and transcultural points of view, best described in terms of the nonreductive dialectics of wholes and parts involving a simultaneity, of unity in diversity, of identity and difference of opposites—a dialectical process I have described in detail in the last chapter of *Unriddling the Quantum Enigma* (2020).

What an observer finds *dualistic* in his reference frame he should problematize to be a cross-section instead of a broader reality characterized by a nonreductive dialectical process in all reference frames involving a pattern of change through continual splitting and reintegration. What an observer finds *atomistic* in his reference frame he should problematize to be a cross-section instead of a broader reality characterized by *superpositionality* in all reference frames. What an observer finds *separable* in his reference frame he should problematize to be a cross-section instead of a broader reality characterized by *inseparability* in all reference frames. What an observer finds subjectlessly *objective* in his reference frame he should problematize to be a cross-section instead of a broader reality characterized by subject-included objectivity, of *relativity*, in all reference frames. What an observer finds *deterministic* in his reference frame he should problematize to be a cross-section instead of a broader reality characterized by *probability*, of infinite possibilities of determinism, in all reference frames. What an observer finds *continuous* in his reference frame he should problematize to be a cross-section instead of a broader reality characterized by *transcontinuity*, continuities that appear discontinuous but in fact express different forms of continuity, in all reference frames. What an observer regards as *disciplinarity* in his reference frame he should problematize to be a cross-section instead of a broader reality characterized by *transdisciplinarity* in all reference frames. What an observer regards as *scientistic* in his reference frame he should problematize to be a cross-section instead of a broader reality characterized by *transculturalism* in all rest frames. These provide a guiding thread, or a set of concrete ideas, about how we can transition from classical Newtonian toward quantum imaginations, including in our sociologies—not dualistically (as a move from A to non-A), but dialectically, as a transition from a partial to its holistic imagination.

The quantum world appears *Newtonian* in the reference frame of any observer, whether or not he or she goes up or down the escalator of reference frames. Classical and incompletely relativistic Newtonianism are seemingly slowed down and larger scale expressions of the *Quantum Newtonian* world in one's own reference frame. Similarly, *moving from Newtonian toward quantum imaginations is not a move from A to non-A, but from a partial vision to a broader, holistic vision that sublates the part vision in itself.*

In what follows I offer the attributes of the quantum way of imagining reality in light of the relativistic interpretive solutions I have summarized above and reported in more depth and detail in *Unriddling the Quantum Enigma* (2020). Here, however, I will try to illustrate the attributes in an applied way, by showing the implications each has for understanding society, sociology, the sociological imagination, and as an alternative framework for conducting our new Khayyami studies.

1. Relating Personal Troubles and Public Issues: From Dualism to Simultaneity (Not "Duality," Nor "Complementarity")

The classical Newtonian way of imagining reality was founded on a formal, dualistic logic where A cannot be non-A at once. Scientific experiments with and interpretations of light's behavior contributing to the quantum revolution, however, advanced the view that light is characterized by what is called a "wave-particle duality," behaving like both A and non-A, as both a wave and a particle. And this duality was then found to be an attribute not only of light, but also in principle of all matter.

However, such a "duality" itself was subsequently interpreted in two different ways. According to one interpretation, usually referred to in terms of the so-called "Complementarity Principle" (a term coined by Niels Bohr), light is *potentially* "dual," but in *actual* experimental contexts, it is observed/measured (or not) as being *either* one *or* the other, as either particle or a wave, but not both at once. According to another interpretation, one I have called that of "Simultaneity," light is considered to behave *at once* as both, all the time, everywhere.

The quantum way of imagining reality has been heralded as one that has challenged the dualistic ways of thinking in the classical Newtonian science. However, it is important to note that in the efforts made a language of "duality" has been retained whose subconscious connotation following the Complementary Principle is still that something is A at one time and non-A at another time, A in one place and non-A in another place. This interpretation can be inferred from the commonly expressed enigma that, say, in the double-slit experiment, light behaves as a wave whereas in the photoelectric experiment it behaves as a corpuscular photon. Such a language is itself logically problematic and has been in my view contributive to the cognitive enigma arising in quantum science since at the same time that it states light is both particle and wave, it actually treats its meaning in a way that the attributes become separably manifested across different experiments.

In *Unriddling the Quantum Enigma* (2020), I have argued and demonstrated that the notion of complementarity is untenable and derived from an equally false "wave-particle duality of light" narrative. As I briefly noted earlier in this chapter and is more fully explained in that book, light remains an electromagnetic wave throughout, and the so-called 'duality' is a relativistic effect resulting from the fact that light manifests for us as observers in our own macroscopic reference frame as a localized wave flashing by, while in the photon's own reference frame it is a wave spreading out in all directions. In other words, we do not have a case of an object switching between a particle and a wave behavior, but a wave that manifests in two different reference frames *at once* as localized and spread-out, and depending on the relative speeds of the motions involved for the observed object and observers, the effect is less or more pronounced; but technically it is an effect attributable to motions of all matter. Objects are at once localized and spread-out depending on the reference frame in which they are observed.

According to the Simultaneity principle or interpretation, the photon is at once both A and non-A, paradoxically a whole and a part of itself, so to speak, simultaneously being somewhere and everywhere, at once localized and spread-out. In the falsely conceived complementarity interpretation such a simultaneity is ignored and treated as existing only in potentia, while in actual experimental contexts, it is expected that light at any given moment behaves in either one or another mode, but not both. This, I have argued, is a false interpretation that brings back the dualistic way of imagining or thinking about reality from the back door.

What does such a logical reimagination of reality away from Newtonian dualism in favor of a quantum vision emphasizing the simultaneity of objects existing at once as localized and spread-out contribute to our quantum reimagination of society, sociology, the sociological imagination, and Khayyami studies?

Our classical Newtonian visions of society have etched in our subconscious minds society and social reality as being an ensemble of "individual" billiard balls whose interactions from without in personal and group or institutional settings become the subject matter of our sociologies. A quantum reimagination of such a Newtonian vision would imply that an individual is a localized expression of another spread-out reality that extends far beyond his or her local lifetime, having also a potentially world-historical presence as far as the human race is concerned, and even beyond, as a microcosm of the universe, a view that has been noted as well in genuine spiritual teachings.

How spread-out in world-historical spacetime an individual is or can be may be a matter of empirical experience, with some individuals having less and others more such presence, depending on what experiences they undergo during their lifetime. It may turn out that for some the spread-out presence more or less ends at physical death, and with others their influence and presence continues for a while or for much longer and wider.

One does not have to engage in spooky or supernatural discourse to imagine the rational side of such a consideration. We do not know of many who lived in Neyshabour a thousand years ago, but we know and are still quite curious (more than any others) about one particular man born there, Omar Khayyam, for one reason or another. But one does not have to be famous to leave long-lasting traces. Some hard working folks helped build the Stonehenge, or the Pyramids, or left the footprints of Lucy. The wave ripples of their corpuscular presence are still with us.

The individual and world-historical simultaneity of human nature implies that any person cannot really understand himself or herself without understanding his or her belonging to the human race and more broadly as a particle of a universe, and, significantly vice versa, that is, the person cannot understand himself or herself, his or her personal troubles, nor the public issues of his or her society, apart from the story of his species in world-historical as well as cosmic contexts.

When a physicist says we are star dust, this knowledge is bound to make us feel differently about ourselves if we are not too distracted by the bombardment of our TV commercials or the seemingly odd behaviors of business or political demagogues these days. The transformative implications of such an individual and world-historical simultaneity of each person is also significant. To the extent that a person succeeds, while arriving at a simultaneously personal and world-historical/cosmic self-knowledge, in bringing about radical changes in himself or herself, he or she has simultaneously succeeded in bringing about changes and ruptures in the inherited fabric of his or her personal and broader social and world-historical spacetime, and by logical implication of his or her powers in effecting not just broader social, but also cosmic transformation considered in other spacetime frames of reference. The scientist who convinces others that it is better to focus on preventing the next fatal crash of a huge meteorite on Earth, or to prevent the destruction of the human habitat due to human-caused global warming, will certainly prove that point, a simple individual thought having consequences for the entire planet and the Solar System of which it is a part.

Quantum sociology, therefore, is and must be inescapably and inherently a simultaneous exercise in world-historical and personal self-knowledge. A sociology of self-knowledge should not be seen as just another passing fad, but a new common denominator of any research, involving quantum reimagination of sociology as well, whether or not we call it as such. The promise of Mills's sociological imagination, in fact, was just that—that is, one cannot really be sociologically imaginative and complete any research project without engaging with both the micro and the macro, the personal troubles and the public issues, of whatever subject matter one chooses to study. To the extent that Mills so insistently and successfully transformed our sociologies to take seriously the paradigmatic significance of studying the personal troubles and public issues of our lifetimes in relation to one another, to that extent he was advancing, advertently or not, a quantum vision of society and of sociology. By doing so, he was telling us that each of us is at once a localized and a world-historical being, understanding ourselves being impossible without taking *both* sides of the dialectic into account as a common denominator of any research we undertake.

However, the implication of the above for the reimagination of the central tenet of Mills's sociological imagination, one that abandons a chunky, classical Newtonian, view of personal troubles and public issues, is that such a project should go beyond simply linking what is otherwise presumed to be separate micro and macro folds, implying that one may deal with personal troubles not arising from public issues, or public issues not manifesting in personal troubles. As I stated in the first chapter of this book, we could approach the relation of personal troubles and public issues still as billiard balls, conceived as being external to one another. This would be the equivalent of the "Complementary" notion that assumes one can separate the local and the global attributes of our nature and lives from one another, assuming there could be personal troubles that are not at once also public issues, or public issues not also at once manifested as personal troubles.

In quantum sociological imagination, one starts from the premise of the simultaneity in which all personal troubles are world-historical products, and all world-historical public issues consequential and manifestable in personal, everyday lives, here and now. By problematizing taken-for-granted personal troubles in the here-and-now, any individual seeker of truth in favor of a just global society will have the best and most organic way of arriving at understanding his or her history and cosmic existence. Conversely, all human world-history and cosmic insight will be most concretely and deeply understood when it leads the seeker to see their relevance in the concrete, here-and-now, realities of his or her everyday/night life.

Again, the transformative power of such a quantum reimagination of society, sociology and the sociological imagination can be considered in terms of how radical and critical problematization and transformation of one's own personal everyday life in the here-and-now can have far-reaching implications for the transformation of human species considered in world-historical and cosmic contexts. Conversely, new radical insights about the nature of human species, world-history, and cosmos can and must have their manifestation in and implications for the conduct of his or her everyday life.

If you feel depressed, it is not just your personal trouble, but indicative of something having gone wrong in the way human species has organized its life. If you see something wrong about your society, it has in one way or another caused a trouble in your personal life as well.

Khayyami studies can provide a wonderful opportunity for exploring, in a quantum sociological imagination framework, the life and works of a single individual whose deeply private and secretive acts of writing poetry inducing radical and creative work on himself simultaneously influenced world-history and human curiosity about the nature and purpose of human existence in a cosmic setting.

Here we have someone purposely eschewing public life and political ambitions—an inclination which must have been also shaped by the colonial context in which he lived—yet becoming in time a world-historical public intellectual on whose thoughts and poetry politicians of diverse persuasions and backgrounds are inspired to draw, duplicitously or not, to pursue their everyday personal and career lives.

Khayyam's presence was not just a personal reality wave localized in his life and time's spacetime, but is a world-historical wave of intellectual and creative force that offers interesting opportunities for exploring how an enigmatic personal life experience could be explained by applying a quantum sociological imagination framework to our research. His expression of sorrow and feeling depressed about his life and times is, simultaneously, an expression of sorrow and depressed feelings by a humanity that is supposed to be the pinnacle of creation but is wasted away living for a past and tomorrow devoid of the joys of the here-and-now.

When he tells others who call him a philosopher that he is not what they say he is, he still wonders why now that he has come to this sorrow's nest, he should *himself* not know at least who he is. In doing so he is not expressing just a personal trouble, but the existential question of an entire human species. Is not this the reason why many generations of readers from all walks of life and cultures across many generations have found his poems speaking to their own experiences?

Here, we can draw on the notion of simultaneity of part-whole dialectics as expressed in the simultaneity of local-global, or personal/world-historical, presence of each of us, to introduce a new quantum way of framing Khayyami studies as far as the problem posed by the lack of certainty regarding the authorship of the attributed Robaiyat are concerned.

Here, from the first attribute of the quantum sociological imagination framing our Khayyami studies, we can then draw a very important conclusion and guiding thread for its entire process. Khayyam's name was rendered in Arabic and even some Persian texts also as "Khayyami." We can use this interesting personal and historical coincidence to devise a nondualistic *quantum language* when referring to him *as both a localized person and a world-historical wave*, one that at the same time, simultaneously, conveys the associations with a specific person and what has been attributed to him as a movement or tradition in a world-history context. In other words, "Khayyami" could mean both the person and whatever has become attributed to or associated with that person for one reason or another.

I will show that employing such a sociologically imaginative quantum device involving a language of simultaneity when referring to Khayyam's life, works, and legacy—especially when it comes to the study of the attributed Robaiyat—can have significant methodological, substantive, and practical consequences for framing and conducting our Khayyami studies.

So, when we refer to Khayyami from now on, we will simultaneously mean to refer to a local, actual person's life and works, and whatever has been attributed to him in a spread-out wave form in a world-history context.

2. Relating Personal Troubles (or Not) of Many Selves: From Atomism to Superpositionality

The classical Newtonian way of imagining microscopic reality characterizes it as consisting of corpuscular objects whether atomic or subatomic who subject one another to external influences from without. Such a view obviously implies that an object has a definite presence in spacetime in distinction from others, such that it cannot exist in two or more places at the same time.

In contrast, quantum interpretations of the microscopic world have accepted the notion that not just light but all matter is generally (in potentia and/or actually, as noted regarding the previous attribute) characterized by "wave-particle duality" which necessarily implies that an object, being corpuscular and also spread-out as a wave, can be at once in two or more places. This assumption is a necessary result of holding the wave-particle 'duality' attribute in mind.

If something is spread-out everywhere in the universe but at a moment's observational measurement is manifested in a definite somewhere in the universe, a view espoused especially by the Complementary interpretation of 'duality,' this means that potentially it exists in many places superposed, even though the probability of being in some places may be more than others, depending on the particular wave attributes of the object.

So, if you contrast the classical Newtonian view that microscopic reality is universally made of separable chunks of sub/atomic objects with the quantum view that objects can be, at least potentially (Complementarity) and also actually (Simultaneity) at the same time somewhere everywhere, the radical difference between the classical and quantum ways of imagining reality becomes evident.

Even if we use a subject-omitted analogy of the billiard balls game, i.e., in the classical imagination, the balls are clearly separate from one another, colliding, joining, deflecting, one another, from without. In the quantum imagination, each ball is potentially or also actually a fuzzy thing, spread-out principally everywhere in the universe, perhaps more likely to be found somewhere than elsewhere, but is still everywhere. This means it is superposed, not only in terms of its own possibilities of being somewhere everywhere, but also in terms of interpenetrating with other objects that share similar superposed attributes.

So, the previously imagined separate 'atoms' colliding with one another from without share spacetime possibilities of being superpositionally somewhere everywhere as well. In a given spacetime event, both atoms may exist, that event being at the same time A and non-A, and B and non-B. It is both A and non-A, since the object A may be there or not. It is both B and non-B, since, also, the object B may be there or not. And a combination of the two various options may also exist where A can be B, or not.

The issue I raised above regarding the problematic nature of using the logical language of "duality" to contrast with dualism may also be consequential here. The quantum view that microscopic objects are at the same time localized and spread-out implies that one cannot find them in one experiment as particle non-waves and in another as wave non-particles. Therefore, it is problematic to suggest that something exists everywhere in one time but somewhere at another time (say, when it is observed, which in quantum science language has been referred to as "collapsing the object's wave function").

The issue I raised above regarding the problematic nature of using the language of 'duality' to contrast with dualism may also be observed here. In the interpretive vision of Complementarity where light, despite being *potentially* particle and wave, is treated in *actual* experiments or observations as being either one or the other, allows for retaining still an atomistic view of reality when observation and measurement are present. It is then assumed that when observation and measurement are not present, a quantum state as described in the previous paragraph exists, where an object is spread-out everywhere, and not in a specific spacetime, as particles are presumed to be.

However, the interpretive vision of Simultaneity whereby the object is considered to be at once, always, *in potentia as well as actually*, localized and spread-out, an effect resulting from what I have identified to be relativistic effects (2020) of an object being observed in/from different reference frames, this implies that the quantum state as described above is retained across the experiments, all the time, everywhere, whether the measurement and observation is present or not—although the measurement itself adds its own influence to the interaction being observed, which should be taken into account in a subject-included model of objectivity.

Again, note the significance of the difference between the two interpretive pathways above. One (Complementarity) leads to the notion that when observed and measured, world can collapse into and continue to be atomistic and subject to the generally Newtonian interpretation, such that superpositionality is not likely to be confronted as a state in the macroscopic world, though existing in potentia in microscopic world. Another (Simultaneity) leads to the notion that reality is always quantum, superpositionality exists in all reality, microscopic or macroscopic, although subjected to differences brought on by the added element of macroscopic observers doing their measurements who would view reality from the standpoint of their own macroscopic frame of reference.

The interpretive strategy of Complementarity, according to which light or object is considered to be, while in potentia both corpuscular and wave, in actual experimental contexts either one *or* the other depending on whether it is measured, may lead to a back-door way of accommodating an atomistic view of macroscopic reality, even though in the microscopic world atoms are imagined to be superpositionally fuzzy, cloud- or field-like, interpenetrating, and overlapping things, rather than corpuscular objects clearly marked out from one another with more or less vacuum in between. In contrast, the Simultaneity interpretation according to which light or object is considered to be at once localized and spread-out depending on the reference frame in/ from which it is observed offers an interpretive opportunity for considering that light and objects always, in microscopic *and* macroscopic worlds, retain their quantum superposed attributions, and whether they are perceived as localized or not depends on the frame of reference and vantage point of macroscopic objects such as us, observers, contributing to the interaction through observation and measurement.

So, depending on the two interpretations we previously noted in the duality of light attribution, we can also speak of two Complementary and Simultaneity interpretations for the superpositionality attribution, so to speak. In one interpretation, superpositionality is a potentiality, in actual reality being retained *or* not depending on being observed/measured or not, being macroscopic or not. In another interpretation, superpositionality is potentially *and* actually retained at once in objects, though its perception depends on the frame of reference and interpretation of those trying to observe, measure, and interpret the attribute. The above inconsistencies also point to another enigmatic observation made by physicists over the decades, namely that somehow these quantum attributes govern the microscopic world but seem not to be observable and applicable to the macroscopic reality, said to be still more or less explainable by classical or relativistically-corrected Newtonian laws.

In *Unriddling the Quantum Enigma* (2020), I have problematized the notion "wave-particle duality of light" and its associated notion "Complementarity Principle" for involving false narratives and notions. I have also addressed the enigmatic proposition of superpositionality as being an attribute of unobserved microscopic world only, a proposition that has persisted in the debates on the quantum enigma. Alternatively, I have suggested how indeed one can argue that the attribute of superpositionality is also a quantum attribute of all matter, though manifested differently depending on the reference frame in/from which it is observed. Consequently, the quantum imagination and superpositionality is also applicable to the macroscopic world, provided that we dispense with certain Newtonian presumptions that have habitually survived or subconsciously crept back into our arguments.

My view is that in fact the quantum notion of superpositionality is not one that is applicable merely to the microscopic world, but *also* valid and essential for a truthful and proper understanding of the macroscopic world, a world that also includes our social reality, and by implication should implicate our sociologies and sociological imaginations, and frame our Khayyami studies as well.

When considering the implications for our sociologies, sociological imaginations, and Khayyami studies, of the Newtonian notion of atomism and its contrast with and transformation into the alternative quantum notion of superpositionality, the following broad propositions can be considered.

First, to be consistent even in our classical Newtonian visions of reality, which have had their merits in making us aware of the parts constituting wholes comprising reality, there is no reason why we should argue that an atomistic view of individual is more valid than a subatomic view of our individual lives as being ensembles of *selves*. It is our own habitual lenses, reinforced and protected by one or other ideological interests, that have led us to take for granted our individualities as solid billiard balls, being not further divisible into selves.

I have extensively elaborated on this issue in my previous work (1999-2020), drawing on various Eastern and Western intellectual traditions, to argue that in fact it makes more sense to consider social agencies to be subatomic selves than presumed individuals. Adopting such subatomic social lenses would offer more plausible explanations for when we see the very same person behaving in radically different ways in diverse social spacetimes, doing so not necessarily consciously and intentionally at all times. Having a subatomic lens of recognizing selves as acting agencies rather than presumed individual solid billiard balls can also provide significant clues toward diagnosing psychological pathways to healing, not just in clinical settings, but also in understanding the everyday lives of the person, still living or long passed away, such as our Omar Khayyam.

However, if we further divide our individual lives into their real, subatomic self sub-particles, we need to be still guarded about not further deepening our Newtonian ways of seeing even those selves and subatomic particles as separate units separably existing, rather than, as quantum sciences today propose, as superposed waves as well. It is possible to contrast Newtonian ways of seeing our subatomic selves with quantum, superposed ways of imagining them. A self still remains, from an alternative quantum point of view, both a localized personal self as well as a spread-out social entity, potentially extended in a world-historical spacetime as I suggested above when presenting the first proposition of simultaneity of individual/world-historical presence at a level of abstraction that did not yet problematize the multiplicity of the individual's selfhood.

This leads us to ask how the quantum notion of superpositionality may be understood (in contrast to its one-sided, Newtonian atomistic, counterpart) when we consider the self or selves-group (individual and broader) acting agencies constituting, constructing, and reconstructing our social realities in local, regional, and world-history contexts?

Let us consider our Khayyami studies to illustrate this point.

Consider, for instance, that you are confronted with several Khayyami quatrains (using our quantum language, this would now mean quatrains that are attributed to him in the past, being possible that they are his as well). One is the expression of a sad, deeply doubtful soul, or self. Another is of a hopeful soul, or self. And yet, another of a happy and ecstatic soul, or self.

A Newtonian sociological imagination would be puzzled, treating these quatrain atoms to be so separably supposed, leading one to be puzzled as to how they could all be traceable to the same, presumably solid and singular historical Khayyam. What, or where, are any of such quatrains? Does its substance exist just in that quatrain, or is it present in a superposed way also in one or another of his philosophical, religious, scientific, or literary writings, or even in a particular event or narrative reported by his contemporaries? Can one find a trace of it spread-out even in certain known then contemporary events, or forms of art or architecture, and so on?

In order to find his genuine Robaiyat, then, should we be looking only into the available quatrains, or also into his other writings, or, say, even his reported birth horoscope? Where can we exactly locate our answers or clues about the questions we ask in terms of spacetime? Is his poetry only in his quatrains, in his philosophical writings, his treatises on algebra or geometry, or even in his astronomical calculations? Can we find his calendar reform innovations or involvements in his quatrains, or in his treatise in *Nowrooznameh*? Is it possible that his Robaiyat is spread-out through such other writings in a superposed way? Can the seemingly separate quatrains expressing seemingly separate feelings of sadness, hope, happiness, and ecstasy, be localized expressions of a soul in search, evolving, through a lifetime, as he reflects on the meanings of his life and its purpose in a world-history and even broader cosmic, existential, context?

The point here is that once we consider the quantum notion of superposition and do not limit it to being applicable to microscopic objects only but also to macroscopic, including inner self and broader personal and social, objects—suggesting that something could be in many places at once, a notion that is itself more fundamentally derived from the localized/spread-out simultaneity of light and all matter—then we may not be confronted with seemingly disjointed and nonsensically scattered pieces of poetry or writing that offer at first no clues on the surface about their interconnections. We would then not discard the question in an *a priori* fashion and declare a research impasse, but turn the seeming enigma or anomaly itself into questioning what could explain the puzzle at hand. It should not take a FitzGerald to ask whether there could be hidden links between the seemingly separate presumed billiard-ball quatrains, consciously intended or unconsciously existing. We may even discover in due course of our research that the notion of the "Rubaiyat" as a system of interconnected quatrains was not really a notion invented by FitzGerald, but one he felt existing across the seemingly scattered quatrain originals he was reading— that FitzGerald noticed a pattern that was already present, and intended to exist, in the quatrains as originally created by Omar Khayyam.

Using our quantum sociological imagination lens, when considering the "inner life" and "external career" of our Khayyam, therefore, we would not see them as separate atomic balls colliding with another to understand them, but we would regard them as overlapping, interpenetrating, aspects or spheres of our object, superposed with one another, with those found in others, and with broader public issues amid whose milieu they coexist. We would not dismiss a private trouble, thinking it is not related to the public issues, and therefore not worthy of our "sociological" or "philosophical" attentions, but instead question not whether but how and why they manifest themselves in superposed ways in interpersonal, and broader social, natural, and built-environmental realities.

Note how the above is pointing us to a "restitching" project at hand. If the Khayyami facts and data have become fragmented and studied as such in the past within a classical Newtonian worldview shaped by dualistic and atomistic thinking, then we need to move in the direction of restitching them back into a whole. This would not be a Newtonian restitching, presuming that the pieces or patches are separate and chunky to begin with, but that we recognize their being likely pieces of a puzzle in each of which one can see a whole tent present in embryo.

In other words, the pieces of the puzzle that had been superposed with one another and for one reason or another became fragmented, are each still at once a localized and a spread-out object, retaining clues as to how each belonged to a broader whole before breaking down into pieces, like a jug. Each piece may then be found to have sufficient clues, as left-over data of the larger whole of which they came from, so that they can be "restitched" like a jigsaw puzzle back to one another in order to understand not only the whole of which they were a part, but also where each of them came from before they were made, bought, and sold in the jug-maker's shop.

So, when we say in this series that we are studying Khayyami quatrains, and then devote a book to the seemingly odd pursuit of Khayyam's birth date by studying his horoscope previously explored by others, we are not really starting with something "outside" those quatrains, but are studying the quatrains in a specific fold of abstraction from their expression. After all, even if we are interested in discovering the "genuine" Robaiyat, and their attributability to the historical Khayyam, should we not know truthfully when their supposed composer was born and when he died, even leaving aside any other discoveries we may make along the way by treating the questions of Khayyam's horoscope interpretation and that of his native as superposed, and not atomistically separable, quantum objects?

So, going back to the quantum notion and exploratory device "Khayyami" that I introduced in the previous section regarding the quantum simultaneity attribute, by using this notion in relation to the attribute of quantum superpositionality we mean to note, first, that being attributed to Khayyam is not a monolithic this or that, yes or no, thing, expressed by a sad or happy, certain or doubtful, despaired or hopeful, self, but that we would consider any data or information about Khayyam's personal life and writings as equally worthy of our investigation, letting the process of research and analysis show whether or not the pieces fit or not one another amid the life and works of Khayyam and his times.

Second, that in such an effort we would try to consider each data, each passage, each quatrain, as being not a separate and localized atom, but also a spread-out meaning that overlaps and superposes with other pieces of information about him, considering it possible that each piece may offer clues to other pieces in a superposed way because they may be fragments of a previous whole that need to be holistically restitched to one another in the same hermeneutic spirit in which they were conceived.

Likewise, conversely, we would consider that a poetic insight may not present itself only in a readily-accessible and localized quatrain or poetic form, but one that may exist in spread-out form in his other writings, or even in reliable second-hand reports passed down the historical line from his contemporaries.

Overall, then, we abandon an atomic view of any piece of information received about Khayyam, dismissing any in an *a priori* way as belonging (or not) to the historical Khayyam. Using the quantum notion device "Khayyami" allows us to justify paying equal attention to any data received from the past that has been attributed, for reasons we cannot prejudge, to Omar Khayyam.

3. Relating Public Issues World-Historically: From Separability to Inseparability

Einstein's general theory of relativity and its derivative theory of gravitation in terms of spacetime curvature led us to imagine how things that seem separate macroscopically are actually (not just potentially) inseparable, although their interaction is subject to the delay brought on by the speed of light in which signals or effects can travel. However, just because it takes time for the Sun's light to reach the Earth should not lead us to imagine them as being separate, but note the spatiotemporality of the effect from the vantage point of observing/measuring objects such as ourselves living on the Earth. So, the inseparability should be assumed macroscopically as well.

It is important when considering the attribute of quantum inseparability to distinguish two options; one, Complementary inseparability, where it may be assumed that inseparability applies in actual terms to microscopic world but not necessarily to macroscopic reality; and, another, Simultaneous inseparability, according to which all reality, microscopic or macroscopic, is deemed to be comprised of inseparable events, even though the interactions are subject to delays as conditioned by the speed of light limit, the simultaneity of coincidences also being in need of relativistic interpretation.

The distinction between the two Complementary and Simultaneous ways of interpreting the "wave-particle duality of light" thus implicates also how the attribution of macroscopic inseparability may be alternatively interpreted. If in the "Complementarity" version we say objects are potentially both, but actually one or the other, this would lead us to a view of reality in which the unobserved/unmeasured microscopic reality is potentially inseparable, but in the macroscopic world, separability is deemed possible since things can be separated from one another. In the second alternative interpretation, that of Simultaneity, we would arrive interpretively at a quantum imagination of reality in which inseparability is always present, microscopically *and* macroscopically.

In my recent work (Tamdgidi 2020) I have argued that the notion "wave-particle duality of light" and its associated "Complementarity Principle" are false narratives, which necessarily lead to a dichotomous imagination of two "levels" of reality where quantum "laws" apply to one (microscopic) but not to another (macroscopic) "level." Instead, I have argued that my proposed notion of "localized/spread-out simultaneity of objects" is more consistent and defensible in leading us to imagine inseparability as an attribute of the macroscopic world as well.

The implication of inseparability of reality for understanding social reality is significant, since in its classical Newtonian variant, surprisingly still predominant in our contemporary sociologies and sociological imaginations, it is deemed possible to know personal troubles and/or public issues within supposedly "national," "civilizational," or even, at best, "world-systemic" units of analysis, where the analysis is not taken to its quantum, nonreductively dialectical, logical conclusion that there is only one social reality, the world-historical, no matter how far we go back or forward in time.

I have explored the notion of world-history as a singular unit of analysis elsewhere (Tamdgidi 2002, 2006a), advancing a nonreductive dialectical conception of past history of imperiality in contrast to materialist approaches, arguing for both the relative historical validity and the transitory nature of the primacy of economies and their analyses in world-historical social science. I argued that the dialecticity of such a conception allows for politics, culture, and economy to have similarly played primary parts in the rise of distinct forms of imperiality in world-history corresponding to ancient, medieval, and modern historical eras across multiple, but increasingly synchronous and convergent, regional trajectories. The nonreductive dialectical mode of analysis reverses and relativizes the taken-for-granted universalistic modes of analysis of imperialism in terms of class, allowing for considerations of political domination, cultural conversion, and economic exploitation as historical forms of deepening imperial practice violating self-determining modes of human organization and development. Power-, status-, and class-based relations and stratifications are thereby reinterpreted as distinct forms of imperial practice that now assumes a substantively generative position vis-à-vis those structural forms. The notion of "imperiality" (in contrast to "imperialism") is then used to denote both the macro-structural and the micro, intra/interpersonal, dynamics of the historical phenomena still shaping our everyday lives.

A quantum notion of society as an inseparable, world-historical, reality offers a different vantage point to understand the transitory and relative nature of our personal troubles and public issues. Such a notion in effect introduces a superposed conception of our social experiences across historical time and space, such that at the same time that I, for instance, reflect on my experience living in the US, I am able, as a migrant from Iran, to imagine myself to be living in two places, in two times, two cultures at the same time. Migrants living in literal or cultural borderlands are more open to experiencing such superposed, spooky modes of living where they can directly experience the duplicity of imperial powers promising to impose democracy on others by starving the "other" people's lives as part of their coup-engineering (or what is today called "regime change" sanctions warfare) packaged as wishful policy-making, and do so in real-time, simultaneously, across vast distances in time and space. It is the Newtonian imperial mindset that considers having more migrants around is a liability rather than a contribution to quantum experiences of solidarity and sharing of the human experience as an actualization of human species being.

The quantum ability to reexperience, to reimagine, personal troubles and public issues in a world-history context is a gift that in-depth studies of Khayyam's life and works can creatively contribute to our Newtonian sociologies and sociological imaginations in favor of moving them in quantum directions. Khayyam's world-historical self-reflections, as limited as our records of them may be, are telling of a people's experience having undergone their own homegrown Persian, as well as regional Arab and Turkic imperial experiences in conversation with perceived values of an original Islamic message that itself became increasingly distorted amid the imperial expansions of one or another ruler.

Of interest can be how Khayyam negotiates the worth and the lessons of all such experiences bearing their complexities, amid a wider existential story of how we as humans come to know why we are here and where we are going. It is the inseparability, and sameness, of the passing away of kings and beggars, and the meaning of their lives, that permeates the beauty of the Khayyami poetry as received over the centuries across cultures and languages while all evidence points to the enigmatic fact that he did not even publicize any or most of them during his own lifetime.

But such inseparability in his life and poetry from ours cannot be properly understood apart from understanding the inseparability of the various spheres of his writings, and whether and how they in fact are interrelated in a superposed way across seemingly separate philosophical, religious, scientific, astronomical, literary, and poetic domains. This is so, because such substantive inseparabilities could also be telling of how inseparably he regarded his search for the knowledge of God, Islamic learning, philosophical reflections, scientific pursuits, and creative writings.

What is different—even more wonderful than that of C. Wright Mills, in my view—is the inseparability of Khayyam's sociological worldview from his cosmic vision. For him, public issues go beyond the social issues of his time or even of world-history, and engage with cosmic public issues having to do with existential reasons for our coming and going. It is only our narrow Westernized, disenchanted, and secularized notions of the sociological imagination that leads us to view such an expansive imagination of our personal troubles and public issues as being exotic and different. However, if we wish to put ourselves in the shoes of Khayyam and those living his time and culture, we cannot really separate the personal and the public from the broader cosmic, spiritual, and existential contexts in which Khayyam interrogates the dialectics of personal troubles and public issues facing humanity as a species being living a polo game whose whyness remains inaccessible to him, still.

So, here too we have a quantum restitching (or reentanglement) project at hand. We cannot advance Khayyami studies in a quantum sociological imagination without making efforts in restitching his life and works to the world-historical context of human life and its cosmic and existential enigmas. We have to not only be flexible in restitching the various personal views, feelings, sensibilities, and selves we encounter in him amid the personal troubles of his life, not dismissing one or another in advance in an *a priori* way, but also be imaginative enough to relate them to the broader, singular story and public issues of humankind in world-historical, cosmic, and existential contexts, of which he and we ourselves are inseparable parts.

4. Relating the Sociological Imaginations of Others to Those of Ourselves: From Subjectless Objectivity to Relativity (Subject-Included Objectivity)

Perhaps the most shocking conclusion—shocking, of course, to the classical Newtonian worldview—resulting not only from the findings of quantum science, but also from Einstein's theories of relativity, has been the notion that the reality of an object cannot be determined apart from the observational position and measurements used for that determination, since those observational positions and measurement instruments themselves are parts of what is being studied and are subject to relativistic effects. Spacetime is neither neutral, nor absolute, nor can one measure anything, microscopic and macroscopic, without changing the *observed* object in the process.

Enigmatic aspects of the role played by observation and measurement have been reported to include (when choosing the Complementarity interpretive option), in the double-slit or the photoelectric experiments for instance, those of changing the particle or wave nature of light or electron/matter upon the choice of experiments made. In the double-slit experiment, or variations thereof, it has been claimed that observation/measurement of the particle may be responsible for the changing of the history of its trajectory backward in time. For instance, if the split wave is observed when already past the two slits, the observation is said to collapse the process back in time to the pre-slit phase and make the particle behave all over again as a particle, since that is how it is detected by the screen (rather than being contributive to an interference phenomenon).

In *Unriddling the Quantum Enigma* (2020), I have explained in detail how additional interpretive errors combined with the false narrative "wave-particle duality of light" and its associated "Complementary Principle" to result in such enigmatic experimental reactions in quantum science. However, as I noted earlier in this and the previous chapters and have further elaborated on the same in my recent work as noted above, the notion that understanding the nature of an object depends not only on its own but also on that of the observer's motion in a relativistic way even in macroscopic realm points to the view that a subjectless notion of objectivity did not have scientific merits even in the classical Newtonian worldview.

The fact that quantum science findings have confirmed the so-called "measurement problem" in microscopic spacetimes, therefore, should not surprise an Einstein applying his theories of relativity, but should confirm the meritless nature of a subjectless model of objectivity as an ideological belief system. However, where Einstein departed from the quantum interpretation was the notion that there are hidden variables independent of observation that one has to still reckon with. Some have considered such a challenge from Einstein, and the subsequent efforts by theorists to disprove Einstein in the quantum entanglement debates, as an opportunity to discredit the notion of hidden variable in general, despite the reservations that Einstein had to the contrary until the end of his life.

It is true that in an imagination of reality in which everything is related, and is not universally chunky, one cannot in principle maintain the old subjectless notion of objectivity any longer. The observer is intricately involved and implicated in the reality being investigated, a reality which, because it includes the observer, must change when the observer and his or her measurements and observations change.

However, it is not clear why the measurement problem and hidden variables should be a zero-sum game, such that believing in one should necessarily lead to universal overturning of the other. Reality preexisted humanity in the form we exist today. Attribution of hidden variables to that reality, and whatever in reality that has not been interactively observed and measured by humanity, is a rather commonsensical proposition. However, to the extent that reality *becomes* interactively observed, measured, and in the process transformed, whatever the results of such observations may be, the new reality inevitably has to comprise not only what is 'out there' but also what is 'in here' and how we as observers go about interacting with the material and understanding it.

As such, of course, we could not claim to know the thing itself, but only through how it becomes a thing for us. But this is not a new proposition, and should have been taken for granted even in the classical Newtonian worldview. By analyzing Moon rocks, you change the Moon to the extent that a piece of it is transformed in the lab. The photon from a distant galaxy you receive and analyze changes that galaxy, to the extent you transform a photon of it in your lab. It is the same for macroscopic and microscopic research, and the research problem, and the Uncertainty Principle is still applicable to the macroscopic reality that becomes subject to human research. By transforming the Moon rock while testing it you can never be certain that what you study is exactly what it was before you tested it. But, that does not mean we have to abandon the notion of hidden variables. And the test of truthfulness, or not, of what you discover is in eating the pudding, not in what you may (wrongly) claim to be the thing was in itself.

It is important to note here that the uneasiness that arises from the so-called "measurement problem" has a lot to do with what notions of measurement we hold on the subject matter, depending on what worldview we adopt when interpreting it. The classical Newtonian worldview was ideologically biased in favor of a perspective in which it was assumed that it was possible to measure reality "objectively" without any consideration for the observer doing that measuring and the change that observation brought about in what was being studied. So, obviously, it was troubled by confirmed quantum science findings that announced such a subjectless notion of objectivity to be in error. So, it confronted it as a "measurement problem." We should also not forget that the reaction itself was also a result of the assumption of a dualism between microscopic and macroscopic realms.

One can trace this dualism in different ways of interpreting objectivity also to the two alternative, Complementarity versus Simultaneity, interpretations of the so-called "wave-particle duality" of objects I noted regarding the first attribute above. In the Complementarity interpretation, it is assumed that observation and measurement reestablishes a classical Newtonian reality by and large, so that we can go on and do our sciences as usual, as done in the past. This is what the Copenhagen interpretation advises us to do, when it comes to macroscopic research projects. In contrast, in the Simultaneity interpretation where the quantum reality and attribution is always retained for all reality, macroscopic and microscopic, the relativistic notion of subject-included objectivity will need to be maintained at all times. In one interpretation, objectivity is assumed to exist and be attainable without including the observers and the observation, even when observation is taking place. In the other interpretation, objectivity is attained while always taking into consideration the role played by the observer and his or her measurement influence and frame of reference, because the observer is also an interactive agent participating in the reality being studied.

In this sense, the notion of objectivity transitions from a subjectless notion to one in which the subject is and must always be included. In this sense the quantum notion of objectivity is inherently relativistic. The Complementarity notion of objectivity suggests we should have a subject-included objective approach to microscopic reality, but abandon it in macroscopic research and do its scientific business as usual using a subjectless mode of objectivity. The Simultaneity notion of objectivity in contrast suggests that in all research, microscopic and/or macroscopic we *have to* apply a subject-included objectivity model.

To be objective in the quantum sense, therefore, we have to, inescapably, include ourselves in the subject matter of our studies. Our sociologies cannot really avoid being reflective sociologies, and sociologies of self-knowledge. Reflexivity must be what C. Wright Mills called, a "common denominator" of all our studies across the natural and social sciences and the humanities, even though in his approach he was more inclined toward advocating the sociological imagination more in the study of "others'" personal troubles in relation to "their" public issues.

But, in our quantum sociological imagination, we insist that we, ourselves as observers and investigators, must always include ourselves in our research, and be *always* self-reflective, both in the personal sense of what we study, and the broader sense of our own times' public issues. We recognize, therefore, that our biases are not avoided simply because we choose to artificially push them under the rug through our supposed, impossible to achieve, self-deceiving, "blinded" (or even more self-deceiving "double-blinded") peer reviews, but through the ever more, open, transparent, all-accessible, "double-transparent" peer review models that make particularly ourselves aware of any biases or partialities we may carry, advertently or not, in our research endeavors. We do also have a scientific (as well as human) right to apply the same inquiry to others reviewing us.

In classical Newtonian visions of peer reviewing, in other words, the cart is pulling the horse; we "peer review" (which is really an euphemism for becoming docile self-censoring "review agents" amid a panoptic, still Newtonian, academic system) in order to censor (or not) the publication process. In quantum visions of peer review, publication becomes *itself* a means for the widest, wisest, most public and transparent, and least cherry-picked, peer review practices, liberating knowledge production from a duplicitous, never-ever-blindable, peer review models by putting the horse of creativity back where it belongs, pulling the cart—in the process exposing the political and duplicitous natures of how the panoptic "modern" peer-review regimes prevalent in academia serve the preservation of status quo knowledges, careers, and academic organizations serving imperialities at home and, more broadly, abroad.

The implications of advancing quantum models of objectivity for developing our sociologies, sociological imaginations, and Khayyami studies are thus enormous and inescapable. The notion of objectivity in social science, including sociology, can be consistently maintained only if we include ourselves in our studies, being always continually aware of how we go about selecting our problems, setting priorities in our research goals, and conducting our research. This is important not only in the interpretive sense of involvement, but also in its transformative sense—that is, how the very object of our studies can be changed and influenced by the way we go about choosing (or not) our problems, conducting (or not) our inquiries on particular subjects, and what attitudes we take (or not) in the practical conclusions we draw in our sociological research.

In our quantum sociological reimaginations of Khayyami studies, not only the personal troubles of our Khayyam or the public issues of his time matter but also our own personal troubles and the public issues of our own times should be inescapably taken into consideration. This also applies to any knowledge or data we have received in the course of the centuries about Khayyam's life and works. We can never ignore, for instance, how our views of Khayyam have been shaped by how his life and works, his "Rubaiyat," were portrayed for us by an Edward FitzGerald, whether or not he actually realized how his Orientalization of Khayyam served the cause of imperiality and cultural coup-making and spiritual "regime change" induction in a "distant" land. In order to understand the portraits, we have to indeed also consider FitzGerald's personal troubles and the public issues and contexts of his time amid which he undertook his interpretations and translations—considering his arrogant and self-pleasing views on what tropes such as "wine" mean for the culture being semi-colonized by way of his translations to be a part of the extent in which we appreciate (or not) his work.

Similarly, we cannot avoid our own contemporaneously constructed lenses when studying any social reality in the past, present, or emerging futures. This does not mean that we abandon the methodological requirements of abstraction and concretion in our research. It may be wise to focus first more on Khayyam's own attributed writings before consulting those of others, but ultimately we have to go around the circle and include in our studies the ways in which the knowledges and/or myths about Khayyam's life and his works have been constructed by specific others who are themselves inseparably situated in specific socio-cultural contexts of their times, past or present.

Colonialities were not something only Khayyam experienced in his own way amid inherited Persian, Arab, Turkic, and other imperialities shaping his past and contemporary times, but also one that we also experience, albeit in newer (or different) forms today in the way we go about understanding our experiences of being subjected to British, Western, and US imperialities-induced personal troubles and the public issues of our times in Iran's semi-/ neo-colonial contexts in the past and present. Nor should we ignore the efforts made in recent decades to resist continued imperial designs for Iran amid the volatile region of which it is an integral part. Khayyam's legacy having been reduced to an Orientalized, inebriated, cup and jug in hand, image of carelessness about the world is not just an innocent, incidental by-product of a well-meaning FitzGerald still influencing our Khayyami studies, but a seemingly effective, Islamophilic way of marginalizing self-critical voices arising from Iran's subaltern milieu, both at home and abroad.

In Khayyam being depicted as such, those of us coming from his shared historical and cultural backgrounds are depicted (or aspire to become) also as such, and by internalizing such imaginations of ourselves, we perpetuate old and new forms of coloniality and imperial power in the fabric of our everyday heres and nows. Khayyami studies are, simultaneously, studies of ourselves, and their questioning and transformation, exercises in questioning and changing ourselves. And in the very act of doing so, we can change backward in time the very way our histories and our here-and-nows have been and are being continually re/constructed.

So, here, our restitching efforts in the quantum sociological imagination of Khayyami studies should include those of restitching his life and works, his personal troubles and time's public issues, with our own personal troubles and our time's public issues amid a singular world-history context. Any source or data we encounter, whether contemporaneous with Khayyam, or contemporaneous with us, or contemporaneous with the numerous, countless unknown scribes or poetry lovers who over the centuries cared enough to make records of any information they had found about Khayyam, should be regarded a part of his legacy, and treated with the same critical eye of exploring their contribution from a quantum sociological imaginative framework.

5. Reimagining Causal Patterns Creatively: From Determinism to Probability

Quantum theory has been regarded as the most tested and consistently affirmed in science. At the same time, it is based on the finding that reality is by nature, fundamentally, not deterministic, but probabilistic. The view is not that there are no causal forces at play; causes may determine the outcome of specific microscopic or macroscopic processes. The view is that such interactions are not absolute and universally predeterminable, but that they are inherently probabilistic and subject to forces that include those exerted by observers and their measurements.

When we consider the notion of "predictability," we imply the presence of an observer or subject that is making that prediction. So, the predictability of the motion of an object implies the nature of involvement of that observer and subject in the course of its motion. The quantum way of imagining reality in which the observer is assumed to be a part of the object being studied necessarily undermines a notion of the predictability of that object absent the knowledge and will of the observer involved.

I may *choose* to remain "passive" and presumably do nothing to an object when studying it in order to understand how it moves or changes by itself. But this is because I *chose* to do so, such that if I otherwise did get involved, I would realize that I also was part of the process of its change. I may even discover that by being proactive, I may eliminate the problem in the first place, freeing myself from the need for studying it. My lack of involvement under the name of "objectivity," in other words, is itself a subjective choice on my part and as such I cannot claim the existence of an absolute state of predictability, simply because I chose not to participate in its outcome.

There may still be, and certainly are, fields in nature, microscopic or macroscopic, in which we have not attained the knowledge (or even the suspicion of existence) of some processes, and in that sense things may be and are happening on their own, and thus may be and are predictable based on precedence. But, this does not mean that they may not become subject to our observational and transformative action, thereby undermining the notion that they were predictable on their own. At times, even, without knowing it, we may affect the object of our research.

Once I gain the ability to know and change an object consciously and intentionally, I can claim that it is predictable, because my creative ability to know it and change it in a testable way has made it a predictable event. An illness was predictably destroying life. Now, I can predictably cure it. But, this predictability has come about because I recognized the probabilistic nature of what could happen across various scenarios of life and death for my patients, and I chose to become a healing probability, realized.

Further studies may in fact indicate that what I was regarding as an "objective" fact is a result of subjective actions by others. Just because some claim "poverty" to be a result of human nature and its laziness, does not mean it is so, even if you find lazy people, poor or rich, personal or corporate, roaming around. Further study will indeed show that the emergence of such attitudes are results of particular social and economic design and engineering schemes that resulted in social systems in which wealth and poverty are two sides of the same coin. The "predictability" of such behaviors "objectively" is then found to be that of say, classical Newtonian, social systems, probabilistically created (or miscreated) by agencies according to whom economic behavior is presumed to shape cultural and moral behavior, and not the other way around (which may still be a Newtonian model, offering a different mechanistic viewpoint).

The agencies could have been alternatively quantum in thinking and imagination, and regarded economy, polity, and culture in terms of simultaneity, considering an economy that is based on oppression and repression of one part by another of humanity to be not a good choice, since a developing economy cannot take place via dictatorships imposed by an imperial power on other nations through one coup or "regime change" scheme or another, soft or hard, overnight or decades-lasting—ridiculously presuming that the cultural ideal of democracy can be imposed on a people from without. If you design a society based on a dualistic model of economy being separate from polity and culture, one that, moreover, is based on the mutual conditioning of wealth and poverty, you are creating the "objective" conditions of poverty in practice while claiming in words to be seeking wealth and prosperity for all. This is because, in such a system, the acquiring of wealth *depends on* the deprivation of wealth from others.

The findings of quantum science, however, go beyond the notion of subjective probability and point to the inherent probabilistic nature of reality, observed or not. The quantum notion of probability, first of all, is different from the subjective one suggesting that it is our lack of precise knowledge that leads us to come up with probabilistic knowledge of society; according to such a view, if we had complete knowledge about our subject matter, presumed to be inherently involving determinable causal relations, we would be able to certainly determine and predict its movements.

The quantum notion of probability points to the inherent indeterminability and unpredictability of microscopic reality, no matter how much knowledge we may attain about it. Our own effort in studying that reality by measuring it is itself also contributive to such a probability, since the act of measurement itself adds to the causal forces unpredictably shaping that reality. This, the so-called "measurement problem," finds its expression in the Heisenberg Uncertainty Principle, in the notion that we can never measure both the location and the speed of a subatomic particle. To know its location, our measurement affects its speed; to know its speed, our measurement affects its location. How the object is "in itself," therefore, cannot be really known. This has offered the grounds for the Copenhagen Interpretation of quantum reality and enigma, in fact, which has suggested that we can never know the nature of microscopic reality, and what we do know has been shaped by our measurements. In its extreme formulations the Copenhagen Interpretation has denied the existence of microscopic reality altogether, suggesting that what we regard as that reality are basically our own concepts, mathematical formulations, and theoretical schemes about the quantum world.

As I have argued in *Unriddling the Quantum Enigma* (2020), the notion that the so-called "measurement problem" applies only to microscopic reality and research is itself, also, a false narrative resulting from our subconsciously inherited classical Newtonian worldviews as ideological constructs. The measurement has always been, and will always be, a problem, be our research microscopic or macroscopic. Our ideological lenses inherited from classical Newtonianism had falsely assumed that the same does not exist in macroscopic realities and investigations, so those of us still subconsciously holding on to the old viewpoint felt deeply shocked to find, while conducting new experiments on light and subatomic particles, that there is no way we could avoid the problem.

The quantum science findings simply showed us, clearly and based on undeniable evidence, what we should have learned long ago about macroscopic reality and research—namely that a notion of subjectless objectivity is an ideological illusion that serves, nonetheless, specific functional needs in maintaining the socio-economic, political and scientific status quo in modern times. In the same way, the notion of determinism and predictability borrowed from classical Newtonianism has ideologically masked the fact that social reality is also inherently an infinitely malleable, flexible, probabilistic, and creative medium to understand and transform which the creative artistic/artful attitude—one that draws on the best philosophical, spiritual, and scientific wisdom while avoiding their shortcomings—may be the most proper attitude.

My comments above on the Newtonian presumption of subjectless "objectivity" as a supposed law of scientific inquiry, rather than the quantum notion of it as including the observers and the human agency as part of the research process, is meant to provide a plausible explanation for the supposed enigma of the dualism of macroscopic predictability and microscopic probability of the *same* reality being studied. The macroscopic predictability and mechanical determinism is itself a socially constructed artifact of our own narrow scientific and observational lenses, which actually best explains why the distorted, playerless, form of classical billiard balls game analogy has been found to be applicable for its representation. If you take the billiard ball players out of the picture, you have, by choice, redefined your game as a mechanical and predictable operation; if you include them, with all their subjectivities, creativity, and spontaneity that comes with human agency, it would be impossible to simplistically predict how or even whether a game may begin, how the strikes may happen, whether they are interrupted, or concluded, and who loses or wins the game.

Similarly, it has been our choices of whether and how we can or should or do participate in understanding or changing our realities, including the social realities within and without, that have led us to the illusion that in the macroscopic sphere we should assume that social reality is a Newtonian one. Even for macroscopic realities seemingly independently existing light years away, or nearer, their predictable behaviors must be judged both in the context of the frameworks used in our studies of them. The reason probabilistic reality is shocking and enigmatic to some is that they had taken for granted, as influenced by and using a classical Newtonian subjectless billiard balls game point of view, that reality was deterministic to begin with.

It is important to continue keeping in mind that the two contrasting Complementarity and Simultaneity interpretive strategies regarding the 'dual' wave-particle nature of light also result in different ways of approaching the matter of causal determination in reality. According to the Complementarity interpretative option, which allows for the actual either/or possibilities for each attribute to manifest in macroscopic spacetimes, a classical Newtonian causal determination model may remain attractive, since it allows folks to argue that in the macroscopic realm things still happen in a predictable and deterministic way. Obviously, such a perspective would be more favored by those who wish to maintain the status quo since their vested interests are served by it.

However, in the Simultaneity interpretation, reality in general, microscopic and macroscopic, is regarded as being probabilistic in nature, although the spatiotemporal unfolding of the alternative historical alternatives for the objects under consideration may vary relative to the frame of reference adopted for such observations.

According to this perspective, one does not even have to, and should not, wait for objective conditions for change to come. The infinite possibilities of a better society and personal life begin in the here-and-now, and all it would take is to not take things for granted as is, and try to be creative in living better alternative ways of life not projected as a wish into an uncertain tomorrow to come, but in the details of everyday life, in relation to oneself, to others, and to the natural/built environment.

But the self-fulfilling prophetic implications of adopting a Newtonian attitude toward our studies of nature, society, and mind, should not be ignored.

If we approach our nature, society, sociologies, sociological imaginations, and Khayyami studies in a predeterministic, predictable, habitual, and mechanical ways, we will certainly end up with Newtonian social organizations, universities, sociologies, sociological imaginations, and Khayyami studies that are not only boring, but are also self-defeatingly repetitive, mechanical, and uncreative. We can continue to restitch (or not) the same passages and quotes from this or that contemporary, from this or that translator, ignoring in the meantime the major pieces from Khayyam's philosophical or scientific writings, or ignoring his *Nowrooznameh (The Book on Nowrooz)* altogether again. Such predictable modes of studying Khayyam will "certainly" result in the same findings and repeated conclusions. We will certainly find ourselves living another one thousand years not learning who Khayyam was.

Quantum sociologies do not conduct social research with a presumed notion or law to frame empirical facts. They don't presume that economy, polity, culture, or anything, always and universally determines social development. They may find patterns in what has happened in the past, but this does not mean such a pattern had to happen, or must continue to happen in the future, or does happen today. Quantum sociologies do not assume a single act, a single person, a single poem, could do nothing to change the course of world-history; it might. They approach reality, including social reality, in a creative, open-ended, way, seeking to understand the probabilities of its nature in as serious a way as it would have approached it with certainty.

If a quatrain is Khayyami, that is, if it has been for one reason or another attributed by some collector or scribe hundreds of years ago to Omar Khayyam, which means it may be his, or not, the probabilistic quantum approach would still call for a serious consideration of it so as to determine whether it has any relevance and worth in understanding the subject matter as a result of the study itself. This approach would consider it also interesting and noteworthy that particular quatrains have over time become attributed to Khayyam, and others not. It asks, why? It becomes curious about things otherwise others take for granted. Why did this complier, this scribe, this collector, include these poems in the Khayyam section of their collection? The Khayyami wave on which such quatrains ride may itself be significant subject matter of research, perhaps pointing to a pattern in the collective consciousness, or subconsciousness, of people across generations in the greater Iranian region where a specific form of cultural identity, and sets of values, become collectively associated with such Khayyami quatrains and the historical Omar Khayyam.

So, we do not presume the Khayyami quatrains to be authentic or not in an *a priori* way; we subject them to probabilistic studies and analyses, treating them as seriously as any quatrain indubitably attributed to the historical Khayyam. From a quantum sociologically imaginative point of view, we let go of any preconceived notions we may have about Khayyam's life and works and let the process of critical inquiry into the data and information received to decide where it takes us. We will do our best to avoid falling in habitual, repetitive, tried patterns of thinking and imagining, and be open to new probabilistic, creative opportunities that may arise in the course of our investigations to follow new leads, to using and following new threads and patterns, to restitch in new probabilistic ways the various elements of our Khayyam studies together. We will recognize, instead, that what we already presume to be the "facts" of Khayyam's life and works have themselves been probabilistic narratives woven, for better or worse, by one or another weaver in the Khayyami tradition, having become in time so frozen and taken for granted that we wrongly regard them to be the "truths" of his legacy.

Approaching sociology and the sociological imagination in a quantum way as a framework for Khayyami studies would render it as open to surprise, avoiding mechanical yes or no predeterministic answers to questions; it takes nothing for granted as accepted truths about who Khayyam has been reported to be, or his attributed writings have been assumed to mean, even when he has been assumed to have been born and died, or what his contemporaries or those coming after have presumably offered as judgments about his character.

6. Reimagining Causal Chains Also As Causal Leaps: From Continuity to "Transcontinuity" (Also Known As "Discontinuity")

As noted in the attributions of classical Newtonianism, it was assumed that there is a continuous causal chain operative in reality, such that A causes B, which causes C, which causes D, and so on. The assumption has been that in both spatial and temporal terms causes are effected in local ways, such that A cannot jump, or leap, over B and C to cause D directly, but has to go through the intermediary local events in the continuous causal chain.

According to quantum science findings, however, microscopic reality seems to not follow that pattern always, appearing as if causal influences, themselves probabilistic, defy local events and take place in leaps, or "discontinuous" ways.

As also noted in *Unriddling the Quantum Enigma* (2020), I prefer to use the alternative term "transcontinuity" for what is called "discontinuity" in quantum science literature to describe an attribute of quantum reality. The reason I do so is to avoid a connotation that may inadvertently contradict the attribution of inseparability that is also claimed for quantum reality. In other words, a universe that is characterized by inseparability does not, logically, contain events that imply the opposite, separability, which is what the notion of "discontinuity" may imply, causing unnecessary confusion.

The term "transcontinuity" instead points to a different, quantum, way of imagining *continuity*—that is, a continuity that seems to leap over intermediary local steps in a presumed causal chain. In that sense, it is different from the classical Newtonian way of considering continuity in causal chains, but does not throw the baby of inseparability away with the water of trying to show the difference across the worldviews, so to speak.

Transcontinuity does not negate the notion of inseparability. What it does is to suggest that there is what appears to be a "leaping" way in which cause and effect take place such that some intermediary local events are (or seem to be) bypassed or leaped over to connect the two events to maintain the inseparability of what David Bohm called the undivided universe.

Again, it is helpful to note that the two different, Complementary versus Simultaneous, ways of interpreting the wave-particle 'duality' of light or matter also lead to different ways of imagining transcontinuity. In the former interpretation, transcontinuity is assumed to be something that happens only in the microscopic world, while the macroscopic world is regarded as following the more "familiar" deterministic pattern involving local causal chains and continuities. In the other interpretation, that of Simultaneity, all reality, including both microscopic and macroscopic realms, are characterized by continuity as well as what appear to be transcontinuous, non-local causal patterns.

In traditional literature, at times the language of quantitative and qualitative changes was used to refer to this pattern of change. And, as has been the case, such events have not been observed only in microscopic realms, but also, in fact, have been most readily observed in macroscopic events. The gradual quantitative changes suddenly resulting in qualitative changes have by no means been a microscopic narrative, but most readily used and observed in everyday life.

Much of the current studies in implications of quantum science for the study of nature and evolution and coevolution have been devoted to understanding how such leaps have occurred in nature. The transcontinuous changes by leaps in social-historical development in terms of slow or rapid, at times revolutionary, changes can also be considered as macroscopic manifestations of what others have considered to be a new idea in quantum science studying only microscopic spacetimes.

So, the issue is not, in my view, a matter of contrasting continuity with discontinuity, and associating them dichotomously with macroscopic and microscopic worlds respectively, but that of contrasting *different patterns* of continuity in all reality, microscopic *and* macroscopic, amid a reality characterized by universal inseparability. What this calls for, therefore, is a revisitation of events quantum science confronted as displaying "discontinuity," in an effort to understand how such a process of so-called "discontinuity" could be possible in a world of inseparable events. This may provide an opportunity to understand what appear "discontinuous" in terms of "transcontinuity."

The notion that societies, and sociologies, can undergo transformation through leaps, seemingly defying longstanding continuities, should not strike us as odd. The same can be considered in the context of Khayyami studies.

No one may have predicted that an English translation of Khayyami "Rubaiyat," even as "free" as it was, could launch not only an international fame for Khayyam, but also lead to both rational and at times Orientalized and Islamophilic depictions of Khayyam in the public imagination. Imperial interests have often been deeply and significantly served by the trivialization of colonized cultures, by distorting their meanings and symbolic language, depriving them of their critical voices and alternative insights in favor of perpetuating the imperial status quo. Khayyami studies can provide ample examples for how such imperial cultural distortions and manipulations take place in both overt and covert, subliminal ways.

Some may regard both trends as continuities arising from certain "essential" features in the "Rubaiyat" by which an Edward FitzGerald swore. Others see the trends as having more to do with the Victorian culture of mid-nineteenth century England, than having anything to do with Khayyam's own thoughts. However, there is no question that a "leap" of sorts took place since FitzGerald, introducing Khayyam to the world in a way that had not happened before, with some claiming that Khayyam's fame had much to do with the translation, and what was being (authentically or not) translated.

Spending too much time with FitzGerald and not with Khayyam's own works and life sources may be itself a trap, playing in the hands of imperial political and cultural analyses, keeping us in a vicious cycle of believing it was FitzGerald who made Khayyam famous, and not the other way around, in fact. As pieces of the stitches to be considered, these connections certainly warrant also critical revisitation. But care must be taken to not become obsessed again with FitzGerald and *his* "Rubaiyat" at the cost of continued neglect for long-ignored and urgently needed pieces of Khayyam's own puzzle. Otherwise, we may end up with continuities of repetitive and often misguided studies that mistake Khayyam's life and works for what was absorbed and "freely" translated in limited ways in FitzGerald.

Khayyami studies being aware of causations in terms of transcontinuities would not abandon searching for causes per se, but would be careful not to derive them only from the more easily accessible "local" contexts, both in terms of space and time. They would be open to possibilities of new research method and orientation and their applications that can result in qualitatively new leaps in understanding of seemingly old and taken for granted "facts" about Khayyam's life and works. This does not mean that the new trends arise from nowhere in a separable context from what has gone before, but new insights would allow new ways of interpreting prior events and ideas in his life that cast qualitatively new light on the subject matter. Khayyami studies also can, and deserve to, be subjected to qualitatively new and creative ways of conducting research about his life and works.

Another way transcontinuity can be observed in Khayyami studies is by seeking to understand the apparent continuities or discontinuities in Khayyam's attributed works across philosophy, religion, mathematics, astronomy, literary writing, and poetry, and even architectural objects remaining from his period. We should particularly be on guard against exploratory strategies that may assume that Khayyam could suddenly abandon a theme or topic of intense interest in, say, his philosophical works, when he preoccupies himself with problems in geometry and algebra, for instance. Or, we may take for granted the apparent discontinuities between his scientific, literary (such as in *Nowrooznameh*) and poetic endeavors. What may appear discontinuous there, in other words, may be found to be, in a deeper fold of hermeneutic analysis, to be signs of a wonderful transcontinuity in progress in his life's work. We should particularly be cognizant of the fact in an Islamic worldview characterized by a deep sense of unity ("towheed") in God's creation, the inseparability of existence must also express itself in the inseparability of ways of inquiry in the mind, heart, and sensibility of the most serious and deeply Islamic critical thinker that was Omar Khayyam.

The key here is to problematize taken for granted continuities presumed to exist in knowledges about his life, works, and times, with the consideration in mind that seemingly unrelated causal linkages may manifest themselves in the course of research that result in new and deeper transcontinuities in the way pieces of Khayyam's life and work puzzles can be differently restitched together beyond what at first glance predictably meets the eye.

7. Reimagining Sociology: From Disciplinarity Toward Transdisciplinarity

Quantum science has, enigmatically, resulted on one hand in the questioning of disciplinary boundaries, especially regarding whether or not physics and related natural science disciplines should "encounter consciousness," and, on the other hand, in its continued reliance on disciplinary boundaries and identities in carrying out scientific work and on fears and stigmatizations of trends that one way or another challenge that order.

In *Unriddling the Quantum Enigma* (2020), I have tried to show how this dualism has itself been reflective of the dualism still gripping and defining the main expressions of the quantum enigma itself, namely the paradox that we have scientifically affirmed theories of the quantum world that seem inconsistent with the still-relevant (classical or relativity-corrected) Newtonian theories of the macroscopic world. If scientists are still divided and wondering about how from such a quantum, presumably non-Newtonian, microscopic world a Newtonian macroscopic world arises, then presumably we would find some scientists still holding on, consciously or not, to their Newtonian approaches to understanding macroscopic reality, including society, social forms of organization, universities, disciplines, and perhaps even manifested in the continuity of "disciplined" Newtonian approaches to Khayyami studies.

So, we would then find a subject matter such as that found in Khayyam who may have seen his seeking of truth as a unitary exercise in religion, philosophy, science, creative writing, and poetry, become increasingly ripped apart and chunked away by this or that mathematician or geometrist, astronomer or philosopher, theologian, creative writer, poet, or translator. So, each ends up confidently saying what the subject matter is—say, a tail, a wall, a trunk—neither recognizing the elephant in the room. Khayyam and his life and works may also offer an illustrative instance of how an elephant whole is mischaracterized by fragmentary and partial attitudes of various thinkers or persons. Even in the Khayyami Robaiyat we have quatrains in which the poet self-consciously speaks of how each sect has its own supposition of him, insisting that he himself knows best who he is.

There is no question that an important result of the advent of quantum sciences and the failures in resolving its enigmas has been a greater openness by quantum scientists to participate in and encourage transdisciplinary research. But such work does not seem to be, yet, a mainstream trend almost a century since the quantum revolution. Even now, the boundaries of disciplines are still maintained with force or by consent, fear, or self-censorship, and clearly the efforts to involve other disciplines often leave out social sciences and humanities, even in situations where socially critical nuclear physicists are involved.

Unfortunately, not all mainstream physicists and scientists have shared the sentiment of transdisciplinarity as an innovative intellectual movement. Still some believe one has to "shut up and calculate," believing that the microscopic and macroscopic imaginations of reality can never be unified, and others who treat engagements with the quantum enigma as recreative and secondary pastime, and not a part of serious, tenure-worthy, research. And there are some who take it seriously while being cautious not to rock the boat, so to speak, if still academically employed and concerned about their tenure, promotion, or reputation. And there are also other serious quantum physicists who believe the broader meaning and practically liberating results of quantum science cannot be obtained without a thoroughly transdisciplinary approach.

When amid a quantum revolution in science viewing reality as holistic and interdependent we find that the natural sciences still more or less timidly ask whether consciousness should be encountered or not, this signifies not only the expression, but perhaps even a cause, of why the so-called quantum enigma has endured over many decades.

The reaction some may have to the event of a sociologist writing about the quantum enigma, as found in my *Unriddling the Quantum Enigma* (2020), may also illustrate why in a quantum imagination of academia in terms of transdisciplinarity, such a shock, or uneasiness, should not happen. The "transcontinuity" of sociology and physics leaping over the intermediary disciplinary causal chains of their own discipline neighborhoods should be expected in a worldview in which the disciplines are not corpuscular entities bound by the walls of easily locatable departments on a campus map, but spread-out ways of going about understanding a single reality, such that their knowledges overlap, superpose, and probabilistically inform and entangle with one another in creative and unpredictable ways.

The continuities of such "objectivist" and positivist approaches to science, sociology, and Khayyami studies also need their own explanation, for they certainly fulfill a function in the pursuit of the types of knowledge and those sorts of sociologies and social policies that help maintain the status quo of their universities, their states, their ideologies, and their empires, no matter how much they may deny harboring such "subjective" biases or interests in their "objective" pursuits of truth.

Quantum sociologies, sociological imaginations, and Khayyami studies dispense with *a priori* valuations of whether a particular discipline or academic culture has the exclusive right or relevance to any subject, including the study Khayyam's life and works. They approach transdisciplinarity in the spirit of no discipline or field of science having a monopoly over the truth. It approaches its study not in terms of disciplinarity, interdisciplinarity, or even multi- or cross-disciplinarity per se. These have had made their contributions, for sure; but still, they presume separately existing fields of specialty or "levels" of knowledge that need to be brought into conversation with one another, in a Newtonian way, from without.

The quantum approach is transdisciplinary in that it regards reality as a unitary one whose fields and folds are inseparably and non-dualistically intertwined in terms of identities in difference, one that inescapably includes the observer/researcher as a part of the reality being studied. In that sense, transdisciplinarity transgresses all artificial disciplinary boundaries, lives and thrives on disciplinary borderlands, finding it necessary to cross artificially set boundaries, while not eschewing but critically embracing, in an appreciative way, any knowledges that have been contributed by inter/multi/cross/disciplinary sciences, setting its tasks to in fact demonstrate how the pursuit and findings of such seemingly separate disciplines are manifold expressions of a unitary, integrative, and common transdisciplinary search.

For this reason, we should do our best in our quantum sociological imaginations of our Khayyami studies to tackle topics that may seem alien to us and not a part of our specialties. Just because we are not astronomers, and even less into astrology, should not prevent us from studying Khayyam and his horoscope. We should try to understand as best as we can the essential reasons why Khayyam wrote his philosophical essays, wrote on algebra or geometry, engaged in creative writings, was concerned with the cultural significance of the Iranian New Year (Nowrooz), and composed quatrains. Such an approach will certainly be more challenging and difficult than limiting ourselves to one or another domain of Khayyami works. But, it may, in unpredictable ways, provide qualitatively new opportunities and vistas for understanding our subject matter.

8. Reimagining Science: From Eurocentrism to Transculturalism

It has been a hallmark of quantum science and the efforts in grappling with its enigmas that many scientists and spiritual thinkers have come closer in appreciating each others' works and in adopting a transcultural attitude devoid of presumptive superiority of only one way of knowing.

At the same time, there are still those in mainstream academia who make sure they drop in the label "pseudoscientific" against perceived "others" often enough in fear of losing their academic position, tenure and promotion, in order to distinguish their own, often self-admittedly "wild" speculations about quantum reality tinged always with the promise of some kind of (presumably final) scientific verification of them in a near or distant future.

The transcontinuities of transculturalism also should not be surprising to quantum ways of imagining the reality of global research and scholarship. What may appear as a discontinuous scholarly behavior from a Middle Eastern background always caught in the dialectical tensions of the East and the West exploring the quantum enigma, will be unriddled when one adopts a quantum view of ourselves as an inseparable human species traveling somewhere in an undivided cosmos, one that has *always* been characterized by a transcultural reality despite the ethnocentric points of view of those who regard the spread-out common culture of humanity a corpuscular possession of their own imperial islands bound by supposedly fixed walls and borders.

If the unriddling of the quantum enigma requires conscious and intentional sensitivity to taking into account the hidden, included-middle, borderland regions of the disciplines and cultures, should it be surprising that helpful suggestions may be offered from within the discipline of sociology, a traditionally transdisciplinary "in-between" field, or from the "middle-eastern" borderlands where one has to confront in each cell of one's body and soul the creative (or not) dialectical tensions of the East and the West, for millennia, during a lifetime, every day?

What cannot be denied is that the blurring of the hard lines between science, spirituality, philosophy, and art, has been a hallmark of the quantum revolution and era, even though it may still not be clear whereto their dialogue may be heading.

Quantum sociologies, sociological imaginations, and Khayyami studies are inherently transcultural pursuits, and do not in *a priori* ways eschew any particular intellectual tradition simply because it is different from ours. As in the case of living in the borderlands of disciplines and academic cultures of natural sciences, social sciences, and the humanities, in the wider context of human cultural traditions, it thrives on living in the borderlands of world cultures, regarding them not as separate billiard balls of ways of knowing, but as manifestations of a unitary human pursuits in a world-history context.

Khayyami studies conducted within a quantum sociological imagination are inherently projects involving superposed restitching of disciplinary and cultural patches of otherwise inseparable knowledge, fragmented over the centuries amid the horrible earthquakes of land, cultures, wars, and social unrest and calamities. The quantum restitching of Khayyam's life and works must be regarded necessarily as a creative, unpredictable, open-ended, project, one that pays as much attention to obvious continuities as to less obvious transcontinuities in the data and information passed on from the past. The project is at heart that of restitching the enigmatic story of how Khayyam's personal troubles and the public issues of his time related to one another, and how the same relate to our own personal troubles and public issues today, here and now.

The move from Newtonian toward quantum reimaginations of our common reality, of sociology, and of our Khayyami studies is not a move from A to non-A, as if between two mutually exclusive and dualized/dichotomized things or "levels," but that of moving from a part to a broader whole that includes the part but is much greater than the part. The Newtonian imagination is a quantum vision that is collapsed and frozen in one of its possibilities at a specific scale of its spatiotemporal continuum, and quantum vision includes Newtonianism as one of its possibilities but is much greater than that. So, one is the same and different from the other. Their relation is that of identity and difference, as in the dialectics of part and whole.

The quantum vision liberates the imagination from regarding the Newtonian vision as the only possible and valid vision, without dismissing that one possibility as being in and of itself irrelevant on its own grounds; but the validity of Newtonianism's collapsed possibility is limited to that collapsed possibility. The Newtonian imagination is only a collapsed possibility of a much wider quantum imagination representing a wave function of infinite possibilities in how we go about understanding and changing our social realities, our sociological imaginations and our Khayyami studies.

In the foregoing, I have included the attributes of transdisciplinarity and transculturalism in the quantum attributes model, or their parallel contrasts in the classical Newtonian model (disciplinary scholarship and cultural scientism, as presented in the previous chapter). Some may prefer that the focus remain on the "real" subject matter than the process of going about researching it, which these two attributes address and imply. Some may even bring up the traditional academic argument that "consciousness" should be left out of "serious scientific research" and thus of these attribute lists.

I think it is important to note again that the very notion of traditional "objectivity" as inherited from the classical Newtonian model is at contention between the two outlooks, and therefore it is essential not to dichotomize the "real" subject matter and the way of going about understanding it from one another in this comparative consideration. I even daresay that those who may object to including the attributes of transdisciplinarity and transculturalism in the quantum (and their corresponding ones in the classical Newtonian) respective lists may still harbor their own subconscious Newtonian habits of thinking about what the two models should and should not include and how they should be contrasted with one another. This is so, because it is in the very nature of the quantum challenge to the classical Newtonian way of going about doing science to dichotomize the object and subject as if they are separable from one another.

After all, who has been telling us that there is such a thing as a quantum enigma, other than physicists working in definite academic disciplinary and socio-cultural contexts? How did they come to regard one way of doing science as being "normal" and another one as "enigmatic"? A scientist has wrongly believed, asleep to classical Newtonian way of thinking, that there is such a thing as a subjectless objectivity, and when he or she finds out, amid undeniable experiment results, that there is such a thing as a "measurement problem," he or she is obviously quite shocked and enigmatized. But, why should we be mesmerized by that scientist's shock, and feel that we have to follow him or her, simply because he or she has a degree or tenure?

Enigmas and enigmatic experiences do not emerge from thin air, but in the minds, feelings, sensations, and lives of specific individuals working in definite ways in their concrete institutional and socio-cultural settings. In fact, from a quantum point of view, it is even more important to consider the difference the standpoints and perspectives of actors make, while working through their institutional and socio-cultural settings, in understanding and in fact shaping the realities they seek to understand.

Let me offer two examples here.

Consider the fact that in sociology, especially in its more critical trends, it has become *for decades* a matter of common sense that social reality is constructed. Considerable literature has emerged in the field in how that construction is made, in order to avoid approaches that reify social reality, presuming that social reality has an objectivity apart from the process which establishes such realities through what Peter Berger and Thomas Luckmann called externalization, legitimation, and socialization; that is, how social actors create new social relations, how they become legitimated as objective social orders, and how these social orders are then continually reproduced through processes of primary and secondary socialization.

Sociologists even take for granted as a research challenge that, say, in the interview process, the "reality" of the ideas or sentiments held by the interviewee often changes. In other words, what quantum scientists are so shocked about as far as microscopic reality is concerned has been considered a matter of taken-for-granted knowledge in sociological research. It has been likewise a matter of common sense, as well as social scientific interest, that in public opinion research and polling, the measurement efforts can actually affect the public opinion and even political voting patterns as pollsters go about doing their work, a process that has become even more intensified and visible in the age of the internet, social media, and fake news.

My point here is to note how disciplinary boundaries can play a part in compartmentalizing enigmatic experiences itself, such that what is enigmatic to one discipline may have already become a common sense knowledge in another discipline, or at least in the more critical trends in the latter, as far as sociology is concerned. What a quantum scientist regards as enigmatic in the "measurement problem" has been taken-for-granted for social scientists and sociologists, even if they differ about the extent and nature of that process.

A physicist may now counterargue by saying that, well, we are talking about physical reality, and you, social reality. And my response to that would be, yes, indeed, that is precisely the point—how disciplinary boundaries may lead physicists to argue that social reality is not "real" enough to constitute a legitimate subject matter, so they end up not feeling the need to learn from the research and experiences of colleagues in other disciplines to see whether the quantum enigma is equally enigmatic in other fields.

Oddly, you still find universities where sociology does not exist even as a discipline for its lack of being considered a science, and some science prize-givers apparently do not think sociology is worth being even called a discipline, let alone being offered a prize. We are not even speaking of classical Newtonian habits of treating a field of study as being considered worthy of a disciplinary label, not even being treated as a chunk. Such habits are indeed not even classical Newtonian, but pre-Newtonian, and themselves engage in self-fulfilling prophecies where certain domains are awarded at the expense of ignoring others, and in the process end up being self-defeating for advancing socially relevant scientific knowledge. Just think about it, a prize structure to advance science is established which, in its very structure, awards studies that reproduce disciplinary boundaries and hierarchies, and thereby self-defeats the scientific purpose for which it is launched.

In the literature that I have read on the quantum enigma and the encounter of physics with consciousness, and the speculations made about the nature of consciousness and how it emerges, I have yet to find engagements with literature in the tradition of symbolic interactionism and sociological theories of the self and knowledge, for instance. At best, there is some references to the Pavlovian dogs, or Skinnerian psychology, which are perhaps what are recalled from physicists' earlier undergraduate education gained in their general sociology electives taken long time ago. So, a physicist would not even wonder, unless critically minded, that there could be hypnotic ideological conditioning, advertently or not, consciously or not, going on in the very science (even most abstract) he or she is learning, teaching, writing, or making science documentaries about. Psychology, sociology, philosophy, art, and the humanities are alien disciplines for such a physicist, unless undertaken in spare times.

The fact that reality is hierarchically compartmentalized into physics here and society there while consciousness is exiled altogether to the humanities or even away from academic work with modes of knowing thereby becoming fragmented across separate academic disciplines and cultures is a result of the workings of a broader paradigm, that is classical Newtonianism, or even pre-Newtonian (that is, before even the Western Renaissance, although in other parts of the world experiencing their renaissance such disciplinary overlaps were taken for granted, as one can find in the works of Khayyam or Avicenna), which regards atomism, separability, and inflexible predictability of disciplinary boundaries essential frameworks for imagining reality. Sadly, even in proposed or guided alternative universities by physicists, we find the same habits of leaving out the social sciences and the humanities, as if poetic imagination, or social self-reflexivity in understanding the interplay of public issues and personal troubles, have nothing to do with the students.

So including the disciplinary or transdisciplinary natures of scholarship, or scientism and transculturalism as well, as attributes of Newtonian and quantum models respectively is essential for understanding how they differ from one another and also for understanding how a scientific encounter is experienced as commonsensical or enigmatic. For the same reason, the reactions to the effort being made in this book and series in developing and applying a quantum sociological imagination framework for Khayyami studies may appear odd to those thinking that the boundaries of the disciplines are etched in stone and meant to be kept separate. I hope that this study will provide opportunities for such observations to be critically self-evaluated and changed in favor of fostering transdisciplinarity in Khayyami studies.

As another instance regarding the transcultural attribute, I can share the example from my studies of mysticism as I explored, for instance, in the teachings of the Caucasian mystic, G. I. Gurdjieff.

In Gurdjieff's cosmology, there is no dualism between matter and mind. He says everything is material; even God is so, such that He can be weighed and measured. For Gurdjieff matter is vibration, and depending on its location in what he calls the Ray of Creation, we may have finer or coarser vibrations. The fact that the term "matter" is used, in other words, should not be misunderstood as somehow portraying him as a materialist in the traditional (philosophical) sense of the term. He is basically avoiding the dualism of matter and mind, matter and vibration, since everything is made of the same stuff. So, matter is mental, and mental is material.

One does not have to agree with Gurdjieff to see the point I wish to share here. My point of sharing this example is to indicate that the questioning of dualistic thinking has been a common and continuing theme in Eastern spirituality and science. You cannot read Rumi in the original Persian without confronting how seriously he takes the problem of moving beyond dualism. There is no way one can understand Khayyam's life and work—not in the way he has been Orientalized and distorted starting with the well-intentioned and otherwise stylistically pleasant works of translators such as Edward FitzGerald—without appreciating the way he transcended, and called for transcending, dualistic thinking. Even to this day, specialists dismiss Khayyam's poetry as a pastime, as if what he was trying to do through poetry was not, at the same time, a scientific, religious, and philosophical practice.

So, just because Western physicists suddenly discover, when experimenting with light, that it has a "dual" nature (a term whose use itself is in fact problematic since, as I noted before, it still subconsciously allows for dualistic thinking while, obviously, it intends to note that something can be both wave or particle, that it can be both mass or energy, and so on) and thus becomes enigmatized by such a discovery because their Newtonian way of thinking had conditioned them to think that way before, it does not mean that other cultural ways of knowing in the world's spiritual and scientific traditions had not already come across that truth in their own way, through quite elaborate and detailed scientific, philosophical, and artistic traditions which have been expressed, "enigmatically," often in poetic forms.

After all, as noted before, what form of knowledge could be more suitable for the expression of nondualistic notions than that of poetry, which allows for multiple meanings to be probabilistically embedded at once in a single line or even word, such as "wine," "drunkenness," "love," and "beauty"? But then, how could a Western scientist who is, consciously or not, still Newtonian in his or her way of thinking, not disregard such Eastern poetry as not being also a scientific effort in knowing the world?

So, when considering the Newtonian or quantum attribute models or ways of imagining reality and delineating, it is by no means redundant, but in fact essential, that we include the ways of knowing (such as disciplinarity or cultural scientism in the classical Newtonian model and their contrasting parallels, transdisciplinarity and transculturalism, in the quantum model) as part of the "package," so to speak, of what each model represents. This, in turn, makes it possible for us to avoid reifying enigmatic experiences in diverse social, cultural, and disciplinary contexts, by *always* asking "enigmatic for whom?" "Whose Enigma?"

The questioning of the *a priori* causal determination of how society shapes personal selves is a result of the distinction I make between what I call Newtonian and quantum sociological imaginations. I use the term 'Newtonian sociology' to denote that conventional and still prevalent perspective in sociology that associates 'society' with an ensemble of interacting 'individuals' or groups of 'individual' actors. In this view, the so-called 'individual'—possessing a more or less singular self or self-structure in everyday life except for rare and extreme clinical situations—is treated as the basic acting 'atom' or unit of the broader society. 'Individuals' in this sociological imagination are the equivalent of 'bodies,' similar to billiard balls in the Newtonian vision of the universe. The laws point to the orderliness and predictability of the motion of matter as a result of external forces exerted by bodies on one another. To explain the state of motion of a body, all it takes is to describe the forces exerted upon it from without.

However, the Newtonian laws do not in and of themselves take into account the possibility that the presumed bodies may be self-moving, self-motivating, and self-determining, a result perhaps of the diversity of forces arising from *within* the bodies—or that they may themselves be subjected to inner fragmentation and contradictory inner forces each of which may also tend to move the body as a whole in one or another direction. If the bodies were internally divided, diverse, and self-moving, then the externally conceived motion of bodies as stated in Newton's laws would not make their motion predictable—or, at the very least, the diverse inner forces and tendencies of bodies have to be also taken into consideration in explaining their motions. Their inner forces taken into consideration, the bodies would otherwise seem to be strangely acting, unpredictable, chaotic, and contradictory.

A consequence of this insight for traditional models of sociology of knowledge, of which the Millsian sociological imagination may be considered an expression, is that the thesis of "social origins of knowledge" is rendered not to be universally applicable in its crude interpretations, as if society and knowledge (including that of the investigator him/herself) can be separated in terms of a dualistic A versus non-A logic. Neither the knowledge of those studied, nor the knowledge of the one(s) studying, can be regarded as universally originating in a presumed "social reality," since that social reality, when considered in terms of the whole-part dialectic, encompasses the knowledges studied and studying, empowering those studied and the observers studying, as being also capable of generating new causal forces of determination shaping social reality.

Therefore, the traditional Newtonian model of subjectless "objectivity" of knowledge cannot be universally presumed, but any relation of determination between knowledge and society has to be discovered through specific analysis of particular conditions present in the subject matter of study and not presumed in advance. It is for this reason that I have advocated a sociology of self-knowledge model (in contrast to the traditional sociology of knowledge model) whereby the determination of causality between "knowledge and society," "observer and the observed," etc., need to be discovered anew in any given particular investigation rather than universally presumed in advance. Most importantly, the role played by the observer, i.e., by the investigator himself or herself, is reconsidered in what I have called (2002, 2020) a "postdeterminist" fashion—i.e., in a way that allows for the observer himself or herself to participate in the understanding and even the reality-forming transformation of the "object" (or subject matter) under study.

The issue of the role of the observer in not only understanding, but also even shaping, of the "reality" under study, is important. What I wish to point out here is that the 'quantum' vision of matter that emerged later in science shed new lights on the micro view of the *same* universe Newton was trying to capture in his precisely deterministic macro laws of motion. In the subatomic, quantum world, things are not as certain as one may suppose. Many strange particles roam around, being not even 'visible' to the most precise scientific instruments; but their presence are theoretically presumed, and without them there could really be no tangible body or matter. The paradox of the whole matter seems to be that the orderliness of the macro-universe and the chaos of the micro-, subatomic, world coexist as aspects of the same reality. Order and chaos depend on one another.

Applying this distinction between the Newtonian and the quantum visions of the universe to society, and sociology, one may arrive at a strange vision of society and social experience—and indeed of sociology. In the quantum vision of society, and of sociology, the basic acting units will no longer be the presumed atomic 'individuals' with presumed singular selves and identities, but of strangely unpredictable and chaotic selves roaming within and across seemingly solid bodies. George Herbert Mead, Charles Horton Cooley, Herbert Blumer, Erving Goffman, and other founders of the symbolic interactionist school in sociology made great strides in transcending the Newtonian structures of Behaviorist models and theorized and illustrated well how and why the self is important in understanding human social behavior and action. Mead (1934) pointed out how having multiple selves is actually a normal affair in human life. Cooley (1983) clarified so well, by inventing his concept "the looking glass self," how our interaction with others is mediated by how we internally *imagine* being seen and judged by them. Blumer (1986) painstakingly noted how and why subjective meanings and human actions are not entirely predictable but change amid everyday interactions. And Goffman (1990) elucidated the complexity of multiple roles actors take or make in the dramas of everyday lives, illustrating the diverse masks and selves they adopt to perform those roles.

However, paradoxically, the recognition by these theorists that the multiplicity of selves is actually a common affair, and that singular and unfragmented selfhoods and self structures are by no means taken-for-granted facts of life, has not led us to fundamentally question our basic definitions of society and of sociology in transdisciplinary and transcultural fashions. We still regard as helpful separating sociology and psychology, or 'sociological social psychology' from 'psychological social psychology'—and these from other disciplines amid a context of continually divided, two or three academic cultures: the natural sciences, the social sciences, and the humanities (Gulbenkian Commission, 1996). Amid a world culture long dominated by Western notions of science and rationality, alternative Eastern views of self and society are also marginalized and Orientalized as merely 'different' and not worthy of equal, if not more, attention as compared to those of Western models of social inquiry, knowledge, and action.

Still we assume individuals possess singular selves, are the presumed actors who otherwise consciously adopt one or more dramaturgical roles in every day interactions, and only in exceptional (or perhaps extreme clinical) situations such selves are seen as being dissociated, leading to what we regard as multiple personality (or, as nowadays called "dissociative") disorders. Such Western assumptions and modes of viewing society, the self, and sociology, seem to contrast sharply with how in genuine Eastern teachings the multiplicity of selves is assumed as a cornerstone of perspectives on the human organism, life, and development potentials.

In a quantum vision of society, what one presumes to be solid 'individual' bodies turn out to be diverse ensembles of multiple selves. Social relations and interactions, then, actually take place among selves and not presumed 'individual' bodies. These selves could interact within bodies (intrapersonal), interact across bodies (interpersonal), and/ or act out in relation to the natural or built environments (extrapersonal). Hence, social relations within or across bodies would be also regarded, paradoxically, as self-relations, and inner self-relations as ensembles also of social interactions. The distinction between the self and society as supposedly separate chucks of billiard balls of reality is then de/reconstructed in terms of a relation of simultaneity, of identity in difference, or difference in identity. It is the nature of particular forms of social organization that leads us to falsely think our relations to others are not at the same time self-relations, and our relations to ourselves, not at the same time social relations.

Newtonian sociological imaginations tend to conceive of 'diversity' only in interpersonal terms, while quantum sociologies are highly aware also of the inner diversity and multiplicity of seemingly 'solid,' 'self-confident,' and 'self-determining' 'individuals.' The 'individuality' of the 'individual' is presumed, whereas in quantum sociology, it is not; it is perhaps rather considered as an ultimate goal of a life-time's work and spiritual development where the chaos of fragmented and alienated selves are overcome in favor of consciously and intentionally integrated individualities.

Newtonian sociology tends to draw predictable impressions from and conclusions about the seemingly visible and easily distinguishable 'diverse' nature of a given population, such as a classroom. In quantum sociology, no such presumption can be made, since the object of study itself is treated as unpredictable and not predetermined; it postpones judgments regarding the presence or absence of diversity to the specific context of the life of a concrete population or person, and only in relation to the criteria applied to the determination of their diversity. The Newtonian attitude tends to preemptively stereotype a given population as being diverse or not. The quantum attitude is open to surprise, to subtle realities and forms of diversity beneath seemingly 'obvious' uniformities.

In quantum sociological imagination, one could have both black and white selves, male or female selves, abled and disabled selves, while *appearing* to be one or another. In this sociological imagination, a person could be oppressed at work, and yet, at the same time, quite an oppressor at home. One could be poor and rich at the same time. One could be masculine and feminine at the same time. One could be a liberating and a incarcerating teacher at the same time. One could be an attending and an absent student in class at the same time. One could be an absent yet quite involved and attending student at the same time. This approach is different from that of being 'color'-blind, gender-blind, or ability-blind, and so on. It is actually the opposite of such blind considerations of diversity; it brings forth 'race'-sharpness, gender-sharpness, ability-sharpness—as far as the powers of perception and discernment are concerned. Quantum sociology would make one readily acknowledge that belonging to this or that 'race,' class, gender, and ability is a proposition to be proven one way or another, and not presumed in advance. It favors the inductive method whereby *a priori* judgments are always subjected to questioning and critical inquiry. It makes one see what lies beneath, is invisible, and readily dismissed.

My reason for using the term "quantum" to designate the kind of reimagination one can derive from the most significant findings of quantum revolution is to signify the broader implications, both real as well as metaphorical, it has for what Mills calls a new "way of thinking," or as an "intellectual universe" or "style of reflection," for our understanding of the universe, society and ourselves. In other words, as Mills rightly argued that the "way of thinking" in Newtonian physics left a deep and enduring impressions on the development of culture, I similarly use the broad label "quantum" for the new imagination that potentially emerged from the quantum revolution, one that we would and should expect to go beyond a narrow 'physics' disciplinary perspective to acknowledge the deep, enduring, and far-reaching implications the quantum revolution has had (or should have) on the way we think about the world and society, including ourselves. There are other connotations that one can build into the notion of "quantum sociology" or "quantum sociological imagination" that I have previously drawn on and will elucidate further in separate writings to follow this series and for which this series in Khayyami studies offers concrete, empirical illustrations.

As a concluding statement I share Figure 3.1 a way of visualizing the same elements that previously (in Chapter 2, Figure 2.1) were imagined in a Newtonian way by way of the chunky, billiard balls game metaphor. Figure 3.1 illustrates how, by reimagining the elements of the sociological imagination in terms of overlapping and superposing circles, one can arrive at a non-dualistic, both/and, conception of elements that was previously imagined in terms of a formal, either/or logic. Personal troubles are a part of public issues, inner life a part of external careers, observer a part of the study, implicated by both his or her own personal troubles and time's public issues.

I have left the outlines for the spheres of world-history and contemporary society/world-system in broken lines simply to indicate the openness of including broader natural and cosmic spheres. However, since the purpose of this visualization is at this point mainly that of contrasting the non-dualistic, quantum sociological imagination with the Newtonian imagination of the same as depicted before in Figure 2.1, I have chosen simply to limit the verbal designations of the various spheres to the comparative purpose at hand.

The reader can notice that a separate visual designation of personal troubles that are supposedly not relevant to the public issues have been eliminated from the preceding figure, suggesting that for the purpose of advancing quantum sociological imaginations all personal troubles should be devoted similar degree and sensitivity of attention as subject matters of research. The same can be noticed regarding public issues.

The overlapping nature of the graphic depiction allows for the public issues to be considered as being simultaneously influenced by specific contemporary as well as wider world-historical contexts. Similarly, the intersecting spheres of the observer agency carrying out quantum sociological reimaginative research is regarded as an inescapable part of her own research, implicating both self-reflections on her own personal troubles and contextual public issues of his or her own time while conducting imaginative quantum sociological research on other persons, groups, or any subject matter.

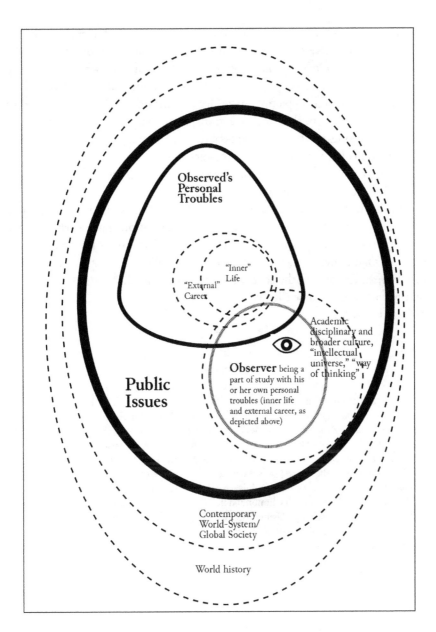

Figure 3.1

Visual Representations of the Quantum Way of Thinking about
the Sociological Imagination

The intersection of the observer and the observed elements in the reimagination is itself significant, implying that one cannot mechanically separate the knowledge gained about the subject matter while (mis)using labels such as "objectivity" when such intersections are inevitable. This points to the overall depiction of desired quantum notion and practice of objectivity where one has to, in a transparent, engaging, and self-critical way, include oneself in the subject matter of research and attain a broader sense of objectivity that can explain, rather than sweep under the rug of advertent or inadvertent omission, whatever biases or points of view that may be motivating and shaping his or her research.

In the next and last chapter of this first book of the series I will try to note the implications the quantum sociological imagination framework can have for pursuing our Khayyami studies. In doing so, I will relax the assumptions we have maintained so far regarding the availability of our resources in this research, and regarding the absence of the important element of secretiveness on the part of the Omar Khayyam whose life and works is the subject matter of such research.

Abstract

This essay, titled "Quantum Sociological Imagination as A Framework for Khayyami Studies," is the third chapter of the first book, subtitled *New Khayyami Studies: Quantumizing the Newtonian Structures of C. Wright Mills's Sociological Imagination for A New Hermeneutic Method*, of the twelve-book series, *Omar Khayyam's Secret: Hermeneutics of the Robaiyat in Quantum Sociological Imagination,* authored by Mohammad H. Tamdgidi.

In the chapter, the author offers a historical overview of how classical Newtonianism as a product of an historical compromise between a receding religiosity and an emerging secularism in the West met its limits and fell into crisis when confronted with the new findings of quantum science. Using the same eight-fold model he used to describe the attributes of the Newtonian way of thinking, Tamdgidi suggests that the quantum way of imagining reality can also be characterized as having eight sets of attributes: 1- Simultaneity (not "duality," nor "complementarity"); 2-Superpositionality; 3-Inseparability; 4-Relativity (subject-included objectivity); 5-Probability; 6-Transcontinuity (which is a term he prefers to call what is commonly referred to as "discontinuity"); 7-Transdisciplinarity

In Tamdgidi's view, we have to always distinguish between *three* kinds of Newtonianism: *classical, incompletely relativistic,* and *completely relativistic.* The *classical* Newtonianism universalizes the eight attributes as listed earlier. The *incompletely* relativistic Newtonianism is the kind prevalent today, confused, enigmatized, still not freed from the classical bounds but not yet fully embracing attributes that it could have independently discovered for itself, ones that it would have found to be "completely" resonating with the quantum science findings (itself stripped of elements contributive to the quantum enigma, such as the "wave-particle duality," "Complementarity Principle," and so on). For the *completely* relativistic Newtonianism he has coined (2020) the term *Quantum Newtonianism*. It is a Newtonianism that treats the reality from the standpoint of any observer's reference frame to be a local reference frame or fold of the broader quantum reality as a whole.

The author suggests that quantumizing the Newtonian in favor of a quantum sociological imagination invites the following considerations regarding each of which he offers illustrations, and from each of which he draws inspiration, about how Khayyami studies can be framed. 1. Relating personal troubles and public issues: from dualism to simultaneity (not "duality," nor "complementarity"); 2. Relating personal troubles (or not) of many selves: from atomism to superpositionality; 3. Relating public issues world-historically: from separability to inseparability; 4. Relating the sociological imaginations of others to those of ourselves: from subjectless objectivity to relativity (subject-included objectivity); 5. Reimagining causal patterns creatively: from determinism to probability; 6. Reimagining causal chains also as causal leaps: from continuity to "transcontinuity" (also known as "discontinuity"); 7. Reimagining sociology: from disciplinarity to transdisciplinarity; and 8. Reimagining science: from Eurocentrism to tansculturalism.

Tamdgidi illustrates in a figure how, by reimagining the elements of the sociological imagination in terms of overlapping and superposing circles, one can arrive at a non-dualistic, both/and, conception of elements that previously could only be imagined in terms of a formal, either/or logic. He argues that using the notion of "Khayyami" as a reference both to the person and to the tradition associated with him can offer a sociologically imaginative quantum device involving a language of simultaneity when referring to Omar Khayyam's life, works, and legacy—especially when it comes to the study of the attributed Robaiyat—one that can have significant methodological, substantive, and practical consequences for framing and conducting our Khayyami studies.

CHAPTER IV—Hermeneutics of the Khayyami Robaiyat in Quantum Sociological Imagination: Source Availability and Matters of Secrecy

The prior three chapters of this first book of the *Omar Khayyam's Secret* series were devoted to developing a quantum sociological imagination framework for conducting our Khayyami studies. As noted earlier, to facilitate such an effort, we assumed until now a research undertaking with no limitations regarding the availability or secretiveness of sources. After all, we could still use the quantum sociological imagination framework for any study for which textual sources are abundant and their authors have made considerable efforts in making their intentions and findings transparent and readily accessible in their works.

In our Khayyami studies, however, we cannot assume such perfect research conditions. On the contrary, we are confronted with formidable limitations and difficulties. On one hand, we have the contextually imposed limitations on the availability of resources, even if we assume that our author made perfect efforts at writing transparently, straightforwardly, and accessibly. On the other hand, our task is made even more difficult by more or less perceived efforts at secretiveness on the part of our author himself.

Relaxing our prior assumptions and abstractions from such problems, therefore, I will now try in this last chapter of the first book to elaborate in more detail on both of the above challenges confronting Khayyami studies.

1. The Availability of Sources on Omar Khayyam

We wish to understand, as definitively as possible, the life and works of a man who was born in or around Neyshabour, in the present day Iran's northeast province of Khorasan, sometime during the 11th century AD, and who died sometime around the first quarter of the 12th century AD, buried somewhere in or around Neyshabour. His name included Omar and Khayyam or Khayyami, both latter versions having been expressed in his Persian as well as Arabic prose. He was the son of a man named Ibrahim.

What information do we have about the life and works of this man?

My purpose in this section is to draw a preliminary and basic outline of the sources of information available (or not) for our research. My aim at this point is not to delve into the historical, bibliographic, or manuscript conditions or the extent of authenticity of these sources. Those details will be carefully introduced, examined, and evaluated during the substantive explorations of this series in conjunction with careful studies of their contents.

The reason I wish not to go into details here is that such details can themselves be subjected to doubt and in need of reconsideration, and this cannot be done without careful and in-depth substantive explorations of these texts amid the concrete research to which they pertain. Even the times they were written or when they were discovered can be subject to doubts, new insights, and renewed studies, so it would be premature for us to delve too much into the details about them at this point in an *a priori* way. We simply want to draw a very broad working sketch of what types of material we have at hand so that we can determine the basic orientation of our research strategy to be conducted in a quantum sociological imagination framework.

We can broadly categorize the types of attributed information we have received about Khayyam's life and works, be their contents truthful or not (such as references made to Khayyam about having had this or that title, this or that name, or this or that character trait), in part or as a whole as far as each source is concerned, into five basic source categories: 1) primary, 2) secondary, 3) tertiary, 4) architectural, and 5) burial.

1. Primary Sources: Texts That Are Attributed, Unanimously or Not, to Omar Khayyam Himself

Regarding the category of primary works Khayyam himself wrote during his lifetime, that is, the remains of him surviving in textual form, we can consider four possible subcategories (which I will label as A, B, C, and D).

Before identifying these four subcategories, we should note that the texts written down by Khayyam and surviving in these sources may have been subjected to errors, additions, deletions, revisions, and modifications at the hands of copyists down the centuries, as well as corruptions which could have also resulted inadvertently from deteriorations of the materials used to copy these texts. It is one thing to find sources directly written in Khayyam's own handwriting and/or explicitly authorized and signed by him, and another to find sources that, despite containing his writings, have been (re)copied by others in one or more successive steps, not necessarily all coming from one original source, but one copy branching from another and that from yet another, and so on, as it could happen given the traditional ways manuscripts were reproduced and distributed in the distant past.

Say, an original was copied down clearly enough, but by the time it reached the next copyist a century or so later, it was partially corrupted to the point where the new copyist had to guess what the original passage was, so he copied it down in a way that to the next copyist not too far removed in time it appeared as if it was perfectly legible and correct, offered in a "very clean" copy, but the second copy hid a corruption based on a misreading of a deteriorated copy previously surviving.

Such corruptions may be (or not) reversible interpretively, by reexamining the problem passages in light of the meaning of the text as a whole or other reliable texts or a view traceable to Khayyam himself, or by comparing other extant copies of the same text to confirm, first, the fact that indeed a passage was subjected to corruption and, second, requiring a reexamination of the passage concerned in favor of uncovering the originally intended version. We may, or not, end up with varying degrees of reliability of interpretation of the corrupted passages depending on the extent to which we succeed in deciphering and understanding their original contents. However, the very fact that comparisons of multiple copies of the same text point to the possible corruptions and the unreliability of a given passage can itself be significant in our efforts at understanding the surviving textual remains of Omar Khayyam.

Another preliminary consideration has to do with our awareness of the overlapping nature of the four subcategories I am about to list, compared to regarding them as entirely separate or separable billiard balls of knowledge about our subject.

By the above I mean, while some primary sources may be in full attributed to Khayyam, some may have been discovered as parts of works by others. For instance, we have a work by Khayyam on mechanical scale or balance (used to discover the amount of precious materials in jewels without having to disassemble them), because it was incorporated as an excerpt in another work by Abdorrahman Khazeni, who is reported to have been a student of Khayyam. We will include such a section in that source among the primary sources on Khayyam.

However, in contrast, I will not include passages from others in which Omar Khayyam is quoted as saying one thing or another. This does not necessarily imply questioning or doubting the validity of what Khayyam was quoted as saying, or about dismissing secondary sources on Khayyam in general, but about making a classificatory distinction between our primary and secondary (and other) sources in order to define more carefully the parameters of this research project.

The following can be regarded as the four subcategories of the primary sources on Omar Khayyam.

A) As a first subcategory of primary sources, we can include works that Khayyam may have written, intended to be shared or not during his own lifetime or posthumously, of which we do not yet have any records whatever.

We are justified in establishing this subcategory because we have examples (which I will identify later) of sources that had not been mentioned at all by a biographical commentator about Khayyam, but they were actually known to exist or surface later; and by that I do not mean only the case of Khayyam's attributed Robaiyat. In this subcategory I am *not* including any texts yet to be found to which Khayyam himself refers in his writing, of whose contents we do not (yet) have any knowledge; I will consider that a second subcategory. Rather, I am speaking here of sources he may have written of which we do not have any knowledge whatever, not even a name or title.

What Khayyam wrote were subject to the unfolding of historical events, as well as physical survival and discovery, not to mention his own intention to publicize them, or not. Khayyam may have written material, for personal use or intended for others, that were destroyed in the course of devastating upheavals or nomadic invasions or earthquakes that befell Neyshabour (or places where he had kept copies during his travels) during the decades and centuries following his death. Or, they may have survived but have not yet been discovered in old manuscript libraries around the world (such as in today's Turkey, India, or Pakistan), bearing his name or remaining unattributed or unsigned due to the fragmented or corrupted nature of the surviving manuscripts.

B) As a second subcategory of primary sources, we can include works specifically reported by Khayyam (as acknowledged also by others) to have been written by him on definite topics from which we do not (yet) have any complete or definitively labeled "partial" manuscripts. Whether the above sources are lost or not is uncertain as they may still exist in old manuscript libraries or personal collections somewhere and not yet been discovered.

Khayyam is known to have written treatises on the following topics. The expressions in italics are the abbreviations I may sometimes use throughout this series to refer to the sources for the sake of brevity. Also note that the titles given here and thereafter are those customarily used for the works, and in the course of our hermeneutic study they may become subject to revision.

- *On Arithmetic*

رسالة فى مشكلات الحساب

[Resalat fi Moshkelat ol-Hesab (Treatise on the Problems of Arithmetic)]; apparently written originally in Arabic.

- *On Nature*

رسالة مختصر فى الطبيعيّات

[Resalat Mokhtasar fi al-Tabiiyat (Brief Treatise on Nature)]; apparently written originally in Arabic.

- *On Geography (or Topography)*

رسالة فى لوازم الامكنه

[Resalat fi Lavazem ol-Amkaneh (Treatise on the Requirements of Locations)]; apparently written originally in Arabic. Note: This may have been a commentary on climatic conditions associated with natural locations.

- *On Music*

شرح المشكل من كتاب الموسيقى

[Sharh ol-Moshkel men Ketab al-Moosiqi (Explanation of a Problem in the Book of Music)]

Note: This manuscript is to be distinguished from a shorter essay on music, one that has survived (listed further below) and which may (or not) be a part of the above broader work on music. Khayyam's fuller study seems to have been a commentary on the "Book of Music," an important work by the Persian Islamic philosopher Abu Nasr Farabi ("Second Teacher").

C) A third subcategory of primary sources includes the surviving works bearing Khayyam's name that are universally and generally regarded as having been authored by him. Some of these have reached us in seemingly complete form, and some in parts.

On Philosophy and Religion:

• *On the Universals of Existence*

رساله در علم کلیّات وجود

[Resaleh dar Elm-e Kolliyat-e Vojood (Treatise on the Science of the Universals of Existence)], originally written in Persian. This treatise has also been referred to as follows:

درخواست نامه

[Darkhast Nameh ("Requested Letter")]

رساله ی سلسله الترتیب

[Resaleh-ye Selselat ol-Tartib (Treatise on the Succession Order)]

رسالة فی کلیات الوجود

[Resalat fi Kolliyat ol-Vojood (Treatise on the Universals of Existence)]; this is how the title has been expressed in Arabic, even though we know the work was originally written in Persian.

• *On Avicenna's Sermon*

ترجمه ی خطبه ی قرّای ابن سینا

[Tarjomeh-ye Khotbeh-ye Qarra-ye Ebn-e Sina (Translation of the Splendid Sermon of Avicenna)]; this is Khayyam's own commented translation from Arabic into Persian, per request of his colleagues, of an important sermon on God by Avicenna.

• *On Universe and Obligation*

رسالة فی الکون و التکلیف

[Resalat fi al-Kown wa al-Taklif (Treatise on Universe and Obligation) which can also be expressed as (Treatise on the Created World and the Duty to Worship)] originally written in Arabic.

• *On Contradiction, Fate, and Survival*

جواب عن ثلاث مسائل: ضرورت التضادّ فی العالم و الجبر و البقاء

[Jawab an Salasa Masael: Zarurat al-Tazadd fi al-Alam wa al-Jabr wa al-Baqa (Answer to Three Questions: The Necessity of Contradiction in the World, Fate, and Survival)], originally written in Arabic.

• *On the Attributes of Existents*

رسالة فى الوجود

[Resalat fi al-Vojood (Treatise on Existence) or (Treatise on the Attributes of Existents)], originally written in Arabic. This work should not be confused with the Persian treatise on the universals of existence listed earlier; it is, rather, a discourse on the attributes of existents.

• *On the Light of Intellect*

رسالة الضياء العقلى فى موضوع العلم الكلّى

[Resalat al-Zia ol-Aqli fi Mozoo el-Elm al-Kolli (Treatise on the Light of Intellect on the Subject of Universal Science)], originally written in Arabic. This title is not exactly given as such in the original, but is a title that was given by a collection editor in modern times and from then on customarily used by others for the treatise.

• *On Resurrection, Possibility, and Motion*

رسالة جواب لثلث مسائل

[Resalat Jawaban le-Solse Masael (Treatise on Response to Three Problems (Resurrection, Possibility, and Motion))] which focuses on the three topics: resurrection, possibility, and motion. It was originally written in Arabic.

On the Sciences of Geometry, Mathematics, and Algebra:

• *On Circle Quadrant*

رسالة فى قسمت ربع الدايره

[Resalat fi Qesmat Rob al-Dayereh (Treatise on the Division of a Circle Quadrant)], originally written in Arabic. In this work, Khayyam notes his intention to write a major treatise on algebra later on, which he did (see below).

• *On Algebra and Equations*

[Resalat fi al-Baraheen ala Masael al-Jabr wa al-Moqabeleh (Treatise on the Proofs of the Problems of Algebra and Equations)], originally written in Arabic.

• *On Euclid*

رسالة فى شرح من اشكل ما مصادرات كتاب اقليدس

[Resalat fi Sharh ma Eshkala men Mosaderat Ketab Oqlidos

(Treatise on the Explanation of Problems of Postulates in Euclid's Book)], originally written in Arabic.

On the Science of Mechanics:

- *On the Mechanical Balance*

رسالة فى احتيال لمعرفت مقادير الذهب و الفضه فى جسم مركّب منهما

[Resalat fi Ehtial le-Marefat Maqadir al-Zahab wa al-Fezzah fi Jesme Morakkab Menhoma (Treatise on the Art of Defining Quantities of Gold and Silver in a Body Consisting of Them)]. This work written in Arabic has survived as a section inserted in the Book *Mizan ol-Hekmat (Balance of Wisdom)* by Abdorrahman Khazeni who was reportedly a student of Khayyam. The section by Khayyam added to the collection has also been referred to as "Resalat fi al-Qestas ol-Mostaqim (رسالة فى القسطاس المستقيم), which seems to be in reference to the name Khayyam gives to his proposed scale.

On the Science of Music:

- *On Music*

القول على اجناس الذى بالاربعة

[al-Qowl ala Ajnas al-Lazi be al-Arbaat (Statement on the Four-Fold Types)]; this essay on music, originally written in Arabic, may be a part of what Khayyam refers in another work (on Euclid) to have authored on music, one that has not yet been discovered. Since we do not know if this is a part of that fuller work, I also include it in this subcategory of primary sources.

On Society and Culture:

- *Nowrooznameh (The Book on Nowrooz)*

نوروزنامه: رساله در کشف حقیقت نوروز

[Nowrooznameh: Resaleh dar Kashf-e Haqiqat-e Nowrooz (Nowrooznameh (The Book on Nowrooz): Treatise on Discovering the Truth of Nowrooz)]; this manuscript includes an introduction that clearly attributes it to Omar Khayyam. Note: There has been no claim made or found in any manuscript that this work was associated with or authored by anyone else. In my view, disputes regarding its authenticity, which deserve consideration, do not justify excluding it from the primary sources attributed to Omar

Khayyam. Whether or not it is Khayyam's must be a result of its careful examination, and not based on any *a priori* judgment about its attribution to the historical Omar Khayyam.

On Astronomy:

• *Ephemeris Table*

زیج ملکشاهی

[Zeej-e Malekshahi (Malekshahi Ephemeris)]
Note: A short table, single-page long, has survived regarding the map of fixed stars, that has been attributed to the astronomical works of Omar Khayyam who led and/or was a part of a team of astronomers appointed, during the reign of the Seljuk king Soltan Malekshah, to reform the Persian solar calendar. I include this source in this subcategory C of primary sources since it is representative of the primary sources reporting the astronomical activities in which Khayyam had been involved, but about which no other substantial material *in manuscript form* has survived. Khayyam's role in building an (incomplete) observatory in Isfahan, and in reforming the Persian solar calendar has not been doubted.

On Astrology:

• *Problems in Astrology: I think is from Omar Khayyam*

مسایل نجومیّه اظنها من کلام عمر الخیامی

[Masael Nojoomiyeh Azennaha men Kalam Omar al-Khayyami (Problems in Astrology: I Think These From the Words of Omar Khayyam)] A manuscript in Arabic titled as such in the text itself has survived, including questions and answers on astrological topics, attributed to Omar Khayyam. It has generally been ignored, given the manuscript itself is titled in a way that implies a lack of certainty regarding its attributability to Khayyam, and given that scholars have long viewed, based on reading other secondary materials, that Khayyam did not ascribe to astrological beliefs. However, we include it among our sources for further consideration, rather than dismiss it in an *a priori* way.

Poetry:

• *Arabic and Persian Poems (Other than the Robaiyat)*

اشعار فارسی و عربی

Several poems (aside from the Robaiyat) in Arabic or Persian have been undisputedly attributed to Omar Khayyam.

D) The Khayyami Robaiyat:

رباعیّات خیّامی

The Robaiyat (quatrains) attributed to Omar Khayyam. Many quatrains written in Persian have been attributed to Khayyam in various manuscripts down the centuries, their numbers varying in each collection, from a handful to many hundreds. I include this item as a separate, fourth, subcategory of primary sources using the title "Khayyami Robaiyat," because, while the quatrains are attributed to Khayyam, their attributability has been subject to doubt among scholars. So, they could be his, or not, so deserving their own subcategory in the primary sources. Besides, there are at times several renderings of the same quatrain, which may indicate the corruption of the original poem across the hands of multiple copyists who for reasons, advertent or not, modified what original they had received. It is also possible to consider that in an original draft, Khayyam may have jotted down different versions of the same quatrain, as it happens when any author writes down various versions of his or her poems in draft form; so, if the draft fell into others' hands as such, they may have seen even in the originals from Khayyam differently expressed versions of the same quatrain. Treating these quatrains as "primary sources" does not necessarily imply the authenticity of any specific quatrain or any specific rendering of it. Questions surrounding the so-called "wandering quatrains," i.e., quatrains that have been found in other poets' works are also relevant and deserve consideration in our research.

2. Secondary Sources: Old Accounts of Others about Khayyam's Life and Works

Among the secondary sources, the following four subcategories can be distinguished from one another (also labeled as A, B, C, and D). Note that the examples offered in each subcategory are not exhaustive at all, so other items may be included or be found to belong to each subcategory, especially in later time periods, as part of our Khayyami studies in general.

A) Accounts of Khayyam's life and/or works shared by his living contemporaries who had, or reported to have had, in one way or another, direct contact with him. In this subcategory, three sources will be of particular relevance to our Khayyami studies.

One source is the book *Tatemmat Sewan el-Hekmat (Supplement to the Chest of Wisdom)*, written in Arabic by Zahireddin Abolhasan Beyhaqi, who reports having met as a child the elder Khayyam. This book is a very important source of brief biographical information about the intellectuals of Khayyam's period.

Another source is the book *Chahar Maqaleh (Four Discourses)*, also known as *Majma ol-Anvar (Sum of Lights)*, by Nezami Arouzi, written originally in Persian, who regarded himself as a pupil of Khayyam (actually or in reverence), and met him as an adult. In the book, Arouzi offers several reflections on Khayyam that have been of particular relevance to Khayyami studies.

A third source is what Abdorrahman Khazeni, a pupil of Khayyam, tells us about him along with an essay he includes from Khayyam in a compilation on the topic of scales, *Mizan ol-Hekmat (Balance of Wisdom)*. He knew Khayyam as a pupil and as an adult had personal contacts with him.

B) Accounts of Khayyam's life and/or works by his living contemporaries with or without any (claimed or reported) direct contact with him, where we may expect but do not find explicit references to Khayyam.

I am including this subcategory of secondary sources for situations where we may have living contemporaries of Khayyam whom we expect to have said or written something about Khayyam of which we apparently have no record.

I am particularly considering here reported interactions the famous theologian-turned-Sufi Abu Hamed Muhammad Ghazali had with Omar Khayyam, but in Ghazali's own writings, Khayyam is not specifically named, but implied references to "philosophers" such as Khayyam abound.

By introducing this subcategory, I am suggesting that simply because living contemporaries of Khayyam do not *explicitly* refer to him should not prevent us from considering that their writings may include implied references to Khayyam, whose verifiability must be also subject to hermeneutic analysis.

C) Accounts or pieces of information about Khayyam's life and/or works by contemporaries without any (claimed or reported) direct contact with him.

I include this subcategory of secondary sources for hypothetical situations where we may have living contemporaries of Khayyam writing about him without having personally met him. Whether or not we actually have sources in this subcategory may be subject to research and further investigation.

A plausible source in this subcategory may be that of a personal letter written by the mystic and poet of the period, Sanai Ghaznavi, seeking Khayyam's assistance in resolving a personal legal matter. Not knowing whether Sanai had actually met Khayyam should not prevent us from including his letter as a secondary source of this type on Khayyam.

D) Posthumous accounts of Khayyam's life and/or works by others shared down the centuries before the publication of the first edition of Edward FitzGerald's "free translations" of Omar Khayyam in 1859.

The reason I am marking historical periods in Khayyami studies in terms of Edward FitzGerald's work on Khayyam has to do with the observation that sources written before FitzGerald, or found later but dated to the period before him, can offer us important insight about the substantive authenticity of the source in relation to the influence FitzGerald's work exerted on subsequent Khayyami studies.

In this subcategory, which covers the entire long historical period since Khayyam's passing in early 12th century AD to the mid 19th century, we can find a series of short or longer manuscripts referring to Khayyam's life or works, and including material such as his quatrains.

An important source and example is *Tarabkhaneh (House of Joy)*, by Yar Ahmad Rashidi Tabrizi. It is an important collection of hundreds of quatrains attributed to Omar Khayyam, accompanied by reported stories, factual or not, told by others about Khayyam's life and works.

3. Tertiary Sources: Modern and Recent Accounts of Khayyam's Life and Works

This subcategory of secondary sources includes accounts of Khayyam's life and/or works shared in the post-FitzGeraldian era (after 1859) up to the publication of the present series.

This subcategory includes basically anything newly written about Khayyam in modern and recent times ever since the publication of FitzGerald's translation of his quatrains, including those by the translator. Obviously, a vast literature falls in this subcategory.

Again, disputes surrounding the nature of FitzGerald's renderings of Khayyam's "Rubaiyat" should not prevent us from considering the turning point the publication of his free translations marked in modern times regarding the rediscovery and reimagination of Khayyam's life and works in the eyes of the West and as a result of its subsequent influence on the global and domestic Iranian studies and imaginations of Khayyam's life, works, and legacy in general.

4-Khayyam's Architectural Works

A fourth category, physical in nature, that may be worth establishing, whether or not we find examples of them, are any architectural remains from Khayyam's time that may bear some influence from his life and works.

For instance, it has been widely reported and remains undisputed that Khayyam was involved in the construction of an observatory in Isfahan, one that reportedly remained "incomplete." Well, "incomplete" means that some parts were completed and some were not. So, the question can be legitimately raised as to where the "completed" parts of the "incomplete" buildings were or are, if still standing. In other words, there is no reason for us to readily dismiss the possibility of such "incomplete" works still remaining, even though we may not have definitive proof, yet, whether their designs or constructions were influenced by Khayyam's life and works.

This is especially important regarding the complex known as Masjed Jame in Isfahan. Constructed in major parts during the reign of Soltan Malekshah, when Nezam ol-Molk was his chief minister, this complex may still contain at least in part some remains from the observatory that was reportedly left incomplete, one in whose construction Khayyam is reported to have definitively participated. Recent Turkish studies in architectural history of the complex have in particular pointed to aspects of the design and measurements of the part of the complex referred to as the Northern Dome whose high quality and precision required exact geometrical and mathematical skills said to have been possessed at the time only by a scientist of Khayyam's caliber.

We will need to explore this topic further as part of our research in this series.

5-Khayyam's Burial Remains

Although it may not offer any significant verificatory information for the kind of research conducted in this series, as a matter of principle we should also consider a fifth category of sources involving Khayyam's remains existing in physical form.

His burial material and his own body's remains, for instance, whatever is left of him, in any of the graves historically dedicated to him, may offer some information about him, whether or not we choose to pursue investigating them. The information existing, or not, on any reported tombstone(s), may also be important in telling us something about what information others had or not about Khayyam (for instance, the dates of birth or death given, or not, on his gravestone).

Religious constraints notwithstanding and in light of advances made in modern science today (or to be made in the future), where highly precise and exact findings have resulted from the application of genetic and MRI-equipped research on ancient burial remains, Khayyam's own remains could certainly offer, if they still exist and are proven to be actually his, some information about his genetic ancestry, and offer possibilities to discover more about him in the near or distant future. But such studies will be unlikely given religious and practical constraints.

For the purpose of this research, I will include Khayyam's gravestone markings (or absence thereof) as part of the sources, while setting aside the question of examination of his body remains for being obviously impossible at this point and outside the scope of this investigation.

2. Prioritization and Superpositions of Available Sources on Khayyam

Laying aside for now the fourth and fifth (physical) categories noted above, we have basically three, primary, secondary, and tertiary categories of manuscript sources available on Omar Khayyam, some differentiated broadly within as subcategorized above for the purpose of this research.

Given the above broad categorization of our available sources, what research strategy should we adopt, as framed by the quantum sociological imagination, to arrive at the most reliable and definitive understanding of the life and works of Omar Khayyam?

Clearly, the most reliable strategy must be one that lays the most emphasis on the primary material as the source of the most reliable information about the subject matter at hand. Next, we will need to definitely give priority to the secondary sources relative to the tertiary sources available on Khayyam.

However, the separation of primary, secondary, and even tertiary sources should not be absolutized, nor their distinction ignored. The information derived from each of the three categories can shed light on those derived from the other, so while I will establish the basic organization of this investigation on the basic of the examination of primary sources, in the course of their careful examination I will not refrain from considering relevant secondary and tertiary sources while, at all times, maintaining a clear evaluative preference for the value of primary compared to the secondary and tertiary sources.

Considering the primary sources and their four-fold subcategorizations listed above (A through D), while recognizing that there may be little available for our study in the first and second subcategories—namely the material Khayyam may have written about which we have no or little knowledge at hand—the central problem explored in this series narrows down to investigating the relationship between the third subcategory C, that is, the generally regarded philosophical, religious, scientific, and literary writings of Khayyam, on one hand, and the surviving material broadly known as the Khayyami Robaiyat in subcategory D, on the other.

As explained previously, I will use the rubric "Khayyami" as a quantum device, a designation for any robai (quatrain) that has been attributed to Khayyam in the past, regardless of the authenticity of its attribution. The superposed meaning of "Khayyami" can also be used for other pieces of writing, where the question of the authenticity of a text is not absolutely settled, allowing us to treat it as a legitimate site for further exploration.

The central question of the research, in other words, rests on the extent to which we succeed, or not, in discovering definitive *intersections* between the more or less reliably authentic writings of Khayyam in the third subcategory C and the Khayyami Robaiyat in the fourth subcategory D of primary sources. However, we should not lose sight of the doubts cast by some scholars regarding the authenticity, in part or as a whole, of *Nowrooznameh (The Book on Nowrooz)*, in relation to other authentic writings of Khayyam in the third subcategory C, and, by implication, its relation to the Khayyami Robaiyat in the fourth subcategory D.

We are basically confronted with the overall research task of investigating possible intersections, or absence thereof, between Khayyam's philosophical, religious, and scientific writings (plus his few poems written in Persian and Arabic, whose attributions are not generally disputed) and his *Nowrooznameh* on one hand, and between them both and the Khayyami Robaiyat subcategory, on the other hand. The triangular nature of the links to be investigated among the primary sources of Khayyam (the Khayyami Robaiyat, *Nowrooznameh*, and the rest of his authentic writings) thus becomes evident and paramount.

To put the matter differently, we have a spectrum of three sets of texts: on one side stands the most authentic writings of Khayyam (the philosophical, religious, scientific, and a few Arabic or Persian poetic writings), and on the opposite side the most disputed body of quatrains which we will broadly call the Khayyami Robaiyat, and in the middle standing Khayyam's

Nowrooznameh which is undisputedly attributed to Khayyam in the text itself, but for one reason or another some scholars still dispute its being in part or as a whole authored by him.

What this means is that our research task in its broadest sense involves an effort in exploring the links among all of Khayyam's primary sources, with a particular focus on the triangular relation between the Khayyami Robaiyat, *Nowrooznameh*, and the rest of Khayyam's primary writings.

In considering the above, however, we should note three issues.

First, we will have to always keep in mind the first (A) and second (B) subcategories of the primary sources, even though we have little of them available. In other words, if someone says Khayyam did not write much, and the observer, when passing such a judgment, does not list many writing that we know for sure he did write, we are justified in considering that such judgments cannot be made regarding Khayyam's volume of writing without definitively ascertaining whether he actually did not write other material.

Second, on the side of the most authentic writings, we will have to inescapably deal with the internal links between the philosophical, religious and scientific writings as well as the relation of both to Khayyam's few authentically regarded Arabic or Persian poems.

Third, the triangular primary sources are themselves also in need of investigation in relation to all the subcategories of the four-fold secondary material and other tertiary sources at hand as classified earlier.

It is the totality of triangular investigations within and across the primary sources amid wider secondary and tertiary categories, in other words, that will yield most fruit, while always keeping in mind that in this totality, the explanatory and determinative weight of the primary over the secondary (and tertiary) sources should never be overlooked and compromised.

In Figure 4.1, I provide a visual map of the various categories and subcategories of sources to be considered for our study of Khayyam's life and works. I am adopting a superposed, non-dualistic, part-whole dialectical schema in the form of overlapping circles for the depiction of sources mapped onto the substantive areas covered by Khayyam, in order to offer a transdisciplinary imagination of the sources at hand.

As depicted in the figure, God, or the Necessary Existence, may be distinguished from universal "substance" (*johar*) emanating from God, comprised of cosmic, natural, social, and social psychological realms, to which may be associated Khayyam's philosophical, religious, scientific, literary-social, and literary-poetic writings respectively.

The whole-part dialectical schema, however, helps highlight the fact that in each text as broadly distinguished from one another, one may find implied intersections across all the spheres of existence including God, cosmos, earth/nature, society, and psychology, recognizing states of simultaneity across them, where one dimension at the same time superposes with other dimensions. In a quatrain, for instance, all the above spheres may be implied and engaged. And, the same can be said about any of the texts attributed to Khayyam.

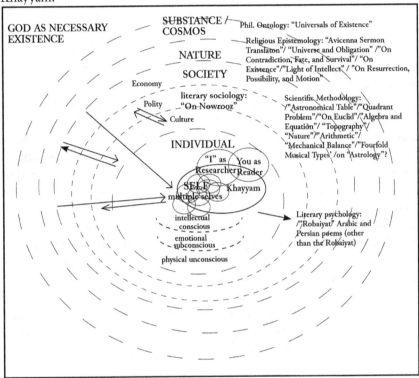

Figure 4.1

Khayyami Studies' Sources Mapped Onto the Substantive
Whole-Part Dialectical Schema

As another instance, in his treatise on *The Universals of Existence*, Khayyam immediately links his conception of the cosmic order of intellects, souls, and spheres, to numbers (and thus mathematics) to human nature and society, and the human individual, his thoughts, feelings, and bodily desires, then moving on to humankind's "duties" of self-purification as epistemological grounds for seeking the truth of God and existence— implying an integral and integrating conception of the spiritual, cosmic, natural, social, individual, and psychological folds. Consequently, one can also map the seemingly fragmented attributed writings surviving (or not) from or about Khayyam, as shedding diverse lights on his works expressing his evolving views on God and the universe on one hand, and on Khayyam's reflections on his own life and biography, on the other.

Note the spheres I have included at the center, superposed with all the wider spheres, representing the life and efforts of the researcher and the reader, such as me and you. Following the sociology of self-knowledge as the framework informing the quantum sociological imagination as outlined in previous chapters, such a depiction is necessary.

In other words, it is important to consider that, besides me as the author, you, as the reader, are also an integral part of this Khayyami study once you become interested and partake in absorbing and evaluating what is being communicated to you. So, from a reimagined quantum sociological framework, your own personal troubles and the public issues of your time and place as experienced by you will also have more or less significant impact on how you absorb and digest, agree or disagree with, regard as important or not, like or not, what is presented in the series. For this reason, I have also included a sphere at the center, superposed with others and partly with the researcher's sphere, to depict such a dimension of the Khayyami study. The same as noted above also applies to me as the researcher of this account.

Note also that, following our quantum sociological imagination framework, a Khayyami quatrain is no longer an isolated ball to be separately juggled and explored in relation to other balls or spheres of information on Khayyam. In the superposed architecture of the view of sources as depicted in Figure 4.1, even when confronting Khayyam's writings on God, on existence, on science, algebra, astronomy, or music, or creative writings on a Persian new year's ceremony such as Nowrooz, even his birth horoscope, we should expect to be also exploring, in their corresponding spheres of analysis, engagements with the substance or even perhaps forms of his poetry.

The converse is also the case, that is, in any Khayyami quatrain we may be able to explore and inquire about Khayyam's views on God, existence, science, algebra, astronomy, astrology, music, or sociological commentaries on cultural, economic, or political matters.

We will therefore not treat all the various categories and subcategories as chunky, separate balls to be struck with one another from without, but will approach them in such a way that despite their apparently fragmented state, they are imagined as being folds of a life in progress, works produced along a lifetime, and commentaries made by others on his life and works amid a wider world-history, cosmic, and spiritual contexts they all share.

Our textual analysis will thereby involve at its heart a restitching effort in a quantum sociological imagination framework to reestablish part-whole dialectics in the study of Khayyam's life and works.

3. Khayyami Studies and the Hermeneutic Method

The study of Omar Khayyam is essentially an effort in textual analysis.

What adds a strong hermeneutic dimension to such a textual investigation is a perception, itself subject to verification, that there are conscious and intentional efforts being made on the part of the author (here, Omar Khayyam) to disguise or withhold certain meanings through diverse compositional strategies. Even if only one or another part of the totality of texts to be studied involve such secretive, symbolic strategies of writing (which should include also, intentional *not*-writing or *not*-teaching to the extent expected by others, which then become misinterpreted by them in terms of an author or teacher being "miserly" in writing and teaching), we are justified in considering the project at hand to be one that strongly requires a hermeneutic approach for its decipherment.

As I noted early on in this first book of the series, the addition of the element of secrecy, which may either be a contingent factor in the message being conveyed or essential to it in a pre-meditated way, poses a three-fold question for any research at hand in addition to the straightforward goal of understanding it: (1) *Is* the author indeed using a secretive style of writing and thus withholding a secrete message he or she wishes to become available, if at all, only to specific audiences? If so, (2) of *what* does the secretive strategy or style consist? And, (3) *why* is it used for conveying his or her message?

Of course, what the secret message is, if it indeed exists, constitutes an altogether ultimate goal for any research exploring the above three questions and wishing to arrive at a truthful understanding of any information the author intended to convey through his or her text.

The Khayyami Robaiyat certainly fit the profile of texts that invite and require hermeneutic analysis. At this point, it is not necessary to start with the assumption that the Robaiyat to be studied are necessarily those by Khayyam. However, there is ample evidence in these quatrains that there are intentional uses of secretive language, that there are secret messages being withheld or conveyed in veiled language, and that the multiple-meanings associated with the signs, tropes, or symbols used cannot be readily understood at their face value, requiring hermeneutic analysis to decipher them. In some quatrains, the poet actually explicitly states that indeed he has a secret that he cannot reveal at the time he is composing it, going into some detail, metaphorically or not, to insist on why and how it cannot, or should not, be readily revealed.

Moreover, the possibility that Khayyam, in other primary sources attributed to him, used a language that requires hermeneutic analysis, or offered clues regarding his interest in using secretive language, should be a matter of continuing interest and investigation throughout our research. The efforts to hide meanings do not have to always take poetic form. Speaking in general ("universal" or "kolli") terms, avoiding details, writing synoptically, using stories or examples to convey meanings indirectly, giving incomplete or even tantalizing information while inviting readers to find the answers on their own, scattering fragments of information for understanding a secret across seemingly separate texts, and so on, also invites hermeneutic analysis.

Hermeneutics is the science of studying texts in order to understand the hidden meanings originally intended by their authors, where they are not readily apparent or given on the surface. It has a long tradition particularly in studies of sacred, literary, and philosophical texts where the practice of secrecy in conveying meanings, spiritual or otherwise, hidden in stories, fables, examples, and symbolic language generally, has been common. It has developed over time a set of methodological and theoretical knowledge and strategies of textual study and analysis in order to pursue the task of interpreting the hidden meanings of texts and "translating" them from veiled to understandable knowledge.

The term itself originates from the Greek word ἑρμηνεύω (hermeneuō) meaning to "translate, interpret," and it has roots in the Aristotelian work Περὶ Ἑρμηνείας ("Peri Hermeneias") or "On Interpretation." However, the etymological root of the term is itself not fully known. It is highly plausible that the term has associations, as commonly believed, to Hermes, the Greek deity known as the "messenger of the Gods," who was known for his ability to translate the hidden meanings and intentions originating in God for humankind.

Adopting a hermeneutic approach to the study of sources by and on Khayyam, then, acknowledges the need for maintaining a central concern with detecting the use of veiled textual strategies, broadly considered, in the texts being studied. Our hermeneutic analysis should not be limited to only the primary sources at hand, or subcategories thereof, however. Once we adopt a hermeneutic approach for our research, we will have to be on guard all the time to detect and consider any piece of information in both the primary and secondary, or even tertiary sources discussing the latter two, to allow for the possibility that any finding could shed light on our efforts at deciphering hidden meanings anywhere among our sources.

A hint amid the most "obviously interpretable" texts in Khayyam's scientific or mathematical writings may provide us with hints at understanding a particular philosophical point advanced elsewhere, such as the meanings of tropes use in his Arabic or attributed Persian poetry. A gesture an old Khayyam makes toward a young child visitor in the company of his father, asking for his knowledge of a collection of Arabic poetry or his knowledge of circles in geometry, or his laying a golden toothpick on a certain page of a book by Avicenna, or purposely going on tangent or a seemingly long-winded explanation when an adversary asks him a sarcastic question about polar stars, may mean something else beyond what appears on the surface.

Therefore, when we say we apply a hermeneutic approach to the study of Khayyam, we mean to apply it to the study of his life and works as conveyed (or not) in the full range of primary and secondary source materials that have historically survived.

As I have emphasized this matter in my other hermeneutic studies—such as, for instance, my study *Gurdjieff and Hypnosis: A Hermeneutic Study* (Tamdgidi 2009)—it is important to make efforts at interpreting textual material on the basis of the symbolic universe created and used by the author, in this case Khayyam, himself. We should be especially mindful that the meaning we attribute to a particular symbol or trope used in the Khayyami source material is relevant to the symbolic universe indigenous to Khayyam's own worldview, to the extent we are able to establish such a worldview based on reliable and available sources. Even if we are persuaded, for instance, to consider what Avicenna meant by using a term or symbol in his writings, we should always be on guard to question whether that meaning is actually what Khayyam also shared.

For this reason, I will be particularly careful to seek, as far as possible, the symbolic meanings amid the language Khayyam *himself* uses from his *own texts* as part of the landscape of his own subjective universe, rather than assuming in an *a priori* fashion that simply because Khayyam admired Avicenna (or anyone else for that matter) he retained and applied the meaning in the same way that Avicenna or others did in their work.

My strategy of seeking Khayyam's own indigenous symbolic universe in his texts is based on the perception that if we look into Khayyam's texts within *his own* symbolic system, we would not be sacrificing the truthfulness of our findings regarding whether Khayyam's meanings coincide or differ from those used by others. If it corresponds, so be it, but if it does not, we are still on safer grounds in understanding the *unique* ways in which he uses a particular concept, idea, story, example, trope, or symbol in his writings. In this sense, my hermeneutic method is Weberian in orientation, in the sense that I am most interested in how the actor, in this case Khayyam, himself is subjectively making and offering sense of his own life and his works, rather than trying to understand him from the point of view of others.

Again, I should note that I am not suggesting abandoning any piece of information that a comparison with other thinkers' works offers on a particular subject; my point is that we should always remain on guard, and not readily assume that simply because Khayyam is using the terms, say, "wine," "dervish," "drunkenness," "saqi" (wine-server), and so on, used by others before and since his time, we should take for granted that he attributed the same meanings to them. This is particularly important when we consider our observational standpoint as hermeneutic analysts removed centuries into the future from his life and historical times, where we could easily assume that what Khayyam meant by "wine" is necessarily that meant by Hafez Shirazi or Molana Jalaleddin Rumi, or a Western translator such as Edward FitzGerald bent on drinking wine, or anyone else nearer to our own time.

The point to emphasize again, then, is that our hermeneutic strategy will be based on interpreting any symbol of Khayyam's subjective universe in the context of *his own symbolic universe* rather than on the basis of presumed affinity with, or difference from, the ways similar symbols have been employed by other thinkers before, during, or following his lifetime, up to the present.

Another important feature of our hermeneutic approach must be the consideration that the *absence* of certain information or discussion in any text can be as important as its presence. Being known as a "miserly" writer or teacher may itself be highly significant and meaningful when considered as part of a life bent on pursuing a secretive, or at least politically or pedagogically cautious, strategy of imparting knowledge, rather than as a sign of personal intellectual stinginess or cowardice.

When some refer to him as not forthcoming with more writing or more teaching, it may be just another way of their acknowledging that he was inclined toward secrecy. In considering such judgments, we should also note that in some cases, the observer may have clearly been even biased, or simply ignorant, misjudging secrecy for miserliness, and in fact the observer's own account may readily reveal that it was the observer himself who was miserly in making the effort to know more about Khayyam since there were indeed publicly available writings or teaching reports of which the observer himself was aware for one reason or another. Our hermeneutic method, in other words, should be able to also transcend actual textual material and consider the broader texture of the author's and other observers' own biographical and historical contexts.

The withholding of discussion or engagement with a particular topic in one text, however, does not mean that it is withheld from another text. In fact, it is possible to consider such a strategy of fragmented rendering of information where it is absent in one text but present in another text, absent in one quatrain but present in another quatrain, as being a hermeneutic strategy for passing on an intended messages that otherwise, if they were offered in the same text, would make the information obvious to the reader— inviting whatever consequences the author may have wished to avoid. Besides, Khayyam may have been secretive about a topic in an earlier writing, but more forthcoming about it in a later writing, when social conditions were more favorable.

For this reason, it is particularly important to be optimally holistic and inclusive in our study of Khayyam's texts, and reject any shortsighted and limiting "disciplinary" considerations in avoiding particular texts of Khayyam for the sake of either convenience or excuses not to take the necessary trouble in learning and engaging with the material at hand.

In hermeneutic analysis it is additionally important not to presume particular strategies for practicing secrecy in textual communication to be set in an *a priori* fashion. We should be open and always on guard to see how the author devises or invents new forms of embedding textual message and symbolic camouflage within or across his or her texts. It would be particularly interesting and noteworthy to find texts in which he actually discusses strategies for "ways of saying" things, which would indicate his or her self-conscious intention to engage in secretive textual creation, yet guide his most interested readers in adopting the proper way of discovering them.

Another consideration that may or not be advertently used as secretive strategy inviting hermeneutic analysis is the following.

Say, an author adopts a, so to speak, Socratic method, of writing, involving raising questions at first that he himself intends at a later point in the text to also answer, and in fact does answer. However, for one or another reason result in the fragmentation of material following his passing, parts of the texts becoming separated across various manuscripts.

So, some who find the fragments including the raised questions, study the material and think Khayyam had lots of unanswered questions about this or that topic and died "incomplete," not having found any answers to them. Others, however, find the other fragments that include texts that suggest the author having found answers. So, those in the first group when confronting manuscripts in the second category come to believe these other answered texts must be inauthentic, and composed by others or Khayyam's adversaries, not being his own; they then regard them as others trying to answer Khayyam by writing this or that quatrain. And the second group, when confronting the fragments in the first category come to believe that they must not be Khayyam's since they are full of wonders and doubts that do not befit a religious man.

Such examples indicate the need for us to be especially on guard in not interpreting corpuscular fragments in isolation, but as part of the widest possible waves his life and works set in motion, since otherwise we will end up thinking Khayyam's elephant to be just a rope, a hose, or a wall.

For this reason and for the purpose of this research on Omar Khayyam, and going back to the previously classified broad sub/categorizations of primary, secondary, and tertiary sources on his life and works, what I wish to point out again in a different way below are two ways of visually "mapping" the available texts in relation to one another.

Note that, as stated in the previous section, our research on Khayyam basically consists of reestablishing, or restitching, so to speak, in a quantum sociological imagination, links within and across all the categories of sources available about his life and works. These range from the linkages we can find between primary and secondary (and some tertiary) sources within and across the subcategories of each of the above, while maintaining a central concern with understanding the triangular linkages between the Khayyami Robaiyat, *Nowrooznameh (The Book on Nowrooz)*, and the rest of attributed Khayyam's writings which focus on philosophical, religious and scientific subjects, as well as his few other Arabic and Persian poems.

First, as I have already noted when depicting the Newtonian way of thinking about the sociological imagination in Figure 2.1 (presented in Chapter II), consider that mapping the primary and secondary (and other) sources on Khayyam's life and works as relations between separate, chunky, elements represented by separate circles would lead to a Newtonian "billiard ball game" visualization of the source elements of our Khayyam study.

The "lists" of "primary versus secondary versus tertiary," or "subcategories A, B, C, D, E," for instance, themselves subconsciously conjure up a divided imagination of the elements as balls or circles whose interaction or linkages are to be explored. The logical architecture of such an imagination is that of formal logic, where A is always separate from B, i.e., a source is considered to be either of the type A or of the type B, a text is considered to be either on the subject matter A or on the subject matter B. In such a formal logical scheme, we have the Khayyami Robaiyat here, the philosophical texts there, the scientific text elsewhere and the literary text yet in another place.

Similarly we may treat "Khayyami" as one who died a long time ago, implying also a divided conception of historical time where past, present, and future are separated as well, and that somehow our knowledges of his life and texts are "objectively" existing apart from the way it has been constructed by others in the past, or being continually reconstructed by ourselves studying his writings or even writings such as this. Each of the primary and secondary sources on or about him themselves are similarly conceptualized as dividing into their own subject matter circles or billiard balls; this also applies, by the way, to each quatrain "unit" of the Khayyami Robaiyat.

In Figure 4.1 (offered earlier in this chapter), however, I mapped the sub/categories of our sources in Khayyami studies in terms of a conceptual scheme based on the superposed dialectics of part and whole, itself following the quantum sociological imagination scheme I presented in Figure 3.1 (in Chapter III). You may consider the point being made at this point by noticing how our research source elements are mapped onto a whole-part dialectical scheme that articulates an architecture of existence ranging from God to personal selves, including the selves of Khayyam or of me the author, and of you, the reader. Let me explain further, then, what I mean here by the employment of the visualization of a part-whole dialectical scheme by means of concentric circles.

By dialectics of part and whole represented in terms of superposing circles I mean to illustrate a conception of elements such that they are recognized to be simultaneously the same and different. In other words, the consideration of the "identity in difference" or "difference in identity" is paramount here. A circle within a broader circle allows for the conception of the two as sharing the same elements (a circle inside occupies a space of the broader circle at the same time, simultaneously) while not sharing in other aspects of the broader circle. Hence, the relation of the two can be schematically visualized in terms of the simultaneity of identity and difference.

A robai (quatrain) expressing a rather personal trouble or emotional experience, for instance, is not just a four-lined poem, but also, at the same time, it may contain—as far as our study of Khayyam's life and works are concerned—a philosophical point involving important ontological, epistemological, or methodological propositions or procedures in itself. It could offer hints about its author's methodological habits of scientific inquiry, mathematical visions of God in relation to cosmic, natural, social, or personal reality, or it could convey a sociological insight, or a public social issue.

Note that I have also allowed for the conception of multiple selves. By this I mean the possibility that in a quatrain a thought, an emotion, a sensation, or a combination of them is consciously expressed and/or subconsciously implied by a self in Khayyam at one age, one period of his life, one moment of his day or night, living in one place or another, while another robai may be an expression of another self in Khayyam living in a different time or place of his life. It is also possible to consider that there is also an "observing" self in Khayyam, aware of both emotions expressed by him in the past across the quatrains, such that in yet a third quatrain he speaks of, say, the bittersweet nature of what he reports about his life.

Conversely, the same can be considered from a reverse direction. That is, in the dialectical conception of our research sources, the Khayyami Robaiyat may be considered to exist not just amid a four-lined quatrain attributed here or there to its poet, but in the very fabric of Khayyam's philosophical and religious texts, his scientific writings, his literary narratives, or other poems written in Persian Arabic that do not take the specific form of four-lined quatrains.

The Robaiyat, then, in this alternative conception, are treated at once as both a congealed (or corpuscular, so to speak) four-lined poetry, and a defused, spread-out wave of thinking, feeling, or sensing present in other seemingly "separate" philosophical, religious, scientific, and literary texts— even transcending the textual realm and the texture of his life as reported by his contemporaries, becoming reflected in specific architectural remains or in one's burial aspirations, perhaps, or, through his textual remains, reports of others down the centuries. The fact that the wave increasingly loses its ebb and flow across time and space does not mean that it is not a result of a motion ushered by Khayyam, thus being a "Khayyami" wave.

We can, therefore, similarly map our primary, secondary, or even tertiary and other, source elements in terms of the dialectics of part and whole. In this conception, it becomes possible to consider, accept, reject, or rethink, a commentary made by a secondary source about Khayyam during his time, centuries later before and after FitzGerald's "free" translations, in the context of not just one or another of the attributed Robaiyat, but also in relation to all of Khayyam's primary writings. A comment made by a biographer about Khayyam's cosmic self-awareness becomes then relatable to what may have been stated in his reported birth horoscope in another secondary source, and/or to a particular robai, or to a method he used to solve a particular problem in geometry, algebra, arithmetic, music, or even a mechanical balance designed to find the amount of authentic precious material amid an indivisible assembly of jewelry.

In the part-whole dialectical map in Figure 4.1, you may note that I have placed particular texts of Khayyam in one circle while drawing arrows to other circles. This is to show that in a given text intended to be primarily focused on a given topic, he may also share information or discuss subjects that pertain to other topics. This is meant to facilitate the visualization of our efforts in understanding how various primary or secondary texts on Khayyam's life and works relate and contribute to one another toward building an integrative understanding of whatever he intended to convey through his writings or life events.

If we encounter texts by an author who does seem to be intending to convey his views about himself and the world secretively, whether the reasons for secrecy are contingent or essential to his message, the issue of secrecy itself may be sublated as a component of the author's message that needs to be itself understood in its dialectical personal/historical context.

In other words, the introduction of the element of secrecy, requiring hermeneutic analysis, does not abolish the value of sociological imagination as a requirement of our research, but adds another layer or element to the message of the author being conveyed through the secretive text, leading us to ask what sort of personal troubles or public issues necessitated or explain this element of secrecy as a substantive and/or formal component of the text that invites sociologically imaginative hermeneutic analysis.

It is in light of the above that I think an imaginative quantum sociological approach to the hermeneutic study of Omar Khayyam's life and works is not only warranted, but also offers the best venue for exploring the historically surviving textual fragments that can be mapped, as done in Figure 4.1—

restitching a substantive landscape of subject matters ranging from the very personal and private as expressed in his attributed poetry, on one hand, to the very large and public issues expressed in his philosophical, religious, and scientific texts about humanity's place in the universe and existence, and in relation to his God.

We may even perhaps discover that, centuries before C. Wright Mills, Khayyam had introduced and practiced his own highly creative variety of Eastern sociological imagination through his texts and particularly his poetry, weaving an imaginative tent that includes the cosmos in the macro and his most private inner thoughts, feelings, and sensations, in the micro folds of the dialectic of his personal troubles and the public issues of his times, expressed in a universal poetic language that is understandable by all.

4. On Secrets and Being Secretive

Let us suppose Khayyam did have a secret during his lifetime. In conducting hermeneutic analyses of his works we may legitimately wonder and ask this. What right do I or we have in revealing it?

In other words, was his secret intended to be something personal, meant to simply die away with him, or did he intend to pass it on as a part of whatever legacy he wished to leave for future generations? If the latter was the case, did he intend the secret to be forever wrapped in veil as a perpetual, one may call Socratic, process of raising questions about him, his times, the world, cosmos, God, and so on, and if so was this perpetual secretiveness and questioning important components of the legacy he intended to leave behind?

If that was the case, if we find or claim to have discovered his secret, would we then be justified in revealing it, sharing it, and disseminating it as such? Would we be committing a "closing" of the Khayyami tradition of experiencing wonder and mystery about ourselves and the world by offering our own interpretations of the answers Khayyam gave to the questions he posed? Would that run counter to the very purpose and spirit of his intended secretiveness and socratic pedagogical style?

Or, in contrast, should we assume that he wished his secret to be indeed revealed beyond his own troubled times provided that necessary personal efforts on the parts of those who seek it are made? If so, then what method of explanation or mode of exposition should those who discover the secret adopt in sharing it with others?

I think the above are all important, legitimate questions to ask. What right do I have as a scholar to reveal what I have discovered in my research to be Khayyam's secret—assuming that my understanding of the secret corresponds to what Khayyam actually had in mind?

As I conducted this research, I often came back to this question. How I resolved it for myself was that, instead of trying to offer *a priori* answers to it I will let the process of research itself offer convincing answers to the question, one way or another. In other words, the question whether or not it is proper to reveal Khayyam's secret (if we discover that he had one, and what it was) can be best answered by relying on Khayyam's own text, and understanding how Khayyam himself may have gone about answering, or offering hints about answering, the questions he posed.

An ironic or paradoxical implication of adopting such a strategy, however, is that we would have to be engaging in the research on Khayyam secretively ourselves, for, we would really not know whether it is proper to reveal Khayyam's secret without having brought the research to a plausible conclusion. Indeed, this explain why you as reader are reading this account of my findings now than earlier, during the time it has been in the works.

As odd as the constraints posed by such considerations and research strategy may sound, it is the case that, as we shall see, we find quatrains where the poet specifically forbids revealing his secret until the pearl is completed in the privacy of the oyster's work in the shell. The quatrain I have chosen to epigraph this first book is itself clearly telling of such a sentiment, and in a way says in a nutshell, in the artful mind of its poet, what I wish to convey here. The point of the metaphor is that if the shell is opened prematurely, the pearl would lose its chance to complete itself.

Some may regard such ethical questions as irrelevant nearly a thousand years past Khayyam's birth. However, if we follow the spirit of such quatrains in light of the methodological import such advice may contain, it would not be unreasonable to find the advice being given to have quite rational merits. Anyone who wishes to pass on a secret, and goes to considerable lengths to hide it, would want to make sure that what is revealed is optimally thought out before being shared in a rushed way with the world. He may even include instructions, or what I like to call "bread crumbs," for his future readers about what to do or not when trying to decipher his work. Even in his scientific texts, Khayyam adopts such a strategy, so why not do the same in his poetic pursuits?

Obviously, while the above may partially explain the time it took me to complete and publish this work, it should be obvious now that I would not have written and be sharing this series on Khayyam if my study of his life and works had not convincingly demonstrated to me that he indeed invited all to seek, find, digest and share as best as they can the secret he wished to impart, but do so not in a rushed way, but in a way that Khayyam's artwork deserves.

Of course, just because I will offer my own views that Khayyam had a secret, itself comprised of layers of constitutive secrets, does not mean that others should take it for granted and not pursue efforts on their own to address the questions arising from Khayyam's life and works.

On my part, I will demonstrate in this series that Khayyam indeed had and kept a secret that was not simply for personal ends, but one that he wished to impart as his legacy posthumously.

This partly served his need to survive life-threatening and oppressive conditions of his times. But the secretiveness was not simply caused by considerations for external cultural or political conditions of his time or in fear of personal danger to himself, but that the secret itself, intrinsically, due to the nature of the inherent message intended to be passed on, had to be secretively and Socratically delivered wrapped in a highly skillful, creatively designed and constructed canopy of poetic patchworks so that it could result in such effects on his audiences as Khayyam, the wonderful teacher and writer that he was, intended it.

Was the secrecy coincidental, or of the essence, to whatever it was that Khayyam intended to pass on to future generations? In other words, was this secrecy due to, say, the troubled political conditions of his time and his fear for his life, and/or due to the intrinsic requirements of whatever it was that he wished to leave as his legacy? Would he have still written a secret-laden work if his times were favorable to him?

If the reason for secrecy was *historical or personal*, i.e., the conditions of his time and fear for his safety, then why not just write a treatise in clear prose and let it be revealed posthumously? However, if what is left as a secret text is itself wrapped in secretive and symbolic language not decipherable by others without significant effort, then should we assume that secretiveness had (also) a *logical* or *pedagogical* necessity, being of the essence of what and how it was that Khayyam intended to pass on? Did he in fact intend that outcome, i.e., to let the secret be, easily or not, revealed posthumously?

To offer a gist of the findings of this series on Khayyam, I can only offer the following broad strokes at this time.

Contrary to the prevailing views that suggest composing poetry was a marginal and recreational pastime for Omar Khayyam, in this series I will advance the thesis that the Robaiyat were in fact the ultimate fruit of his life's work, indeed his *magnum opus*. They represented a deliberate, universal synthesis, condensation, and transcendence of all of his multiple philosophical, religious, scientific, and literary modes of inquiry and expression about the universe of existence and his own place in it in favor of a creative, artistic world-outlook that sublimates the other modes of inquiry into a unified one that alone can bring about inner and broader human liberation.

Based on Khayyam's attributed texts, his contemporaries' reliable reports about him, and all that has been fruitfully accomplished in Khayyami studies ever since his time, I will demonstrate that deeply buried—yet also paradoxically apparent—in the Robaiyat itself as a work of art cultivated in secret by Khayyam are a series of multifaceted inner secrets that together inspired him to privately compose the oddly hypnotic poetry of his Robaiyat.

The Robaiyat as Khayyam's tent stitched from a series of quatrain patchworks also explains both his survival as a free-thinking and critically-minded Muslim amid the oppressive conditions of his time as well as the immortal endurance and global spread of his spirit ever since. I will demonstrate that a research guided by the thesis that Khayyam had such a secret of secrets offers a key to the resolution of nearly all the puzzles surrounding Khayyam's life and works generated over the centuries.

It is important to note here that considering the Robaiyat to be Khayyam's secret is only a beginning step in our journey, as profound as the implications of such a view can in itself be in understanding Khayyam's legacy. Once we consider that possibility, that is, once we ask *whether* the Robaiyat was an important preoccupation of Khayyam's life and works, we still need to understand *what* the Robaiyat is about in terms of their both content and form, which will then also lead us to ask and understand *why*, for what purpose, they were composed. Through this three-fold whether, what, and why inquiries about the Robaiyat (a three-fold inquiry that is actually deeply Khayyami in methodology) runs the central question of why this work was composed, kept, and passed on in secrecy.

While I have offered above a broad gist of the thesis I will advance in the series *Omar Khayyam's Secret*, and some of the associated questions the thesis raises, I think it is important to address another very important question at the outset following the above set of questions about matters of secrecy and secretiveness, one that raises matters of ethical and/or pedagogical concern as far as the study of Khayyam's life and works are concerned.

A stick always has two ends. What was not foreseen by Khayyam in light of social, natural, and other cultural events that followed his passing was that as a consequence of the "secretive" way of imparting knowledge on his part for personal and/or broader social reasons of his time, many misunderstandings emerged and accumulated over the centuries about him posthumously.

In this context, we should be particularly mindful of the devastating impact a series of social and natural events made on Neyshabour and Iran following Khayyam's death, resulting in the destruction and fragmentation of writings or oral biographies and histories that Khayyam may have intended, as anticipated in his will, to be passed down the generations.

And in this regard, one cannot also dismiss the prevalent habits of manuscript transmission, particularly what I call the four-fold "compiling earthquakes" of biased selectivity, alphabetization, wandering, and fabrication that contributed to the manner in which Khayyam's intended legacy were distorted down the centuries, despite what he may have passed on and instructed as part of his will on the day he died.

In any case, it is a testament to the power of Khayyam's spirit and the creative strategies he adopted to pass on his legacy that—*despite* such historical, natural, and recording obstacles and *despite* much misunderstandings and misinterpretations of his teaching across nearly nine centuries after his passing—his memory still lives in the minds, hearts, and sensibilities of those eager to understand his life and works, proving the essence of his creative art with a precision inspired by his philosophical and religious views, scientific mind, and literary skills.

The important additional question I was pointing to is regarding the mode of exposition best suited for sharing the findings of this research, in light of the consideration that being secretive may not be a matter external but essential to the secret Khayyam wished to impart as part of his legacy.

Consider for instance this first book of the series itself. One way to go about sharing my findings in the series is to tell you upfront, in a few lines, the basics of what I discovered. Another way is to take you along the journey of the discovery itself and let you experience it on your own in the same process and stages as how I strangely found my wonderful answers.

The latter approach includes the former, but offers more since the journey itself, as the adage goes, is as important as the destinations reached. This procedure seems to have been the way Khayyam himself chose to pass on his teaching and legacy at the cost of being unjustly blamed for being miserly in his writings and teachings, charges which I will demonstrate in this study to have been groundless, in favor of redeeming the true worth of Khayyam's contributions to human self-understanding amid a wonderful, yet utterly mysterious, universe of existence.

Is it not fair, then, to respect the same in the process of sharing my understanding of his wisdom in this series itself?

Why have secrets? Why be secretive? Why go through the trouble, and not reveal them in a few words and move on, one may ask?

Khayyam's pedagogical style was that of offering hints but not providing answers outright, since he wished that the receiver could employ all of his or her own intellectual, emotional, and sensual energies to discover the "secret" truths of what he wished to impart. The troubling, life-threatening conditions of his time of course also contributed to reinforcing his pedagogical style for sure, but, as I will demonstrate in this series, the nature of what he learned and the truths he discovered lent themselves more to being presented in a particular, Socratic, way than offered ready-made in advance. One does not have to choose between one or the other, personal or public, factors to explain what shaped Khayyam's particular form of intellectual dissemination; both were equally important contributing factors.

Consider the following in the case of this inquiry as well.

Were to offer the "secret" in a few sentences (which is possible, hints at which I may have already provided in the lines, or between the lines, of this chapter itself), doing so will only result in a partial, abstract, knowledge. It may or not meet your satisfaction, but regardless of any judgment you may make about it, it would be an empty notion devoid of the rich experiential attributes merging physical efforts (in terms of dedicating the necessary time, energy, and attention to read and reflect on the material), the emotional curiosities and challenges involved, and the subtle conceptual analyses and syntheses that are required to render the *knowledge* of the "secret"—a concrete *understanding* that one can then employ in one's everyday life. It would be a matter of air knowledge, so to speak, that may appear to be a good idea to readers when they first hear it, but proves to be one that evaporates in an instant of distraction during or following a reading session.

For the air of the "secret" to be fully inhaled in the digestive process of our inner understanding, it needs to be mixed with earth, heat, and water, whose combination only could produce the needed experiential reality of a concrete answer as intended. Of course it is possible that one can turn, especially amid this speed culture we are particularly living in today, to read a later book of the series for a short-cut and a quick answer, but one has to always keep in mind that, as far as the unfolding of the series *Omar Khayyam's Secret* is concerned, the journey is as important as the destination so far as the end of arriving at an adequate "understanding" of Khayyam's secret is concerned. Truth is always concrete, a rich organic unity of diverse aspects, which should ultimately be also practical. The more one engages in the physically, emotionally and intellectually challenging process of searching for it, the richer and experientially more useful will be the result of the inquiry.

My point here is to encourage us to consider that my presentation method for revealing Khayyam's "secret" has to remain respectful of his style of teaching and writing, since understanding that process is itself an integral part of the "secret" he wished to impart through his works, particularly his Robaiyat. And it can be best understood when it is actually experienced.

It is impossible to experience spiritual awakening from the everyday hypnoses of our everyday lives, an awakening which is the central aim of all genuine spiritual traditions of the world, without understanding how the hypnotic process works, how one can fall asleep in everyday life, how one can become aware of one's spiritual sleep, and how to find a way toward real awakening. If we do not grasp this point, we would not grasp why genuine spiritual traditions have used secretive, mystical elements in their teachings, an attribute that one cannot readily separate from their broader religious cosmology and ontology. After all, those who follow a secretive way of imparting their teaching have a grand cosmic example to follow in a mysterious universe created by what they regard as divine force(s) not readily apparent to all. Even God is believed to be keeping secrets for one reason or another; so, why not follow His pedagogical example, they may ask?

There is ample evidence in attributed writings of Khayyam to demonstrate his deep interest in understanding the human condition of living in waking sleep, leading one also to search for understanding how one can awaken from it in favor of realizing highest human potentials amid a sacred cosmology. I will demonstrate that Khayyam was deeply concerned, as are all genuine mystical and spiritual traditions in the world, about the trance of everyday life and how to awaken from the state in favor of spiritual liberation to live a happy life that humankind deserves to have in this life as well. It is impossible to understand Khayyam's many-folded secret and the wonderful way he went about writing about and teaching it, without understanding the role secretiveness *itself* plays in the secret being advanced.

So, based on the above considerations, I hope the reader will forgive me for delivering *Omar Khayyam's Secret* in a secretive (perhaps better say,

Socratic) way throughout this series, since in my understanding this mode of exposition is more respectful in a practical sense of Khayyam's secret itself, and is, in fact, a part or expression of the secret he wished to convey to his world-historical audience that is humanity. The secret will be revealed— hopefully in its strange, wonderful beauty, at a time that is even more odd and majestic—according to a logical progression of critical hermeneutic inquiry into Khayyam's texts and those who have written about him.

Omar Khayyam's Secret inescapably builds on contributions from many Khayyami studies preceding it, the latter considered in the broadest sense of the term ranging from anecdotal to extensive, hitherto conducted across the centuries, in Iran or abroad; without critical considerations of them this study would not have been possible. However, you will find in *Omar Khayyam's Secret* a series of findings and insights about Khayyam's life and works that are entirely new and unprecedented ever since Khayyam passed away about nine centuries ago. In fact, some of what I am about to reveal in this series may not have even been known publicly during Khayyam's own lifetime, beyond his own mind and his most trusted circle of associates.

To put this rather more bluntly, in this series you will be introduced to findings and insights about aspects of Khayyam's life and works that have remained hidden (paradoxically at times in full view, as we shall see, given Khayyam's ingenious strategies for secretive literary writing) for more than nine hundred years. I say "more than nine hundred years" because we may also include in the timeline a part of Khayyam's lifetime during which he kept aspects of his work hidden from public view, literally and/or symbolically.

In consideration of intentional efforts made at secretive writing, we should also consider that objective historical factors that later came into play involving adverse socio-historical events (such as nomadic invasions and wars, etc.), natural calamities (such as series of earthquakes)—not to neglect also the subjective problems having to do with habits (or lack there) of manuscript compilation—prevented the posthumous discovery of the hidden aspects of Khayyam's legacy beyond what he may have intended. However, I will demonstrate in this series that what texts and historical records did survive from Khayyam and reach us despite the enormous external and subjective obstacles noted above are still minimally adequate in the rediscovery and understanding of his multi-layered secret.

The findings of this series on Khayyam's life and works can lead to considerable rethinking of the by now Western (and Eastern) habitual ways of knowing and appreciating Khayyam and his works, particularly his Robaiyat. It is also likely that this series will lead to significant rethinking of the possibilities of cultural translation of texts, especially of poetry, at least so far as translating the Robaiyat are concerned; for, I will demonstrate that translating in ways that convey both accurate meanings and poetic forms of the original are indeed possible. This series will offer a comprehensive translation of the Khayyami Robaiyat to date which will hopefully facilitate further critical studies in Khayyami studies.

From a personal vantage point, this study is an effort in decolonizing myself from a way of understanding Khayyam's life and works that symbolically encapsulates the Orientalist imaginations of Iran and Persia, and the East more broadly, in the minds of the West, and those in the Occidentalist East.

I do not wish that the point I just stated to be regarded as an anti-Western commentary, however, for I believe it is in fact in the open-minded and self-critically new appreciations of what Khayyam did actually intend to offer that the West and the East could meet one another again—beyond anything Edward FitzGerald could have ever imagined—to undo the Orientalist dimensions of the fascination with which Khayyam was received in the post-FitzGeraldian era, one that in fact may help us appreciate the positive contributions even of that Victorian historical reception.

It is in our capacity to let go of habitual ways of thinking about Khayyam, of awakening from our own cherished myths about Khayyam and his "Rubaiyat," that we can indeed reimagine ourselves in both the West and the East to be involved in creatively new and more liberating ways of discovering and absorbing a treasure for all humanity that remained hidden for more than nine hundred years in the bottom of a Khayyami ocean that is astonishingly deep, beautiful, and wonderful.

Abstract

This essay, titled "Hermeneutics of the Khayyami Robaiyat in Quantum Sociological Imagination: Source Availability and Secrecy," is the fourth and last chapter of the first book, subtitled *New Khayyami Studies: Quantumizing the Newtonian Structures of C. Wright Mills's Sociological Imagination for A New Hermeneutic Method*, of the twelve-book series, *Omar Khayyam's Secret: Hermeneutics of the Robaiyat in Quantum Sociological Imagination*, authored by Mohammad H. Tamdgidi. Relaxing his prior assumptions and abstractions from matters of source availability and secrecy as maintained in the previous three chapters of the book, Tamdgidi tries in this chapter to elaborate in more detail on both of the above challenges confronting Khayyami studies.

In the first section, his purpose is to draw a preliminary, basic outline of the sources of information available (or not) for the research on Khayyam conducted for this series. His aim here is not to delve into the historical, bibliographic, or manuscript conditions or the extent of authenticity of these sources. Those details will be carefully introduced, examined, and evaluated during the substantive explorations of this series in conjunction with careful studies of their contents.

Tamdgidi then offers a categorization of sources available for Khayyami studies broadly as follows.

1. Primary Sources: texts that are attributed, unanimously or not, to Omar Khayyam himself. In this category, he identifies the following subcategories: A) As a first subcategory of primary sources, we should include works that Khayyam may have written, intended to be shared or not during his own lifetime, of which we do not yet have any knowledge or records whatever; B) As a second subcategory of primary sources, we have works specifically reported by Khayyam (as acknowledges also by others) to have been written by him on definite topics from which we do not (yet) have any complete or even partial manuscripts. C) A third subcategory of primary sources are surviving works bearing Khayyam's name that are universally accepted to have been authored by him, these include a variety of sources that Tamdgidi lists in the section; D) The Khayyami Robaiyat: A fourth subcategory of surviving primary sources are the Robaiyat (quatrains) written in Persian that have been attributed to Omar Khayyam in various manuscripts down the centuries; it is given a separate subcategory given the disputed nature of their attribution. 2. Secondary Sources: old accounts and information about Khayyam's life and works from the pre-FitzGeraldian era, among which the author identifies also four subcategories as explained in the text. 3. Tertiary Sources: include all the modern and recent sources written about Khayyam's life and works in the post-FitzGeraldian era. Tamdgidi notes further that fourth (possible architecture related works) and fifth (burial related material) categories can also be considered as sources in Khayyami studies.

In the author's view, the most reliable strategy for conducting Khayyami studies must be one that lays the most emphasis on the primary material as the source of the most reliable information about Khayyam. However, in his view, we will have to avoid treating all the various categories and subcategories as chunky, separate billiard balls to be struck with one another from without, but will approach them in their overlapping and superposed nature, in such a way that despite their apparently fragmented state, they are imagined as being superposed expressions of a life in progress, works produced along a lifetime, and commentaries made by others on his life and works amid a wider world-history context they all share.

Tamdgidi then elaborates on his hermeneutic method to be used in the series, noting that he will be particularly interested and careful to seek, as far as possible, the symbolic meanings amid the language Khayyam himself uses from his own texts as part of the landscape of his own subjective universe, rather than assuming in an *a priori* fashion that simply because Khayyam admired Avicenna (or anyone else for that matter) he retained and applied the same meaning in the same way as Avicenna or others did in their work.

Finally, while offering the broad contours and a gist of his thesis advanced in the series, Tamdgidi encourages his readers to consider and understand that his presentation method of revealing the "secret" of Khayyam in the series has to remain respectful of Khayyam's style of teaching and writing, since understanding of that process is itself an integral part of the "secret" Khayyam wished to impart through his works, particularly his Robaiyat.

Conclusion to Book 1: Summary of Findings

In each book of the *Omar Khayyam's Secret* series, I will use the book's conclusion as a space to share the summaries of all the prior sections and chapters of that book, drawing on the abstracts offered for each previously. This way the reader will find in it an overall summary of the findings of that book. However, it is important to note that such abstracts and overall summaries will not substitute for a careful reading of the main text of the book itself, since it is obviously impossible to convey the entirety of the findings of the book in the brief space of a conclusion.

Omar Khayyam's Secret: Hermeneutics of the Robaiyat in Quantum Sociological Imagination is a twelve-book series of which this book, subtitled *New Khayyami Studies: Quantumizing the Newtonian Structures of C. Wright Mills's Sociological Imagination for A New Hermeneutic Method*, was the first book. Each book is independently readable, although it will be best understood as a part of the whole series.

In the overall series, I share the results of my decades-long research on Omar Khayyam, the enigmatic 11th/12th centuries Persian Muslim sage, philosopher, astronomer, mathematician, physician, writer, and poet from Neyshabour, Iran, whose life and works still remain behind a veil of deep mystery. The purpose of my research has been to find definitive answers to the many puzzles still surrounding Khayyam, especially regarding the existence, nature, and purpose of the Robaiyat in his life and works. To explore the questions posed in the series, I advance a new hermeneutic method of textual analysis, informed by what I call the quantum sociological imagination, to gather and study all the attributed philosophical, religious, scientific, and literary writings of Khayyam.

In this first book, following a common preface and introduction to the series, I developed the quantum sociological imagination method framing my hermeneutic study in the series as a whole.

In the prefatory note I shared the origins of this series and how the study is itself a moment in the trajectory of a broader research project. In the introduction, I described how centuries of Khayyami studies, especially during the last two, have reached an impasse in shedding light on his enigmatic life and works, especially his attributed Robaiyat.

The four chapters of this book were then dedicated to developing the quantum sociological imagination as a new hermeneutic method framing the Khayyami studies in the series. The method builds, in an applied way, on the results of my recent work in the sociology of scientific knowledge, *Liberating Sociology: From Newtonian Toward Quantum Imagination: Volume 1: Unriddling the Quantum Enigma* (2020), where I explored extensively, in greater depth, and in the context of understanding the so-called "quantum enigma," the Newtonian and quantum ways of imagining reality. In this first book, I shared the findings of that research in summary amid new applied insights developed in relation to Khayyami studies.

In the first chapter, I raised a set of eight questions about the structure of C. Wright Mills's sociological imagination as a potential framework for Khayyami studies. In the second chapter, I showed how the questions are symptomatic of Newtonian structures that still continue to frame Mills's sociological imagination. In the third chapter, I explored how the sociological imagination can be reinvented to be more in tune with the findings of quantum science. In the last chapter, the implications of the quantum sociological imagination for devising a hermeneutic method for new Khayyami studies were outlined. In this conclusion, the findings of this first book of the *Omar Khayyam's Secret* series are further summarized.

The "Preface to the Series: Origins of This Study," served to shed light on why I launched this series on Omar Khayyam and how it is itself a moment in the trajectory of a broader research project.

The origin of the series on Khayyam goes back to my graduate doctoral research in sociology resulting in a dissertation titled "Mysticism and Utopia: Towards the Sociology of Self-Knowledge and Human Architecture

(A Study in Marx, Gurdjieff, and Mannheim)" (2002). Therein, the more I explored the explanatory value of the overall thesis during my doctoral research, the more I found its echoes in Omar Khayyam's life and works. If Marx, Gurdjieff, and Mannheim represented respectively the one-sided human efforts in utopian, mystical, and social scientific liberation, Khayyam increasingly represented to me an integrative effort at overcoming mutually alienating traditions of utopianism, mysticism, and science as described above. However, the exploration of such a three-fold representation required further research in the deep structures of Khayyam's attributed texts amid wider Khayyami studies, one which I decided to undertake more systematically following my doctoral studies, resulting in the establishment of a research center in Khayyam's name and its scholarly journal and publications.

Following the publication of three books on Karl Marx (2007), G. I. Gurdjieff (2009), and a transdisciplinary study in Karl Mannheim and the sociology of scientific knowledge of the quantum enigma (2020), my continuing interests in reinventing C. Wright Mills in favor of a quantum sociological imagination are explored in this series on Khayyam's life and works, serving as both exploratory and applied contexts.

In the "Introduction to the Series: The Enigmatic Omar Khayyam and the Impasse of Khayyami Studies," I argued that nearly a thousand years after his birth, the life and works of Omar Khayyam are still wrapped deeply in veil, major puzzles about him still abound, and modern Khayyami studies in Iran and abroad, after nearly two centuries of active research, have grounded nearly to a halt, reaching an impasse.

Overviewing a series of puzzles and questions left unresolved about Omar Khayyam's life and works, I invited readers to ask why they may not consider what *they themselves already know* about Khayyam to be based on one or another myth. Acknowledging that not only others', but also our own, knowledges of Khayyam are myths—that they are socially and historically constructed stories about him—can be a good beginning in the true Khayyamian spirit of the term founded on healthy skepticism. Doubting what we know about him in a radical way can be a helpful starting point about developing new understandings of his life, works, and legacy.

It may be that we end up constructing new myths about him, but at least we would be doing so based on more reliable studies, being aware of the social constructedness of our own knowledges or myths about him, and based on efforts that do not pretend to contrast the presumed truths on our parts with lesser-valued myths constructed by others. So, it is not proper for us to assume the existing knowledges about him to be uncontroversially authentic, factual, and official to start with. The very method we use to study him, let alone the substantive knowledges about him, are to be treated as variables, and not as givens, taken-for-granted.

Instead of simply starting with drawing on this or that scholar's portrayals of who Khayyam was and what he wrote, we must start from the scratch by revisiting and rethinking the methodological grounds and frameworks we use in our Khayyami studies. So, in this book, I set myself this task in order to let the exploration itself guide how the rest of this investigation in this and future books of this series will be organized and conducted.

In the first chapter of the book titled "The Promises and the Classical Limits of C. Wright Mills's Sociological Imagination," I suggested that the study of texts to understand their meanings in social context falls in the subdisciplinary field of the sociology of knowledge, broadly defined as a branch of social scientific inquiry concerned with understanding how knowledge and social reality relate to one another. Studying Khayyam's attributed works and those of others about him in order to understand his views and life in historical context, therefore, can be framed as a study in the sociology of knowledge, broadly speaking.

In that chapter, using Khayyami studies as an applied setting, I revisited the Millsian sociological imagination, raising eight issues that I believe express the limits imposed by the classical Newtonian way of thinking on Mills's imaginative framework. I explored the eight issues in terms of the following questions: 1. The problem of dualism: can personal troubles be also public issues, and vice versa? 2. The problem of atomism: which self's personal trouble is it? 3. The problem of separability: whose public issues are these? 4. The problem of objectivity: can we as observers separate ourselves from others' personal troubles and public issues? 5. The problem of determinism: is it always the case that society shapes the individual/self, and that public issues always shape personal troubles? 6. The problem of continuity: are we supposed to find causal relations amid easily locatable and traceable causal chains? 7. The problem of disciplinarity: are we always better off dividing and specializing our knowledges into fragmented disciplines? And 8. The problem of scientism: is science always Western, and still Newtonian?

I asked and explored whether Mills's comments on Newtonianism and the Newtonian "way of thinking" in his book were meant to acknowledge that he himself was gripped by and embraced Newtonianism in his proposed critical return to "classical" pursuit of the sociological imagination, or did he instead mean to question such fundamental structures of thinking, seeking ways to move beyond them in favor of newer scientific, cultural, and sociological imaginations?

In the second chapter of the book titled, "The Newtonian Imagination of Reality, Society, Sociology, and Khayyami Studies," in order to offer a heuristic model of the Newtonian way of imagining reality, society, sociology and the sociological imagination and demonstrate (in a following chapter) how such a perspective is different from the quantum way of imagining them, I used in the chapter the "billiard balls game" metaphor that has been widely used (in my view wrongly) to characterize the Newtonian way of imagining the world.

I suggested that the Newtonian way of imagining, or thinking about, the universe may be broadly characterized as having eight notional attributes—namely, its notions of (1) dualism, (2) atomism, (3) separability, (4) (subjectless) objectivity, (5) determinism (including its associated notion of predictability), (6) continuity, (7) disciplinarity, and (8) scientism—which can be illustrated by using a (what I argue is an ideologically distorted) metaphorical "billiard balls game" way of imagining reality as commonly used for the purpose.

More specifically the attributes of Newtonian imagination I explored were in terms of the following questions: 1. Dualism: can an object be A and non-A at the same time? 2. Atomism: what is the micro unit of analysis of the object? 3. Separability: what is the macro unit of analysis of the object? 4. Objectivity: does the object being observed have an independent reality? 5. Determinism: are causes and consequences in objects certain and predictable? 6. Continuity: is influence exerted through chains of local-causations? 7. Disciplinarity: fragmenting our knowledge of reality? And 8. Scientism: presuming the superiority of Western, Newtonian way of thinking?

I used the above framework to show how such parameters also have shaped our Newtonian conceptions of society, sociology, and the sociological imagination, and may also continue to frame our Khayyami studies if we fail in bringing them to conscious awareness as a precondition for reframing our sociological and Khayyami studies in more fruitful, quantum ways.

I concluded the second chapter by offering a vision of "classical," "Newtonian sociology" that can clarify further the implications the broader

Newtonian vision I outlined above has for shaping the "classical" sociological vision, and the sociological imagination as a framework for conducting Khayyami studies. Introducing a diagram for the Newtonian sociological imagination, I noted that what makes the sociological imagination Newtonian is not simply that it avoids studying linkages between its elements. What makes it Newtonian is its treating those elements in a "chunky" way, in presuming that the elements are separate billiard balls to begin with, that they do not overlap with one another, instead simply needing to be linked with another, to interact with one another from "without," in order to make the imagination work. It does not imagine those elements as already embedded in dialectical part-whole relations of identity in difference.

In the third chapter of the book titled, "Quantum Sociological Imagination as A Framework for Khayyami Studies," I offered an overview of how classical Newtonianism as a product of an historical compromise between a receding religiosity and an emerging secularism in the West met its limits and fell into crisis when confronted with the new findings of quantum science.

Using the same eight-fold model I used to describe the attributes of the Newtonian way of thinking, I suggested that the quantum way of imagining reality can also be characterized as having eight sets of attributes: 1-Simultaneity (not "duality," nor "complementarity"); 2-Superpositionality; 3-Inseparability; 4-Relativity (subject-included objectivity); 5-Probability; 6-Transcontinuity (which is a term I prefer to call what is commonly referred to as "discontinuity"); 7-Transdisciplinarity; and (8) Transculturalism. In my view, we have to always distinguish between *three* kinds of Newtonianism: *classical*, *incompletely relativistic*, and *completely relativistic*. The classical Newtonianism universalizes the eight attributes as listed earlier. The incompletely relativistic Newtonianism is the kind prevalent today, confused, enigmatized, still not freed from the classical bounds but not yet fully embracing attributes that it could have independently discovered for itself, ones that it would have found to be "completely" resonating with the quantum science findings (itself stripped of elements contributive to the quantum enigma, such as the "wave-particle duality," "Complementarity Principle," and so on). For the completely relativistic Newtonianism I have coined (2020) the term *Quantum Newtonianism*. It is a Newtonianism that treats the reality from the standpoint of any observer's reference frame to be a local reference frame or fold of the broader quantum reality as a whole.

I suggested that quantumizing the Newtonian in favor of a quantum sociological imagination invites the following considerations regarding each of which I offered illustrations, and from each of which I drew inspiration, about how Khayyami studies can be framed: 1. Relating personal troubles and public issues: from dualism to simultaneity (not "duality," nor "complementarity"); 2. Relating personal troubles (or not) of many selves: from atomism to superpositionality; 3. Relating public issues world-historically: from separability to inseparability; 4. Relating the sociological imaginations of others to those of ourselves: from subjectless objectivity to relativity (subject-included objectivity); 5. Reimagining causal patterns creatively: from determinism to probability; 6. Reimagining causal chains also as causal leaps: from continuity to "transcontinuity" (also known as "discontinuity"); 7. Reimagining sociology: from disciplinarity to transdisciplinarity; and 8. Reimagining science: from eurocentrism to tansculturalism.

I illustrated in a figure how, by reimagining the elements of the sociological imagination in terms of overlapping and superposing circles, we can arrive at a non-dualistic, both/and, conception of elements that previously could only be imagined in terms of a formal, either/or logic. I argued that using the notion of "Khayyami" as a reference both to the person and to the tradition associated with him can offer a sociologically imaginative quantum device involving a language of simultaneity when referring to Omar Khayyam's life, works, and legacy—especially when it comes to the study of the attributed Robaiyat—one that can have significant methodological, substantive, and practical consequences for framing and conducting our Khayyami studies.

In the fourth and last chapter of the book, titled, "Hermeneutics of the Khayyami Robaiyat in Quantum Sociological Imagination: Source Availability and Secrecy," I relaxed my prior assumptions and abstractions from matters of source availability and secrecy as maintained in the previous three chapters of the book, and tried in the chapter to elaborate in more detail on both of the above challenges confronting Khayyami studies.

In the first section, my purpose was to draw a preliminary, basic outline of the sources of information available (or not) for the research on Khayyam conducted for this series. My aim at this point was not to delve into the historical, bibliographic, or manuscript conditions or the extent of authenticity of these sources. Those details will be carefully introduced, examined, and evaluated during the substantive explorations of this series in conjunction with careful studies of their contents.

I offered a categorization of sources for Khayyami studies as follows:

1. Primary Sources: texts that are attributed, unanimously or not, to Omar Khayyam himself. In this category, I identified the following subcategories: A) As a first subcategory of primary sources, we should include works that Khayyam may have written, intended to be shared or not during his own lifetime, of which we do not yet have any knowledge or records whatever; B) As a second subcategory of primary sources, we have works specifically reported by Khayyam (as acknowledges also by others) to have been written by him on definite topics from which we do not (yet) have any complete or even partial manuscripts; C) A third subcategory of primary sources are surviving works bearing Khayyam's name that are universally accepted to have been authored by him, these include a variety of sources that I listed in the section; D) The Khayyami Robaiyat: A fourth subcategory of surviving primary sources are the Robaiyat (quatrains) written in Persian that have been attributed to Omar Khayyam in various manuscripts down the centuries; it was given a separate subcategory status given the disputed nature of their attribution. 2. Secondary Sources: old accounts and information about Khayyam's life and works from the pre-FitzGeraldian era, among which I identified also four subcategories as explained in the text. 3. Tertiary Sources: include all the modern and recent sources written about Khayyam's life and works in the post-FitzGeraldian era. I noted further that fourth (possible architecture related works) and fifth (burial related material) categories can also be considered as sources in Khayyami studies.

In my view, the most reliable strategy for conducting Khayyami studies must be one that lays the most emphasis on the primary material as the source of the most reliable information about Khayyam. However, we will have to avoid treating all the various categories and subcategories as chunky, separate billiard balls to be struck with one another from without, but will approach them in their overlapping and superposed nature, in such a way that despite their apparently fragmented state, they are imagined as being superposed expressions of a life in progress, works produced along a lifetime, and commentaries made by others on his life and works amid a wider world-history context they all share.

I then elaborated on my hermeneutic method to be used in the series, noting that I will be particularly interested and careful to seek, as far as possible, the symbolic meanings amid the language Khayyam himself uses from his own texts as part of the landscape of his own subjective universe, rather than assuming in an *a priori* fashion that simply because Khayyam admired Avicenna (or anyone else for that matter) he retained and applied the same meaning in the same way as Avicenna or others did in their work.

Finally, while offering the broad contours and a gist of my thesis advanced in the series, I encouraged readers to consider and understand that my presentation method of revealing the "secret" of Khayyam in the series has to remain respectful of Khayyam's style of teaching and writing, since understanding of that process is itself an integral part of the "secret" Khayyam wished to impart through his works, particularly his Robaiyat.

Abstract

This essay, titled "Conclusion to Book 1: Summary of Findings," offers a summary, based on the section and chapter abstracts, of the first book, subtitled *New Khayyami Studies: Quantumizing the Newtonian Structures of C. Wright Mills's Sociological Imagination for A New Hermeneutic Method,* of the twelve-book series, *Omar Khayyam's Secret: Hermeneutics of the Robaiyat in Quantum Sociological Imagination,* authored by Mohammad H. Tamdgidi.

In the overall series the author shares the results of his decades-long research on Omar Khayyam, the enigmatic 11th/12th centuries Persian Muslim sage, philosopher, astronomer, mathematician, physician, writer, and poet from Neyshabour, Iran, whose life and works still remain behind a veil of deep mystery. The purpose of Tamdgidi's research has been to find definitive answers to the many puzzles still surrounding Khayyam, especially regarding the existence, nature, and purpose of the Robaiyat in his life and works. To explore the questions posed in the series, Tamdgidi advances a new hermeneutic method of textual analysis, informed by what he calls the quantum sociological imagination, to gather and study all the attributed philosophical, religious, scientific, and literary writings of Khayyam.

In the first book, following a common preface and introduction to the series, Tamdgidi develops the quantum sociological imagination method framing his hermeneutic study in the series as a whole. In the prefatory note he shares the origins of this study and how the study is itself a moment in the trajectory of a broader research project. In his introduction, he describes how centuries of Khayyami studies, especially during the last two, have reached an impasse in shedding light on his enigmatic life and works, especially his attributed Robaiyat.

The four chapters of this book are then dedicated to developing the quantum sociological imagination as a new hermeneutic method framing the Khayyami studies in the series. The method builds, in an applied way, on the results of Tamdgidi's recent work in the sociology of scientific knowledge, *Liberating Sociology: From Newtonian Toward Quantum Imagination: Volume 1: Unriddling the Quantum Enigma* (2020), where he explored extensively, in greater depth, and in the context of understanding the so-called "quantum enigma," the Newtonian and quantum ways of imagining reality.

In the first book, he shares the findings of that research in summary amid new applied insights developed in relation to Khayyami studies. In the first chapter, Tamdgidi raises a set of eight questions about the structure of C. Wright Mills's sociological imagination as a potential framework for Khayyami studies. In the second chapter, he shows how the questions are symptomatic of Newtonian structures that still continue to frame Mills's sociological imagination. In the third chapter, the author explores how the sociological imagination can be reinvented to be more in tune with the findings of quantum science. In the last chapter, the implications of the quantum sociological imagination for devising a hermeneutic method for new Khayyami studies are outlined. In conclusion, the findings of the first book of the *Omar Khayyam's Secret* series are summarized.

Appendix: Transliteration System and Book 1 Glossary

In the English edition of this series, as needed, I will offer transliterations of proper names originally expressed in Persian or Arabic. I will also offer transliterations, when intended, to accompany the Khayyami Robaiyat in Persian. Any included or quoted longer text originally written in Persian or Arabic will not be transliterated but will be rendered in its own original language. In the bibliography, instead of transliterations, I will include the bibliographic information in the original language in which it was published while providing the information in English translation; if it has been published in English translation, I will provide it instead of my own translation, unless additional notes are needed for correction or clarification.

As explained in the brief transliteration note in the front matter of this book, throughout this series, in order to simplify the rendering of Persian of Arabic texts free of unfamiliar (to the general English-speaking reader) expressions, I will not use diacritics (including those for ʿein ع or hamzeh ء) in the main body and its footnotes, except for where warranted for substantive research purposes, such as when intending to offer full transliterations alongside the Persian originals for the Khayyami Robaiyat. Instead, I invite interested and specialist readers to consult a separate cumulative transliteration glossary of words specific to each book (and earlier ones) that I have placed in this appendix following the transliteration system being introduced.

For instance, the names "Omar" or "Khayyam" are used throughout the series without diacritics, but in the transliteration table, its proper rendering as 'Omar or Khayyām (as well as its original in Persian/Arabic, i.e., "عمر" or "خيّام") will be given. For the word رباعيّات I will use "Robaiyat" (again, without diacritics) which is a more accurate phonetic expression for the word as pronounced in Persian, while providing in the transliteration table in this appendix the full transliteration of the word as expressed in Persian, that is "Roba'iyāt." I will use the spelling "Rubaiyat" only when the specific Western tradition associated with the "free translations" of the Robaiyat by Edward FitzGerald or others similarly undertaken are referred to in the account.

In the case of authors' names or their work titles written in Arabic or Persian—again, in order to simplify the reading experience in English—I will use the simpler transliteration without diacritics, while providing the actual names and work titles in the original language in the bibliography. Regarding sources continually engaged with in the study, I will offer a simple transliteration of the titles followed by its English translation in the main text (or footnotes) while providing the full transliteration also in the cumulative transliteration glossary in the appendix of each respective book.

For instance, instead of using the title "*Tatemmaï Ṣewán él-Ḥekmaï*" for the original Arabic ("تتمة صوان الحكمة"), an important manuscript studied in this series, I will use its transliteration and its English translation as "*Tatemmat Sewan el-Hekmat (Supplement to the Chest of Wisdom)*" in order to convey a simpler and immediate sense of the nature of the source to the English-speaking reader. The full transliteration of the title along with the title in the original language is given in the transliteration glossary in the appendix. As another example, I will render the proper name "Zahireddin Abolhasan Beyhaqi" as such in the main text or footnote while providing its proper rendering in the transliteration table as "Żahireḷddin Abu al-Ḥasan Beyhaqi" and "ظهيرالدّين ابوالحسن بيهقى" in the transliteration glossary in the appendix.

In this English edition of this book and its series, words (with any diacritics) in languages originally using Latin alphabet are rendered as in the original. When quoting transliterated Persian and Arabic words, I will render them (including their diacritics) as found in the source, whatever transliteration system the source has used, which can vary from one source to another. However, my own transliterations of Persian and Arabic texts will follow their pronunciation in Persian. So, Arabic (or any other language) words internalized in Persian language will be transliterated according to their Persian pronunciation, except for the transliterations already in common use.

In the case of a quote in the original Arabic or Persian, I will offer the English translation (noting in parenthesis whether it is from a previously published source, or my own translation); however, whether or not I also offer the original text in Persian or Arabic in transliteration or original language will depend on the context—i.e., depending on the substantive significance of the original text for the purpose of research at hand.

In all of the above considerations, if there arises a substantive need to offer the transliteration in the main text, I will certainly do so. For instance, in offering an opportunity to read the Khayyami Robaiyat in their original Persian pronunciation, it will be necessary to offer a transliteration that is expressive of the Persian pronunciation of the words. Unfortunately, in this regard existing transliteration systems can be misleading since they often rely on Arabic pronunciations of the words, leading to mispronunciations that are not suitable for the proper reading, reciting, and understanding of the Persian poems.

In what follows, I will present my own suggested transliteration system that somewhat overlaps with, but is also significantly different from, other prevailing (mostly Arabic-language based) systems of transliteration. The reason for my offering a different system rather than borrowing from an existing one is two-fold.

First, the main purpose is to designate the transliteration letters and symbols such that the possibility of correct conversions back to the original written texts in Persian or Arabic is retained. For instance, transliterating تتمة as *Tatamat* does not necessarily lead to a correct spelling and writing of the word as it stands in the original Arabic (it would rather result in the rendering of the word as تتمت, which is not the same as found in the original), whereas using the transliteration *Tatemmaï* (as defined in the following system) for the word would offer the possibility of converting the word back to the correct spelling and writing in the original Arabic. This system would thus eliminate the need to offer the actual Arabic or Persian original texts in text (or its footnotes)—unless necessary for other reasons.

Second, the purpose is to offer a system of transliteration using which the original words in Persian (or Arabic words already internalized in the Persian lexicon) can be pronounced as they would be with a Persian accent (while still retaining the possibility of conversation back to the original word in writing, as noted above). Most transliteration systems tend to produce Arabic phonetics and accents; however, for the purpose of this research (especially when it comes, for instance, to the proper pronunciation of words in the Persian Robaiyat) it is important to convey and pass on to readers a transliteration system that more faithfully conveys Persian phonetics and accents for Persian words or even for Arabic words that have become internalized in Persian and are pronounced with a Persian accent.

The Persian alphabet includes the Arabic plus four additional letters (پ ژ چ گ) while some Arabic diacritics are not commonly used in Persian writing. Moreover, several different Arabic letters are pronounced the same in Persian (such as ظ ض ذ ز which are all pronounced the same way as 'z,' or ت ط which are pronounced the same as 't,' or ث ص س which are usually pronounced the same as 's'), differently from the Arabic, where the distinctions of phonetics associated with each letter are noticeably maintained. While the use of the different letters in writing is still necessary even in Persian since they construct different words carrying different meanings, in their pronunciation, especially when (for instance) poetry is concerned, using a Persian accent is indispensable.

For instance, it is more proper for the non-native Persian speaker to read a Persian poem, say a Khayyami quatrain, using a Persian accent rather than an Arabic accent resulting from other transliteration systems. Even the very manner in which the terms robai "رباعی" or its plural robaiyat "رباعیّات"—terms that are in fact Arabic but became a part of the Persian lexicon when the Arabic designation was used for the older Persian words "taräneh" or "sorood"—have been transliterated as "rubai," or its plural "rubaiyat" reflects an Arabic pronunciation rather than ones as pronounced in Persian (which is robai and robaiyat, respectively).

As other examples: the word "Isfahan" is actually pronounced Eṣfahän in Persian; Iran is pronounced like "Earän" not "I ran"; Khayyam is pronounced as Khayyäm—not like "kayam" or ending like "I am" but ending like "from." The "Kh" is pronounced in a guttural way and not as a "K," but such a sound is non-existent in English language, though learning it is a must for anyone seeking to practice correct Persian pronunciation and accent. This is unfortunate since "Kh" is used widely in Persian language, particularly in names, going back to ancient times. The Russian language has this letter, X, and thereby can offer a closer phonetic example (as can be listened to in google translation page for the word "Khayyäm" in Russian, Хайям).

There are perfectly legitimate reasons to establish transliteration systems that differ from Arabic-based systems. It is of course true that there is no single "Persian" accent, as the Iranian population is itself comprised of different ethnic groups practicing their own dialectics and accents of Persian. However, still, one can distinguish a clearly Persian accent originating in the Fars (Färs) or Khorasan (Khoräsän) regions since early times and now spread throughout Iran, including Tehran, and despite its regional accent variations it can be clearly contrasted with the Arabic. The main point here is to encourage non-Persian speaking readers to reproduce the Persian accent in reading Persian phrases and poems rather than practicing an Arabic accent that often results from using prevailing transliteration systems.

In proposing a Persian-friendly transliteration system in the following table, I have tried to construct each transliterated letter from a letter that is close to its expected sound. For instance, I construct the equivalent of the letter ذ using the letter z rather than 'd' (which is common in Arabic transliterations which use the combination 'dh' for ذ). So, I use the letter z to construct all the alphabetical variants from the Arabic that in Persian sound the same as 'z'—that is, for ز ذ ض ظ I suggest ż z̧ ẓ and z respectively. Similarly, I use "s" to built all the letters that in Arabic exist as س ص ث (which are transliterated respectively as ş, ṣ, and s). For ت and ط I respectively suggest t and ṭ respectively. Their distinctions in writing, however, are retained to allow for correct conversions back to the original spelling/writing in the Arabic or Persian.

The overall purpose is to use a transliteration system that results in Persian pronunciation such that even when the diacritics are removed, the sounds intended are closer to the Persian pronunciations than those in Arabic.

Contextual Persian/Arabic Alphabet with Beginning, Middle, or Ending Variations				Letters Used for Pronunciation and Transliteration		Examples	ABC Extended Mac Keyboard Keystroke(s)
آ				ã	Ā	*As in Qorān or Āb:* قرآن *or* آب; *pronounced as in wAter; alef has a "hat." (Notice, Qorān is rendered here in its Persian pronunciation.)*	*option-n + a/A*
ا			ا	ā	Ā	*As in bābā or bāzār:* بابا *or* بازار; *pronounced as in wAter; the "hat" of alef is dropped.*	*option-a + a/A*
أ				á	Á	*As in Áhmad:* احمد *or* أحمد; *pronounced as in bAg; the alef is written with or without a diacritic mark above.*	*option-e + a/A*

Contextual Persian/Arabic Alphabet with Beginning, Middle, or Ending Variations					Letters Used for Pronunciation and Transliteration		Examples	ABC Extended Mac Keyboard Keystroke(s)
´					a	A	As in kalameh: كَلَمه; as in bAg, diacritic mark above letters, added or not.	regular a/A
إ					é	É	As in the first letter of *éḫterām:* احترام or احترام; pronounced as in bEd; the alef is written with or without a diacritic mark below.	option-e + e/E
╌					e	E	As in the third letter of *eḫterām:* احترام; pronounced as in bEd, diacritic mark below letters, written or not.	regular e/E
╶					-e	-E	As in Khayyām-e Neyshābouri: خیّام نیشابوری Diacritic mark below, written or not, linking a name/word to its following adjective (Khayyām from Neyshābur).	lowercase dash + regular e/E
أ					ó	Ó	As in ómeed: أمید; pronounced as in Orchard; the alef is written with or without a diacritic mark above.	option-e + o/O
╹					o	O	As in bozorg: بُزُرگ; pronounced as in Opium; diacritic mark above letters, written or not.	regular o/O
آ إ أ					ä ë ö	Ä Ë Ö	As in ettefāqà: اتّفاقاً; pronounced as 'an' at the end of a word. Although not common in Persian, in Arabic the same diacritic or its variation can appear below or above alef preceded by 'e' or 'o' vowels.	option/shift-y + a option/shift-y + e option/shift-y + o
ا				ا	â	Â	As in kâin: کاین (an abbreviation of که این); pronounced as kin; the alef is written but not pronounced.	option-6 + a

Contextual Persian/Arabic Alphabet with Beginning, Middle, or Ending Variations				Letters Used for Pronunciation and Transliteration		Examples	ABC Extended Mac Keyboard Keystroke(s)
				^	^	*As in raḥmˆn:* رحمن*; the alef is not written, but is pronounced.*	*option-6 + space*
ـب	ـبـ	بـ	ب	b	B	*As in bozorg:* بزرگ*; pronounced as in Bell.*	*regular b/B*
ـپ	ـپـ	پـ	پ	p	P	*As in pedar:* پدر*; pronounced as in Penguin. This letter exists in Persian alphabet, but not in Arabic. In Arabic, usually 'b' or 'f' is used for the 'p' pronunciation (that explains the origin of "Fārsi" which is Arabized "Pārsi").*	*regular p/P*
ـت	ـتـ	تـ	ت	t	T	*As in tamās:* تماس*; pronounced as in Tea.*	*regular t/T*
ـث	ـثـ	ثـ	ث	ṣ	Ṣ	*As in ṣolṣ:* ثلث*; pronounced in Persian as 's', as in Sand; pronounced in Arabic as "th" as in faiTH. Notice here the 's' sound is prioritized rather than the 'th' sound in transliteration since the purpose here is to offer Persian transliteration of Persian and internalized Arabic words.* *Persian speakers do not pronounce this letter as 'th,' unless, of course, they are specifically reading Arabic texts with the intention of reproducing Arabic accents (as in reciting the Qorān, for example).*	*option-c + s/S*
ـج	ـجـ	جـ	ج	j	J	*As in Jamsheed:* جمشید*; pronounced as in Judy or July.*	*regular j/J*

Contextual Persian/Arabic Alphabet with Beginning, Middle, or Ending Variations				Letters Used for Pronunciation and Transliteration		Examples	ABC Extended Mac Keyboard Keystroke(s)
چ	ﭻ	ﭽ	ﭻ	ch	Ch	As in chashm or cheshm: چشم; as in CHurCH. This letter is present in Persian, but not in Arabic, alphabet. In Arabic, usually 'j' is used as a substitute for it.	regular ch or Ch
ح	ﺣ	ﺤ	ﺢ	ḥ	Ḥ	As in Ḥalab: حلب; pronounced as in Home. In Arabic, it has a deeper H sound.	option-x +h/H
خ	ﺧ	ﺨ	ﺦ	kh	Kh	As in Khāk: خاک; this sound is not present in English; pronounced as the letter X in Russian. Khayyām or خيام is pronounced using this letter.	regular kh/Kh
د			ﺪ	d	D	As in Del: دل; pronounced as in DaviD.	regular d/D
ذ			ﺬ	ẕ	Ẕ	As in leẕẕat: لذت; pronounced in Persian as in Zebra; pronounced in Arabic as a DH. Notice that the sound 'z' is used here to transliterate this letter, since is closer to how it is pronounced in Persian.	option-c + z/Z
ر			ﺮ	r	R	As in rāh: راه; pronounced as in Robert.	regular r/R
ز			ﺰ	z	Z	As in zanboor: زنبور; pronounced as in Zebra.	
ژ			ﮋ	zh	Zh	As in Zhivāgō: ژیواگو; pronounced in Persian as in ZHivāgo; this letter is present in Persian, but not in Arabic, alphabet.	regular zh/Zh
س	ﺳ	ﺴ	ﺲ	s	S	As in Sāsān: ساسان; as in Sand.	regular s/S regular ss/SS

Contextual Persian/Arabic Alphabet with Beginning, Middle, or Ending Variations				Letters Used for Pronunciation and Transliteration		Examples	ABC Extended Mac Keyboard Keystroke(s)
ش	ﺸ	ﺸ	ﺶ	sh	Sh	As in Shivā: شیوا; as in Shoe.	regular sh/Sh
ص	ﺻ	ﺼ	ﺺ	ṣ	Ṣ	As in ṣolḥ: صُلح; as S in Persian, but as a deep S in Arabic.	option-x +s/S
ض	ﺿ	ﻀ	ﺾ	ẓ	Ẓ	As in ẓamimeh: ضمیمه; as in Z in Persian, deep mix of Z and D in Arabic. Notice that the sound 'z' is used here to transliterate this letter, since this is closer to how it is pronounced in Persian.	option-x + z/Z
ط	ﻃ	ﻄ	ﻂ	ṫ	Ṫ	As in ṫās: طاس; pronounced as T in Persian, but as a deep T in Arabic.	option-w + t/T
ظ	ﻇ	ﻈ	ﻆ	ż	Ż	As in żolm: ظلم; pronounced as Z in Persian, but as a deep Z or D in Arabic. Notice that the sound 'z' is used to transliterate this letter, since this is closer to how it is pronounced in Persian.	option-w + z/Z
ع	ﻋ	ﻌ	ﻊ	ʿ	ʿ	Precedes a variety of other letters as stand alone (As in meʿmār: معمار) or to give the next element a prior accent, as in Robāʿiyāt, ʿOmar, ʿAli, ʿEmād. It can also appear at the end of word, robʿ.	American Diacs Keyboard option+l or ABC Extended keyboard: "grave accent" key next to number 1 on keyboard
غ	ﻏ	ﻐ	ﻎ	gh	Gh	As in ghareeb: غریب; pronounced in Persian as a deep G, as in GHraib. This sound, in its Persian rendering, is not present in English, but is abundant in French for 'r,' for example.	regular gh/Gh

Contextual Persian/Arabic Alphabet with Beginning, Middle, or Ending Variations				Letters Used for Pronunciation and Transliteration		Examples	ABC Extended Mac Keyboard Keystroke(s)
ف	ف	ف	ف	f	F	As in Fārsi: فارسی; pronounced as in Father.	regular f/F
ق	ق	ق	ق	q	Q	As in Qorān: قرآن; pronounced in Persian as a deep K. This sound, in its Persian rendering, is not present in English, but is abundant in French for 'r,' for example. Q and Gh sound the same in Persian.	regular q/Q
ک / ك	ک / ک	ک / ک	کـ / كـ	k	K	As in kāshef: کاشف; pronounced as in Kin. In Arabic, a hamzeh on top is used for this letter and the upper slant is omitted when used alone or at the end of the word.	regluar k/K
گ	گ	گ	گـ	g	G	As in Galu: گلو; pronounced as in Gas. This letter is present in Persian, but not in Arabic, alphabet. Usually K is used instead in Arabic as a substitute for it.	regular g/G
ل	ل	ل	لـ	l	L	As in lāleh: لاله; pronounced as in Lady.	regular l/L
	ل			ł	ł	As in yowmélddin: یوم الدّین; the 'l' is written but is silent in pronunciation.	option-l + l
م	م	م	مـ	m	M	As in mellat: ملّت; pronounced as in Media.	regular m/M
ن	ن	ن	نـ	n	N	As in nāder: نادر; pronounced as in NaNcy.	regular n/N
و			و	v	V	As in vizheh: ویژه; pronounced as in Violin.	regular v/V
و			و	w	W	As in ówlād: اولاد; pronounced as in Wonderful.	regular w/W

Contextual Persian/Arabic Alphabet with Beginning, Middle, or Ending Variations				Letters Used for Pronunciation and Transliteration		Examples	ABC Extended Mac Keyboard Keystroke(s)
و			و	ō	Ō	*As in mōz:* موز *; written vowel and pronounced as in bOwl.*	*option-a +o*
و			و	oo ou	OO OU	*As in mooyrag:* مویرگ*; written long vowel and pronounced as in rUde, or gOOd.* *Sometimes, in Persian, a double-o or 'ou' is used to convey the same sound, as in Behrooz.*	*regular oo* *regular ou* *regular ou*
و				va ō	VA Ō	*As in gorg va meesh, or gorg ō meesh:* گرگ و میش*; in Persian, pronounced as 'va', meaning 'and' connecting a word to the next word. It is less formally also pronounced as 'ō' also meaning 'and.'* *In these senses, it is used as a stand alone word, separated from preceding and following words.*	*regular v* *option-a + o*
و				ŵ	Ŵ	*As in khŵāst or khŵish:* خواست *or* خویش*; 'v' is written but is silent in pronunciation.*	*option-6 + w/W*
ه	ھ	ﻬ or ﭻ	ﺪ	h	H	*As in mehr:* مهر*; pronounced as in Home. When this letter is used at the end of the word, it is usually pronounced as an "e" or a softer almost inaudible 'H.'*	*regular h/H*
ی ي	ﻴ	ﺌ	ﻰ	i	I	*As in bishomār:* بیشمار *or* بی شمار*; pronounced as in kEY.*	*regular i/I*
ﯽ				ă	Ă	*As in 'alī:* علی*; written as 'i' but pronounced as 'ā.' Usually a small alef is used on top of* ی *to indicate the 'ā' sound.*	*option-u + a/A* *small alef unicode U+0670*

Contextual Persian/Arabic Alphabet with Beginning, Middle, or Ending Variations				Letters Used for Pronunciation and Transliteration		Examples	ABC Extended Mac Keyboard Keystroke(s)
	ﻴ	ﺋ		y	Y	*As in zāyandeh:* زاینده; *pronounced as in blInd.*	*regular y/Y*
ﻪ ﻯﻪ			ﺔ ﻰ ﺪ	-ye	-YE	*As in maghāleh-ye:* مقاله *or* مقاله ی; *a hamzeh over the 'h' or a* ی *after* ﻪ *pronounced as in YEH. This is a variation of -e, the difference being due to its usage when the word ends with a 'h.'*	*regular dash/ ye/YE*
ﻯ	ﻴ	ﺋ	ﻰ	ee	EE	*As in Jamsheed:* جمشید; *pronounced as in sEEn; a long 'i.'*	*regular ee/EE*
ﻉ				ٔ '	ٔ '	*As in 'Alā'é̦ddin:* علاء الدّین. *This sign is called "hamzeh." In this case, it appears stand-alone.*	*American Diacs Keyboard: Option+j or ABC Extended Keyboard: option-e + space*
ﺍٔ				ʾa ʿa	ʾA ʿA	*As in 'abu:* أبو *pronounced as in Ask; alef with a hamzeh above, used in Arabic and not commonly used in Persian (where hamzeh is omitted).*	*a/A + option-e + space*
ﺍ				ʾe ʿe	ʾE ʿE	*As in 'enshā'allāh:* إنشاء الله *pronounced as Entire; alef with a hamzeh below, used in Arabic and not commonly used in Persian (where hamzeh is usually omitted).*	*e/E + option-e + space*
ﺅ				o' o'	O' O'	*As in mō'așșer:* مؤثّر.	*o + option-e + space*

Contextual Persian/Arabic Alphabet with Beginning, Middle, or Ending Variations				Letters Used for Pronunciation and Transliteration		Examples	ABC Extended Mac Keyboard Keystroke(s)
ئ	ؤ	ٔ	ئ	ٔ	ٔ	*A 'y' with hamzeh, or a hamzeh that has its own "tooth." Examples: As in mas'aleh:* مسئله; *masā'el:* مسائل, *shey':* شئ. *It is pronounced usually as a hamzeh, not as a 'y'. (Notice, shey' is spelled according to the Persian, not Arabic, pronunciation of the term.)*	*option-v + space (if needed)*
ة				ẗ		*As in resālaï:* رساله; *pronounced in Arabic as 'ah' if not linked to next word, as in* رساله في, *and as 'at' if linked to next word, as in* رسالة الغفران.	*option-u + h/H*
ّ						*As in KhaYYām:* خیّام; *letter is repeated; if the sign ˝ appears above a letter in Persian or Arabic, it doubles the consonent in pronunciation (the sign is called 'tashdeed').*	*repeat the letter*

Book 1 Cumulative Glossary of Transliterations

In Text	Persian Transliteration	In Original Language
Attar, Farideddin	*Farideÿddin Aïïār*	فریدالدّین عطّار
Azeri	*Azari*	آذری
Chahar Maqaleh (Four Discourses)	*Chahār Maqāleh*	چهار مقاله
Darkhast-Nameh (Requested Letter)	*Darkhŵāst Nāmeh*	درخواست نامه
Farabi, Abu Nasr	*Ábu Naṣr Fārābi*	ابو نصر فارابی
Farsi	*Fārsi (Pārsi)*	فارسی
Hafez Shirazi	*Hāfeż Shirāzi*	حافظ شیرازی
Ibn Sina or Avicenna	*Ébn-e Sinā or Ábu ‘Ali al-Ḥosein ebn-e ‘Abdollāh ebn-e al-Ḥosan ebn-e ‘Ali ebn-e Sinā*	ابن سینا (ابو علی الحسین بن عبدالله بن الحسن بن علی بن سینا)
Ibrahim	*Ébrāhim*	ابراهیم
Iran	*Earān*	ایران
Isfahan	*Eṣfahān*	اصفهان
Islam	*Eslām*	اسلام
Ismaili	*Esmā‘ili (other prevalent transliteration is Ismā‘ili)*	اسماعیلی
Jawab an Salasa Masael: Zarurat al-Tazadd fi al-Alam wa al-Jabr wa al-Baqa (Answer to Three Questions: The Necessity of Contradiction in the World, Fate, and Survival)	*Jawāb ‘an Ṣalāṣa Masā’el: Ẓaruraï ol-Taẓādd fi âl-‘Ālam wa âl-Jabr wa âl-Baqā’*	جواب عن ثلاث مسائل: ضرورت التضادّ فی العالم و الجبر و البقاء
Khazeni, Abdorrahman	*‘Abdorrahmân al-Khāzeni or Ábu al-Fatḥ ‘Abd al-Rraḥmān Manṣoor al-Khāzeni (other transliterations, al-Khāzini)*	عبدالرحمن الخازنی یا ابو الفتح عبدالرحمن منصور الخازنی
Khayyam, Khayyami	*Khayyām, Khayyāmi*	خیّام، خیّامی
Kurd	*Kord*	کُرد
Lur	*Lor*	لُر

In Text	Persian Transliteration	In Original Language
Majma ol-Anvar (Sum of Lights) — This is another name for Chahar Maqaleh (Four Discourses)	*Majma' ól-Ánvār*	مجمع الانوار
Malekshah	*Malekshāh*	ملکشاه
Manteqotteir (Conference of the Birds)	*Manteq ól-ťteir (other prevalent transliteration is Mantiq-ut-Tayr)*	منطق الطّیر
Masael Nojoomiyeh Azennaha men Kalam Omar al-Khayyami (Problems in Astrology: I think is from Omar Khayyam)	*Masā'el Nojoomiyeh Ażennaha men Kalām 'Omar al-Khayyāmi*	مسایل نجومیّه اظنها من کلام عمر الخیامی
Masjed Jame	*Masjed Jame'*	مسجد جامع
Mizan ol-Hekmat (Balance of Wisdom)	*Mizan ol-Hekmaï*	میزان الحکمة
Molana Jalaleddin Rumi	*Molānā Jalāleddin Rumi*	مولانا جلال الدّین رومی
Mosaddegh	*Moṣaddeq*	مصدّق
Neyshabour	*Neyshābour*	نیشابور
Nezami Arouzi	*Neżāmi 'Arouzi (other prevalent transliteration is Nizāmi 'Aruzi)*	نظامی عروضی
Nezam ol-Molk	*Neżām ol-Molk or Ábu 'Ali Ḥasan ibn 'Ali Ṭusi (other prevalent transliterationa include Nizam al-Mulk)*	نظام الملك
Nezari (of Ismailis)	*Nezāri*	نزاری
Nowrooznameh (The Book on Nowrooz) or Nowrooznameh: Resaleh dar Kashf-e Haqiqat-e Nowrooz (The Book on Nowrooz: Treatise on Discovering the Truth of Nowrooz)	*Nowrooznāmeh: Resāleh dar Kashf-e Ḥaqiqat-e Nowrooz*	نوروزنامه: رساله در کشف حقیقت نوروز
Omar	*'Omar*	عمر

In Text	Persian Transliteration	In Original Language
Omar Khayyam	*'Omar Khayyām or Ābu al-Fatḥ Qiyāṣeddin 'Omar ebn Ebrāhim Khayyām Neyshābouri or Ābu al-Fatḥ Qiyās al-Ddin 'Omar ibn Ibrāhim al-Khayyām al-Neyshābouri*	عمر خیّام یا ابو الفتح غیاث الدین عمر بن ابراهیم نیشابوری
Oqlidos or Euclid	*Oqlidos (also transliterated as Uqlidos)*	اقلیدس
al-Qowl ala Ajnas al-Lazi be al-Arbaat (Statement on the Four-Fold Types)	*al-Qowl 'ală Ajnās al-Laẓi be al-Árba'aï*	القول على اجناس الذى بالاربعة
Resalat al-Zia ol-Aqli fi Mozoo el-Elm al-Kolli (Treatise on the Light of Intellect on the Subject of Universal Science)	*Resālaï al-Ẓiā' al-'Aqli fi Moẓoo' al-'Elm al-Kolli*	رسالة الضیاء العقلى فى موضوع العلم الكلّى
Resalat fi al-Baraheen ala Masael al-Jabr wa al-Moqabeleh (Treatise on the Proofs of the Problems of Algebra and Equations)	*Resālaï fi al-Barāheen 'ală Masā'el al-Jabr wa al-Moqābeleh*	رسالة فى البراهین على مسائل الجبر و المقابله
Resalat fi al-Kown wa al-Taklif (Treatise on Universe and Obligation, which can also be expressed as Treatise on the Created World and the Duty to Worship)	*Resālaï fi âl-Kown wa âl-Taklif*	رسالة فى الكون والتكلیف
Resalat fi al-Vojood (Treatise on Existence)	*Resālaï fi al-Vojood*	رسالة فى الوجود
Resalat fi Moshkelat al-Hesab (Treatise on the Problems of Arithmatic)	*Resālaï fi Moshkelāt ál-Ḥesāb*	رسالة فى مشكلات الحساب
Resalat Jawaban le-Solse Masael (Treatise on Response to Three Questions)	*Resālaï Javāb le-Ṣolṣ Masā'el*	رسالة جواب لثلث مسائل

In Text	Persian Transliteration	In Original Language
Resalat fi Ehtial le-Marefat Maqadir al-Zahab wa al-Fezzah fi Jesme Morakkab Menhoma (Treatise on the Art of Defining Quantities of Gold and Silver in a Body Consisting of Them)	*Resālaï fi Eḥtiāl le-Maʿrefat Maqādir al-Zahab wa al-Fezẓah fi Jesme Morakkab Menhomā*	رسالة فى احتيال لمعرفت مقادير الذهب و الفضه فى جسم مركّب منهما
Resalat fi Qesmat Rob al-Dayereh (Treatise on the Division of a Circle Quadrant)	*Resālaï fi Qesmat Robʿ al-Dayerah*	رسالة فى قسمت الربع الدايره
Resalat fi Moshkelat ol-Hesab (Treatise on the Problems of Arithmetic)	*Resālaï fi Moshkelāt ól-Ḥesāb*	رسالة فى مشكلات الحساب
Resalat fi Sharh ma Eshkala men Mosaderat Ketab Oqlidos (Treatise on the Explanation of Problems of Postulates in Euclid's Book)	*Resālaï fi Sharḥ ma Éshkala men Moṣāderāt Ketāb Oqlidos*	رسالة فى شرح من اشكل من مصادرات كتاب اقليدس
Resalat fi Lavazem ol-Amkaneh (Treatise on the Requirements of Locations)	*Resālaï fi Lavāzem ól-Amkaneh*	رسالة فى لوازم الامكنه
Resalat Mokhtasar fi al-Tabiiyyat (Brief Treatise on Nature)	*Resālaï Mokhtaṣar fi âl-Ṭabiʿiyyāt*	رسالة مختصر فى الطبيعيّات
Resaleh dar Elm-e Kolliyat-e Vojood (Treatise on the Science of the Universals of Existence)	*Resāleh dar ʿElm-e Kolliyāt-e Vojood (when expressed in Arabic, "Resālaï fi Kolliyyāt al-Vojood")*	رساله در علم كليّات وجود (رسالة فى كليّات الوجود)
Resaleh-ye Selselat ol-Tartib (Treatise on the Succession Order)	*Resāleh-ye Selselaï ól-Tarteeb*	رساله ى سلسلة الترتيب
Robaiyat (used in Persian pronunciation)	*Robāʿiyāt*	رباعيات
Rubaiyat (used in reference to Western pronunciation)	*Rubāʿiyāt*	رباعيات
Sadi	*Saʿdi*	سعدى
Sanai Ghaznavi	*Sanāʾi Ghaznavi*	سنائى غزنوى

In Text	Persian Transliteration	In Original Language
Sasanian	Sāsāniān	ساسانيان
Seljuk	Saljooq	سلجوق
Shafa or al-Shafa (Healing)	ál-Shafā'	الشفاء
Sharh al-Moshkel men Ketab al-Moosiqi (Explanation of Difficulty in the Book of Music)	Sharh al-Moshkel men Ketāb al-Moosiqi	شرح المشكل من كتاب الموسيقى
Shia d	Shi'ah (at times also transliterated as Shiite or Shi'ite)	شيعه
Soltan	Soltān	سلطان
Tarabkhaneh (House of Joy)	Țarabkhāneh (House of Joy)	طربخانه
Tarjomeh-ye Khotbeh-ye Qarra-ye Ebn-e Sina (Translation of the Splendid Sermon of Avicenna)	Tarjomeh-ye Khoibeh-ye Qarrā-ye Ébn-e Sinā	ترجمه ى خطبه ى قرّاى ابن سينا
Tatemmat Sewan el-Hekmat (Supplement to the Chest of Wisdom)	Tatemmaï Șewán él-Ḥekmaï	تتمة صوان الحكمة
Tehran	Tehrān	تهران
Turk	Tork	تُرك
Turkoman	Torkman	تُركمن
Zahireddin Abolhasan Beyhaqi	Żahirełddin Ábolhasan Beyhaqi (or Żahir al-Din Abu al-Ḥasan 'Ali ibn Zayd Beyhaqi)	ظهيرالدّين ابو الحسن على بن زيد بيهقى
zamaneh	zamāneh	زمانه
Zeej-e Malekshahi (Malekshahi Ephemeris)	Zeej-e Malekshāhi	زيج ملكشاهى

Book 1 References

The purpose of the reference list below is only to provide a listing of the primary, some secondary, and other sources referred to in this book, plus some prior background works by the author that are relevant to this series and its origins. Since in-depth studies of Omar Khayyam's attributed writings will be undertaken in the subsequent books of these series, further bibliographic details about his works and those secondary sources about him will be provided in future respective books of the present series.

1. Preliminary List of Omar Khayyam's Writings and A Few Important Secondary Sources

On Philosophy and Religion

Khayyam, Omar. رساله در علم کلّیات وجود [(in Persian) Treatise on the Science of the Universals of Existence, or درخواست نامه (Requested-Letter) or رساله ی سلسلة الترتیب (Treatise on Chain of Order), or رسالة فی کلّیات الوجود (title expressed in Arabic)]

Khayyam, Omar. ترجمه ی خطبة القرآی ابن سینا [Translation of the Splendid Sermon of Avicenna]

Khayyam, Omar. رسالة فی الکون و التکلیف [Treatise on Universe and Obligation] or [Treatise on the Created World and the Duty to Worship]

Khayyam, Omar. جواب عن ثلاثة مسائل: ضرورت التضاد فی العالم و الجبر و البقاء [Answer to Three Questions: The Necessity of Contradiction in the World,

Determinism, and Permanence]

Khayyam, Omar. رسالة فى الوجود [Treatise on Existence] or [Treatise on the Attributes of Existents)]

Khayyam, Omar. رسالة الضياء العقلى فى موضوع علم الكلّى [Treatise on the Light of Intellect on the Subject of Universal Science]

Khayyam, Omar. رسالة جواباً لثلث مسائل [Treatise on Response to Three Problems (Resurrection, Possibility, and Motion)]

On Science: Geometry, Mathematics, and Arithmetic

Khayyam, Omar. رسالة فى قسمت ربع الدايره [Treatise on the Division of a Circle Quadrant]

Khayyam, Omar. رسالة فى البراهين على مسائل الجبر و المقابله [Treatise on the Proofs of the Problems of Algebra and Equations]

Khayyam, Omar. رسالة فى شرح من اشكال من مصادرات كتاب اقليدس [Treatise on the Explanation of Problems of Postulates in Euclid's Book]

Khayyam, Omar. رسالة فى مشكلات الحساب [Problems of Arithmatic] [Lost or not yet found]

On Science: Nature and Geography

Khayyam, Omar. رسالة فى مختصر فى الطبيعيات [Brief Treatise on Nature] [Lost or not yet found]

Khayyam, Omar. رسالة فى لوازم الامكنه [Treatise on the Requirements of Locations] [Lost or not yet found]

On Science: Music

Khayyam, Omar. شرح المشكل من كتاب الموسيقى [Explanation of a Problem in the Book of Music] [Lost or not yet found, see below]

Khayyam, Omar. القول على اجناس الذى بالاربعة [Statement on the Four-Fold Types], perhaps a fragment of شرح المشكل من كتاب الموسيقى [Explanation of a Problem in the Book of Music]

On Science: Mechanics

Khayyam, Omar. رسالة فى احتيال لما عرفة مقدارى الذهب و الفضه فى جسم مركب منهما [Treatise on the Art of Defining Quantities of Gold and Silver in a Body Consisting of Them]; also known as رسالة فى القسطاس المستقيم [On Right Balance]. A section inserted in the *Book Mizan ol-Hekmat (Balance of Wisdom)* by Abdorrahman Khazeni.

On Science: Astronomy

Khayyam, Omar. زیج ملکشاهی [Zeej-e Malekshahi (Malekshahi Ephemeris)]

On Astrology

Khayyam, Omar. مسایل نجومیّه اظنها من کلام عمر الخیامی [Masael Nojoomiyeh Azennaha men Kalam Omar al-Khayyami (Problems in Astrology: I Think These are From the Words of Omar Khayyam)]

On Society and Culture

Khayyam, Omar. نوروزنامه: رساله در کشف حقیقت نوروز [Nowrooznameh (The Book on Nowrooz): Treatise on Discovering the Truth of Nowrooz]

Poetry

Khayyam, Omar. رباعیّات [Robaiyat]
Khayyam, Omar. اشعار عربی [Poems in Arabic]
Khayyam, Omar. اشعار فارسی [Poems in Persian (other than the Robaiyat)]

Few Important Secondary Literature

Arouzi, Nezami. چهار مقاله [*Chahar Maqaleh (Four Discourses)*]
Beyhaqi, Zahireddin Abolhasan. تتمة صوان الحکمة [*Tatemmat Sewan el-Hekmat (Supplement to the Chest of Wisdom)*]
Rashidi Tabrizi, Yar Ahmad. طربخانه [*Tarabkhaneh (House of Joy)*]
Khazeni, Abdorrahman. میزان الحکمة [*Balance of Wisdom (Mizan ol-Hekmat)*]

2. Other References and Background Bibliography

Blumer, H. 1986. *Symbolic interactionism: Perspective and method*. Berkeley, CA: University of California Press.

Cooley, C. H. [1922] 1983. *Human nature and the social order*. Piscataway, NJ: Transaction Publishers.

Goffman, Erving. 1959. *The Presentation of Self in Everyday Life*. New York: Anchor.

Mannheim, Karl. 1936. *Ideology and Utopia: An Introduction to the Sociology of Knowledge*. Translated by Louis Wirth and Edward Shils. New York: Harcourt, Brace & World, Inc.

Mead, George Herbert. 1934. *Mind, Self and Society*. Chicago: University of Chicago Press.

Mills, C. Wright. [1959] 2000. *The Sociological Imagination*. London: Oxford University Press.

Tamdgidi, Mohammad H. 1999. "Ideology and Utopia *in* Mannheim: Towards the Sociology of Self Knowledge." Presented at a Refereed Roundtable Session of the History of Sociology Section of the 94th Annual Meeting of the American Sociological Association, Aug. 6-10, Chicago.

Tamdgidi, Mohammad H. 2001. "Open the Antisystemic Movements: The Book, the Concept, and the Reality," in *REVIEW: Journal of the Fernand Braudel Center for the Study of Economies, Historical Systems, and Civilizations*, Vol. XXIV, No. 2, 301-338.

Tamdgidi, Mohammad H. 2002a. "Mysticism and Utopia: Towards the Sociology of Self-Knowledge and Human Architecture (A Study in Marx, Gurdjieff, and Mannheim)." Ph.D. diss., State University of New York at Binghamton.

Tamdgidi, Mohammad H., ed. 2002-. *Human Architecture: Journal of the Sociology of Self-knowledge.* Belmont, MA: Okcir Press. (ISSN: 1540-5699)

Tamdgidi, Mohammad H. 2002b. "Ideology and Utopia in Mannheim: Toward the Sociology of Self-Knowledge." *Human Architecture: Journal of the Sociology of Self-Knowledge,* I(1, Spring):120-140.

Tamdgidi, Mohammad H. 2003. "Editor's Note: Social Theories, Student Realities." (Review of the book *Achieving Against the Odds: How Academics Become Teachers of Diverse Students*, co-edited by Esther Kingston-Mann and Tim Sieber, Philadelphia: Temple University Press, 2001.) *Human Architecture: Journal of the Sociology of Self-Knowledge*, II (1, Spring): v-xii.

Tamdgidi, Mohammad H. 2003a. "Marx, Gurdjieff, and Mannheim: Contested Utopistics of Self and Society in a World-History Context," *Human Architecture: Journal of the Sociology of Self-Knowledge,* II(1, Spring):102-120.

Tamdgidi, Mohammad H. 2003/4. "De/Reconstructing Utopianism: Towards a World- Historical Typology." *Human Architecture: Journal of the Sociology of Self-Knowledge* II(2):125-141.

Tamdgidi, Mohammad H. 2004. "Freire Meets Gurdjieff and Rumi: Toward the Pedagogy of the Oppressed and Oppressive Selves," *The Discourse of Sociological Practice,* 6(2, Fall):165-185.

Tamdgidi, Mohammad H. 2004. "Rethinking Sociology: Self, Knowledge, Practice, and Dialectics in Transitions to Quantum Social Science," *Discourse of Sociological Practice*, 6(1):61-81.

Tamdgidi, Mohammad H. 2004/5. "Working Outlines for the Sociology of Self-Knowledge," *Human Architecture: Journal of the Sociology of Self-Knowledge,* III(1/2, Fall/Spring):123–133.

Tamdgidi, Mohammad H. 2005. "Orientalist and Liberating Discourses of East-West Difference: Revisiting Edward Said and the *Rubaiyat* of Omar Khayyam," *Discourse of Sociological Practice,* 7(1&2):187-201.

Tamdgidi, Mohammad H. 2005/6. "Editor's Note: Peer Reviewing the Peer Review Process." *Human Architecture: Journal of the Sociology of Self-Knowledge,* IV, 1&2 (Fall/Spring):vii-xv.

Tamdgidi, Mohammad H. 2005/6. "Private Sociologies and Burawoy's Sociology Types: Reflections on Newtonian and Quantal Sociological Imaginations." *Human Architecture: Journal of the Sociology of Self-Knowledge* IV(1&2):179-195.

Tamdgidi, Mohammad H. 2006. "Anzaldúa's Sociological Imagination: Comparative Applied Insights into Utopystic and Quantum Sociology," *Human Architecture: Journal of the Sociology of Self-Knowledge,* 4(Special Issue, Summer):265–285.

Tamdgidi, Mohammad H. 2006a. "Toward a Dialectical Conception of Imperiality: The Transitory (Heuristic) Nature of the Primacy of Analyses of Economies in World-Historical Social Science," *REVIEW* (Journal of the Fernand Braudel Center), XXIX(3):2006.

Tamdgidi, Mohammad H. 2007. "Abu Ghraib as a Microcosm: The Strange Face of Empire as a Lived Prison," *Sociological Spectrum,* 27(1):29-55.

Tamdgidi, Mohammad H. 2007. "Intersecting Autobiography, History, and Theory: The Subtler Global Violences of Colonialism and Racism in Fanon, Said, and Anzaldúa," *Human Architecture: Journal of the Sociology of Self-Knowledge,* V(Special Summer Double-Issue):113-135.

Tamdgidi, Mohammad H. 2007. *Advancing Utopistics: The Three Component Parts and Errors of Marxism.* London and New York: Routledge/Paradigm.

Tamdgidi, Mohammad H. 2008. "'I Change Myself, I Change the World': Anzaldúa's Sociological Imagination in *Borderlands/La Frontera: The New Mestiza,*" *Humanity & Society,* 32(4):311-335.

Tamdgidi, Mohammad H. 2008. "Editor's Note: Thich Nhat Hanh's Sociological Imagination." *Human Architecture: Journal of the Sociology of Self-Knowledge,* VI, (3, Summer):vii-x.

Tamdgidi, Mohammad H. 2008. "Editor's Note: Toward Sociological Re-Imaginations of Science and Peer Reviewing." *Human Architecture:*

Journal of the Sociology of Self-Knowledge, VI, (2, Spring):vii-xi.

Tamdgidi, Mohammad H. 2008. "Public Sociology and the Sociological Imagination: Revisiting Burawoy's Sociology Types," *Humanity & Society*, 32(2):131-143.

Tamdgidi, Mohammad H. 2008. "Utopystics and the Asiatic Modes of Liberation: Gurdjieffian Contributions to the Sociological Imaginations of Inner and Global World-Systems." Pp. 202-219 in *Asian Regionality in the Twenty-First Century: New Perspectives on the World-Systems*, edited by Ganesh Trishur. Boulder, CO: Paradigm Publishers.

Tamdgidi, Mohammad H. 2008a. "From Utopistics to Utopystics: Integrative Reflections on Potential Contributions of Mysticism to World-Systems Analyses and Praxes of Historical Alternatives." In *Islam and the Modern Orientalist World-System* (Proceedings of the 30th Conference of the Political Economy of the World-System (PEWS) Section of the American Sociological Association (ASA), April 20-23, 2006, Macalester College, Saint Paul, Minnesota).

Tamdgidi, Mohammad H. 2009. "Rethinking Diversity Amid Pedagogical Flexibility: Fostering the Scholarships of Learning and Teaching of the Sociological Imagination." Pp. 169-183 in *Making Connections: Self-Study & Social Change*, co-edited by Kathleen Pithouse (McGill), Claudia Michell (McGill), and Lebo Moletsane (South African Human Sciences Research Council). New York: Peter Lang Publishing Group.

Tamdgidi, Mohammad H. 2009. *Gurdjieff and Hypnosis: A Hermeneutic Study*. Foreword by J. Walter Driscoll. New York: Palgrave Macmillan.

Tamdgidi, Mohammad H. 2010. "Decolonizing Selves: The Subtler Violences of Colonialism and Racism in Fanon, Said, and Anzaldúa." Pp. 117–147 in *Fanon and the Decolonization of Philosophy* edited by Elizabeth A. Hoppe and Tracey Nicholls. Lanham, MD: Lexington Books (a division of Rowman & Littlefield).

Tamdgidi, Mohammad H. 2011. "The Simultaneity of Self and Global Transformations: Bridging with Anzaldúa's Liberating Vision." Pp. 218-225 in *Bridging: How and Why Gloria Evangelina Anzaldúa's Life and Work Transformed Our Own*, co-edited by AnaLouise Keating and Gloria González-López. Austin, Texas: University of Texas Press.

Tamdgidi, Mohammad H. 2012. "Beyond Islamophobia and Islamophilia as Western Epistemic Racisms: Revisiting the Runnymede Trust's Definition in a World-History Context," *Islamophobia Studies Journal* (Center for Race & Gender, U. C. Berkeley), I, 1(Inaugural

Issue):54-81.

Tamdgidi, Mohammad H. 2012. "Editor's Note: To Be of But Not in the University," *Human Architecture: Journal of the Sociology of Self-Knowledge*, IX(1, Winter):vii-xiv.

Tamdgidi, Mohammad H. 2013. "Editor's Note: I Think; Therefore, I Don't—Tackling the Enormity of Intellectual Inadvertency," *Human Architecture: Journal of the Sociology of Self-Knowledge*, X(1, Fall):vii-xxii.

Tamdgidi, Mohammad H. 2020. *Liberating Sociology: From Newtonian Toward Quantum Imaginations: Volume 1: Unriddling the Quantum Enigma*. Belmont, MA: Okcir Press.

Tamdgidi, Mohammad H. 2020. "Private Troubles and Public Issues." In *The Blackwell Encyclopedia of Sociology*. Edited by George Ritzer and Chris Rojek. John Wiley & Sons, Ltd.

Tirtha, Swāmi Govinda. 1941. *The Nectar of Grace: Omar Khayyām's Life and Works*. Allahabad: Kitabistan.

Weber, Max. 1994. *Sociological Writings*. Edited by Wolf Heydebrand, NY: Continuum.

Note: The referred page numbers given in the following index in the print edition of this book may be different from its ebook editions, also depending on the readers' ebook view customizations. However, the live links on the ebook editions correctly resolve to the proper passages with which the indexed words are associated.

Book 1 Index

Q

CPSIA information can be obtained
at www.ICGtesting.com
Printed in the USA
LVHW080734040521
685774LV00007B/24/J

9 781640 980020